The Eighteenth-Century Novel and Contemporary Social Issues

An Introduction

Stuart Sim

Edinburgh University Press

© Stuart Sim, 2008

Edinburgh University Press Ltd
22 George Square, Edinburgh

Typeset in 11/13 Ehrhardt
by Servis Filmsetting Ltd, Manchester, and
printed and bound in Great Britain by
Cromwell Press, Trowbridge, Wilts

A CIP record for this book is available from the British Library

ISBN 978 0 7486 2599 4 (hardback)
ISBN 978 0 7486 2600 7 (paperback)

The right of Stuart Sim
to be identified as author of this work
has been asserted in accordance with
the Copyright, Designs and Patents Act 1988.

Contents

Acknowledgements

My thanks go to Jackie Jones at Edinburgh University Press for her many insightful suggestions about the selection of novels and topics; to Ruth Willats for her careful copy-editing; and, as always, to Dr Helene Brandon for constant support and encouragement – as well as expert help on the subject of genetics in Chapter 7.

Introduction

The eighteenth century has become something of a Cinderella area in English literary studies. While it attracts a substantial amount of critical attention, it is less successful in its appeal to students or to a more general readership. Yet it was a period that saw the emergence of the modern English novel, and although most people will have heard of such works as *Robinson Crusoe* (1719) and *Tom Jones* (1749) in this respect, its public profile is not currently very high.[1] This is an unfortunate state of affairs given the richness and variety to be found in the eighteenth-century novel. From the cultural subversiveness of Daniel Defoe and Samuel Richardson through the philosophically informed wit of Laurence Sterne to the Gothic terrors of Ann Radcliffe and Mary Shelley, this is an area of literature which positively invites reassessment.

The eighteenth-century novel (to be understood here in the 'long' sense historically, running from the Restoration of 1660 to *c*. 1840) is particularly to be admired for its engagement with social issues, and it is fertile territory for the exploration of moral dilemmas. In many cases those dilemmas remain with us, taxing us as much as ever they did. What motivates a fundamentalist terrorist? (see James Hogg's *Confessions of a Justified Sinner*, 1824).[2] What are the justifiable limits of state power? (see William Godwin's *Caleb Williams*, 1794).[3] What can be done to ensure public order? (see Henry Fielding's *Tom Jones*, 1749). What dangers lie in wait for us when we create life artificially? (see Mary Shelley's *Frankenstein*, 1818).[4] Does popular culture corrupt the minds of impressionable youth? (see Jane Austen's *Northanger Abbey*,

1818),[5] or (Charlotte Lennox's *The Female Quixote*, 1752).[6] One of the most productive methods of approaching, and teaching, the eighteenth-century novel is to link it to contemporary social issues such that we can enter into dialogue with it, and that is what is proposed on a larger scale in this book. Eighteenth-century authors were grappling with very similar social problems to the ones we face today, and their fictionalisation of these can help us come to a greater understanding of what is at stake. We may not always agree with their analysis or their projected solutions, but eighteenth-century novelists offer us the opportunity to enter into spirited debate. That has always been one of the great selling points of the novel as a literary form – its ability to inspire social criticism that has wide public resonance, a resonance I claim is not being appreciated to the extent it should be today in the case of the eighteenth century.

The novels selected here represent a cross-section of authors from Aphra Behn in the late seventeenth century to James Hogg in the 1820s, and of novelistic styles and genres throughout the period too. Realism, Gothic romance, historical romance and proto-science fiction all feature, as well as a range of debates from race relations and sexual behaviour through to political sovereignty and fundamentalist terrorism. The novels chosen will be seen to be directly relevant to some of the most urgent socio-political issues of our own time: issues that affect all our lives and do not seem to admit of easy solutions.

A question does arise about the status of two of the works in the selection. Whether Aphra Behn's *Oroonoko* (1688) and Jonathan Swift's *Gulliver's Travels* (1726) qualify as novels in the generally understood sense of the term is a matter for debate, but as extended works of prose fiction they are most often discussed – and taught – within the framework of the early novel, so it is felt to be reasonable to include them.[7] Both narratives relate to topics of intense interest at present – race relations and cultural difference respectively – and it would seem a great pity for them to be excluded from discussion, especially since the novel is hardly the strictest of literary forms. Critics and theorists traditionally have struggled to define it with any great sense of precision: think of E. M. Forster's conclusion in *Aspects of the Novel*, for example, that '[a]ny fictitious prose work over 50,000 words will be a novel for the purposes of these lectures'.[8] Most of the authors we are dealing with here would not have identified themselves as novelists either, as 'novel' was not a generally used term until the later part of the period. Behn gives our survey greater historical breadth, and for Swift to be omitted from any discussion of socially conscious narrative in eighteenth-century Britain would be a considerable loss. It is also worth noting that *Oroonoko* has been published in the past under the title of 'short novel', so a precedent does exist for situating it within the novel tradition.[9] As for *Gulliver's Travels*, the question of its genre has been much debated, but as one critic has summed it up: 'Is *Gulliver* a novel? Probably not, although it is not easy to say (except by arbitrary stipulation) why it is not.'[10] That seems to leave enough latitude to bring it into our survey.

THE TEXTS AND THEIR CONTEXT

The texts to be covered are, in chronological order: Aphra Benn, *Oroonoko*; Daniel Defoe, *Robinson Crusoe*; Jonathan Swift, *Gulliver's Travels*; Samuel Richardson, *Pamela* (1740); Henry Fielding, *Tom Jones*; Charlotte Lennox, *The Female Quixote*; Laurence Sterne, *Tristram Shandy* (1759–67); Ann Radcliffe, *The Mysteries of Udolpho* (1794); William Godwin, *Caleb Williams*; Jane Austen, *Northanger Abbey* (although this will be twinned with *The Female Quixote* for thematic purposes); Sir Walter Scott, *Waverley* (1814); Mary Shelley, *Frankenstein*; James Hogg, *Confessions of a Justified Sinner*.[11] Collectively, they represent an excellent cross-section of the prose fiction of the period, demonstrating its phenomenal breadth and range. The emphasis will be placed on bringing these narratives into contemporary debates on critical cultural issues – race relations, evangelical religious belief, sexual mores in the age of AIDS, public order, state power, contentious scientific experiments and fundamentalist terrorism, for example – with the aim of proving how successful the eighteenth-century novel can be as a medium for social criticism. One of the reasons for that success is that the novel form is able to give extended treatment to issues drawn from the popular culture of its own day: neither poetry nor drama can match it in this regard. The novel form also allows the author considerable freedom to comment on the actions of his or her characters – through the use of a narrator's voice, for example – and thus to reveal the complexity of the socio-political issues that are being addressed.

A brief contextualisation of the works chosen within the more general history of the eighteenth-century English novel seems in order at this point. The novel emerges out of a wide range of fictional and non-fictional sources, and has proved to be a remarkably synthetic form through to the present day. Various commentators have explored its hinterland in news discourse, religious theory, allegory, romance fiction and political theory, amongst many other sources.[12] The works we are considering share that synthetic quality, but they also show how quickly the novel subdivided into a series of sub-genres, with rites of passage narratives vying for readers with the sentimental novel, the novel of sensibility and the Gothic romance, for example (some novels contriving to contain all of these within the one narrative framework). A concern with the individual and his or her relationship to society becomes one of the dominant motifs of eighteenth-century novel writing. What John J. Richetti has referred to as 'the egocentric preferences of the novel' are well represented in our selection, from _Robinson Crusoe's_ intrepid survivor to _Caleb Williams's_ and _Frankenstein's_ alienated and hunted protagonists.[13]

Drawing on postmodern theory, we can identify a conflict between 'little' and 'grand narratives' throughout the eighteenth century, with individuals being subjected to pressures exerted by the dominant ideology of their day. I see this as cashing out in a series of negotiations: women with patriarchy; individuals of both sexes with the class system and its commitment to hierarchy; the ambitious with social convention; political radicals with the _ancien régime_. These negotiations are complex and can test individuals to the limit as they struggle to assert themselves against the prevailing powers in their culture. Robinson Crusoe chooses to defy his father, and the middle-class lifestyle he represents and champions, to express his wanderlust and need for adventure; Pamela has to overcome the twin problems of patriarchy and class if she is to maintain her personal integrity; Caleb Williams finds himself confronted by the full might of what Louis Althusser has called the Repressive State Apparatus for daring to pry into its secrets;[14] Victor Frankenstein pushes science to its very limits in his quest to improve the human condition. On the negative side, Robert Wringhim, in _Confessions of a Justified Sinner_, conceives himself to be a lone crusader against a corrupt and godless humanity, leaving a trail of destruction in his wake.

Whether acting from good or evil impulses, the protagonists of the eighteenth-century novel strikingly often find themselves in conflict with a larger power in this way. That is where much of the interest in these texts lies, in observing how their characters cope with what is often a very unequal struggle that taxes them to the limit, both physically and morally. The moral dilemmas that arise in the novels we shall be studying are no mere abstractions, but ones that affect individual lives very directly – both then and now.

THE GENDER QUESTION

One of the consequences of feminist theory and criticism has been to make us aware of how important women were to the rise of the novel, as authors and as readers, and no work dealing with the period can be unaware of that fact. The notion of a largely male-dominated canon has long since been called into question, and justly so. Women authors are now seen to be central to the development of the eighteenth-century novel and are finally receiving their due credit. Given this, the balance of male and female authors in this particular study calls for explanation. The reason that male authors outnumber female here, by nine to four, is not to be construed as a devaluation of the contribution of the latter. Rather, it is dictated by the topicality of the issues that are being raised. Some texts lend themselves more naturally to discussion in terms of contemporary debates than others do. I have deliberately chosen topical issues rather than more general themes. Thus, although gender issues clearly loom large in both today's culture and the work of the major eighteenth-century female authors, they will appear here in only a subsidiary sense. There is now a substantial body of feminist readings of the gender question in the eighteenth-century novel, and these have been instrumental in demonstrating the presence of some very subversive ideas in the form.[15] But the imperative behind this study is different. The focus here will be on fairly tightly defined current topics such as fundamentalism, racism and government surveillance, and relating them to their eighteenth-century equivalents. Having said that, gender is a critical aspect of the issue of family values in *The Mysteries of Udolpho* and of the impact of popular culture on the young in *The Female Quixote* and *Northanger Abbey*. Then, too, no one confronts the issue of race more directly in the fiction of the period than Aphra Behn. Female authors must not be thought of solely in terms of their contribution to the gender debate; their range is as wide as any male author's, and it underestimates that contribution to see it as purely gender-driven.

USING THE EIGHTEENTH-CENTURY NOVEL

The emphasis of this study, therefore, is on using the eighteenth-century novel to engage with the range of social and political problems that we face now. It is always possible to show just how different a past culture was from our own and those differences certainly need to be borne in mind, especially when we are analysing texts; but equally we can choose to identify the common features and enter into productive dialogue with the past. That is what is proposed here, from *Oroonoko* through to *Confessions of a Justified Sinner*, where we shall find little narrative consistently clashing with grand, individual with system, in a manner that resonates strongly with our own experience despite the gap of several centuries. The issues we shall be highlighting are often as intractable now as they were then, and we have no cause to feel superior to our forebears in our handling of them. Let us see what we can learn from reading the eighteenth-century novel through a selection of such issues, to be outlined at the beginning of each essay before proceeding to the text in question, starting with Aphra Behn's *Oroonoko*.

CHAPTER I

Oroonoko, or, The History of the Royal Slave and Race Relations

THE ISSUE

Race relations is an issue of critical importance throughout Western society, and prejudice against non-white races is still a major social problem in Britain and America. Several racially motivated murders in recent years have shocked public opinion in Britain, for example, casting doubt on the country's claims to be racially tolerant. It has also proved to be notoriously difficult to secure convictions in such cases, which has not helped the situation, with the black community often complaining that the police are not as thorough in investigating crimes against them as they are against other sectors of society. Organisations such as the British National Party (BNP) feed on such prejudice with its belief in the superiority of the white race, and use it to maintain a visible presence within British political life, even to the extent of winning seats in local council elections around the country. Of late, they are trying to market themselves as a more mainstream political party, claiming that it is immigration and overcrowding, rather than race, that are their primary concrerns, although critics regard this as no more than a diversionary tactic designed to fool unsuspecting voters. Movements similar to the BNP can be found in Western Europe, notably in France, with Jean-Marie Le Pen's Front National having a high profile in the French system, and trading quite unashamedly on latent prejudice against non-whites in the country. Multiculturalism may be the ideal in Western European countries, but that does not mean that the official line has persuaded all citizens of its value.

In North America, race still infiltrates all aspects of life, with the mutual suspicion between the black and white communities coming to a head in the high-profile O. J. Simpson case, where the racial divide was particularly clearly marked. For most of white America the not guilty verdict in Simpson's criminal trial in 1995 for the murder of his white wife was a travesty of justice, whereas for most of the black population it represented a victory over a judicial system traditionally strongly biased against them. As far as many in the black community were concerned it was the Los Angeles Police Department, a notoriously racist institution, which was on trial, not Simpson. The latter's subsequent conviction for the same offence in a civil trial, which carried far less stringent punishments (a large fine, which Simpson has not yet paid), failed to alter their perceptions that he was the victim of race hatred. The situation was all the more complicated in that Simpson had been a famous sports star who had gone on to become the acceptable face of black America to white America, being much sought after for advertising endorsements and even appearing in several Hollywood films. For all that he had become a success in a white man's world, the black community could only see this as contingent and feel that when it came to a crisis, as in the murder charge, the white authorities would quickly revert to seeing Simpson as a stereotypically violent black male. Certainly, his legal team in the criminal trial were highly skilled in constructing his defence around just such perceptions – and with the desired outcome for their client.

The latent racism in British society, and the contradictory attitudes it can engender, became a public issue in early 2007 as a result of the *Celebrity Big Brother* reality television show. Footage was shown of two contestants on the show racially abusing one of the others, an Indian film actress, Shilpa Shetty. One of the abusers, Jade Goody, a minor celebrity because of previous appearances on the programme, was voted out of the Big Brother house by viewers, and polls were conducted shortly afterwards to try to determine how representative such views were. These generally concluded they were not, and the government felt compelled to intervene in the controversy, with the Chancellor of the Exchequer, Gordon Brown, who happened to be on an official visit to India at the time, urging Britons to 'vote for tolerance'.[1] More than 40,000 complaints about the programme were subsequently received by Ofcom, the UK's broadcasting regulator, indicating that it had caused widespread public offence and that it was thought some action should be taken against the broadcaster, Channel 4. The latter's claim that the programme had been valuable in bringing the race issue into public debate was generally dismissed as ingenuous at best.

But the incident was also picked up by the Commission for Equality and Human Rights, whose chairman, Trevor Phillips, was less convinced by what the public outcry, backed by sensationalist headlines in the tabloid press, really signified: 'This programme has laid bare the dark heart of private prejudice that all too often sits behind the public veneer of tolerance and it tells us we still have work to do to feel at ease with our diversity.'[2] Channel 4 was accused of broadcasting the footage in a cynical attempt to boost sagging viewing figures, and these did increase significantly from 3.5 to 8.8 million in just a few episodes. Whether that renewed interest constituted proof of innate tolerance or intolerance amongst the audience would be harder to say. Another commentator felt it had simply highlighted the 'everyday racism' that generally went unremarked in British culture.[3] The fact that Jade Goody is of mixed race origin, and thus is a potential target for racial abuse by the less enlightened members of British society, only adds to the general confusion. It could even be said that the reaction against her, particularly by the tabloid press, might have contained a racist element, deeply ironic though that would be.

THE TEXT

Aphra Behn, *Oroonoko, or, The History of the Royal Slave*

Aphra Behn's *Oroonoko* (1688) is one of the first sustained studies of racial prejudice in Western fiction, and if we are going to claim her for the novel, then this is where race enters that tradition as a major theme. The lovers, Oroonoko and Imoinda, both high-born black Africans, are taken as slaves to the English colony of Surinam in South America. Oroonoko leads a revolt of the slaves against their masters, but later surrenders on promise of fair treatment by the colony's governor. Instead, he is betrayed, kills Imoinda to prevent her being sexually abused and is executed with extreme cruelty by the English colonists, for whom he has become a threat to their way of existence – a potent symbol of the massive injustice and inhumanity of slavery as a system.

The 'gallant slave' Oroonoko contrasts sharply with the brutish Europeans, who can never be trusted to keep their word and consistently renege on their promises in a manner that Oroonoko's sense of honour never will allow him to do.[4] Although Behn makes it clear that the Africans are capable of underhand behaviour too (the King of Coramantien sells Imoinda into slavery when she refuses his advances in favour of Oroonoko), her sympathetic treatment of them overall establishes that there is no moral justification for one race enslaving another. As Laura Brown has remarked, *Oroonoko* must be 'recognised as a seminal work in the tradition of antislavery writings from the time of its publication down to our own period. . . . Historians of slavery have never neglected *Oroonoko*.'[5] Given that so much recent criticism of Behn concentrates so emphatically on the gender aspect of her writings, in *Oroonoko* as elsewhere, it is perhaps time to join such voices as Brown's and bring the race issue to the fore in literary critical terms.[6]

Behn is at pains to demonstrate the humanity of the Africans, a humanity that the Europeans wilfully refuse to recognise – except in the special case of Oroonoko, who invariably impresses all those he meets no matter what their race. The maltreatment, stemming from an unthinking belief in white superiority, that has contributed so much to the current impasse between the black and white races, in both the UK and in the US, is made plain by the narrative, and it only takes an event like the O. J. Simpson trial to show how deeply engrained the attitudes of distrust on both sides still are. Slavery may no longer exist, but the attitudes that underpinned the system persist and infect relations between the races to this day.

Oroonoko in particular gives evidence of great nobility of character. Despite a career spent in the military service of his nation, Coramantien, he displays 'that real greatness of soul, those refined notions of true honour, that absolute generosity, and that softness that was capable of the highest passions of love and gallantry'.[7] And all this at a precociously early age. Admittedly, the way Behn describes Oroonoko suggests that the white race is still being held up as the standard for both manners and physical beauty. For a start, Oroonoko's character development has had some European help:

Some part of it we may attribute to the care of a French man of wit and learning, who finding it turn to very good account to be a sort of royal tutor to this young black, and perceiving him very ready, apt, and quick of apprehension, took a great pleasure to teach him morals, language and science.[8]

Oroonoko has also had the benefit of contact with English and Spanish traders, which endows him with yet another layer of sophistication such that he 'addressed himself as if his education had been in some European court'.[9] It begins to sound as if Oroonoko is a walking advertisement for the benefits of Western cultural imperialism: 'a European aristocrat in blackface', in Laura Brown's rather cutting phrase.[10] In appearance he displays many Western characteristics as well, with a 'Roman' nose, thin lips (rather than 'those great turned lips, which are so natural to the rest of the Negroes')[11] and long hair that he keeps straight by means of dressing it with a quill. Even his blackness is different from that of his countrymen: 'His face was not of that brown, rusty black which most of that nation are, but a perfect ebony, or polished jet.'[12] Behn undoubtedly means well, although she can sound very patronising to a twenty-first-century audience. Had Oroonoko been more typical of his race, one wonders if the narrator would have taken much notice of him at all. Oroonoko comes across as an all but honorary white (as to some extent O. J. Simpson became in the aftermath of his sports career), but in reality the colour bar is not broken that easily nor European prejudice so simply overcome. It is skin colour that is the major barrier to acceptance, not features.

Imoinda, too, is measured against Western aesthetic standards, being the 'female to the noble male, the beautiful black Venus to our young Mars', and attractive enough to have 'an hundred white men sighing after her and making a thousand vows at her feet, all vain and unsuccessful'.[13] One does wonder what would have happened had any one of them *been* successful in his efforts to woo her: mixed marriages are difficult enough in most Western societies even now, but in Behn's time were practically unthinkable. There is more than a suggestion that the female narrator is as enamoured of Oroonoko when she encounters him in Surinam, and there is a distinctly erotic quality to her descriptions of his person, but the fact that he is a slave at the time makes the situation even more problematic than it was with Imoinda and her putative white suitors.

Given their superior personal qualities it is unsurprising that Oroonoko and Imoinda are drawn to each other, but their love idyll is shattered by the intervention of his grandfather, the nation's ruler, who forces Imoinda to become one of his many wives, even though he is extremely old and, following Behn's many hints on the topic, most likely impotent. When Oroonoko and Imoinda finally become lovers, she insists that 'she remained a spotless maid till that night, and that what she did with his grandfather had robbed him of no part of her virgin honour'.[14] Even Oroonoko's sexual standards are above those of the rest of his circle, with no suggestion that he will follow the looser morals of the court: 'contrary to the custom of his country, he made her vows she should be the only woman he would possess while he lived; that no age or wrinkles should incline him to change, for her soul would be always fine and always young.'[15] The practice in the court is that royal males take several wives, discarding them as they age in favour of younger brides, so yet again Oroonoko is exhibiting a European sensibility.

Oroonoko's first experience of European double-dealing comes when he is invited aboard an English ship, whose master is an old acquaintance with whom he has traded in slaves in the past (only one of several ironies in a story ostensibly challenging the notion of slavery, including the fact that Oroonoko presents Imoinda with 150 slaves as a token of his love for her). After entertaining Oroonoko and his party, the captain sets sail while they are still drunk, claiming them as slaves in their turn. Thus does Oroonoko find himself transported to the colony of Surinam, where, providentially, he is reunited with Imoinda, now a slave also. On route he is chained in irons, but such is his influence amongst his countrymen that he has to be unshackled before they will agree to end the hunger fast they have embarked upon in protest at their capture. Not for the last time in the narrative an Englishman finds his authority undermined by the moral integrity being displayed by one 'whose honour was such as he never had violated a word in his life'.[16]

Even when in captivity in the colony Oroonoko cuts an impressive figure, and his sheer charisma impels the English colonists to accord him special treatment:

[H]e was received more like a governor than a slave. Notwithstanding, as the custom was, they assigned him his portion of land, his house and his business up in the plantation. But as it was more for form than any design to put him to the task, he endured no more of the slave but the name, and remained some days in the house, receiving all visits that were made him without stirring towards that part of the plantation where the Negroes were.[17]

The new name Oroonoko is given by his captors, Caesar, is further proof of the high regard in which he is held; reinforced by the narrator's effusive comments that 'he wanted no part of the personal courage of that Caesar, and acted things as memorable, had they been done in some part of the world replenished with people and historians that might have given him his due'.[18] Considering that the narrator is writing Oroonoko's life story after he has led a slave revolt against the English settlers of whom the narrator is one (and has initially feared rape at the hands of the insurrectionaries), this is striking testimony to his powerful personality. This is a culture which reveres classical heroes, and no higher compliment can be paid Oroonoko than to compare him to one of the greatest of Romans. He even conspires to be an Enlightenment man *avant la lettre* in his attitude to the Christian religion, stating that he 'would never be reconciled to our notions of the Trinity, of which he ever made a jest; it was a riddle he said, would turn his brain to conceive, and one could not make him understand what faith was'.[19] Significantly enough, this draws no criticism from the narrator, who simply notes it in passing.

Oroonoko's charisma even wins over the local population, who are as drawn to him as the narrator and the English colonists are, thus enabling good relations to be established between the Indians and the settlers (the latter being wary of the former, 'their numbers so far surpassing ours in that continent').[20] In all respects he proves himself to be a superior being to anyone with whom he comes into contact, his honour and intelligence shining through at all times – as well as his bravery, which extends to killing tigers single-handed. When eventually he is betrayed by unscrupulous colonists, the injustice of his treatment at their hands is all the more shocking.

The narrator is at pains also to make it clear how justified the slaves are to rise up in revolt, and that Oroonoko considers himself honour-bound to assume their leadership. Stung by Imoinda's distress at the thought of their unborn child being a slave too, Oroonoko is spurred into action on behalf of his fellow countrymen, and in consequence he made an harangue to 'em of the miseries and ignominies of slavery, counting up all their toils and sufferings under such loads, burdens and drudgeries as were fitter for beasts than men, senseless brutes, than human souls. . . . '[W]e are bought and sold like apes or monkeys, to be the sport of women, fools and cowards, and the support of rogues, runagates, that have abandoned their own countries for rapine, murders, thefts, and villainies.'[21]

It is a searing indictment of the colonial enterprise, which is revealed as the exploitative system that in reality it was, and Oroonoko once again is seen to occupy the moral high ground in comparison with the European settlers, thus further enhancing his already considerable personal stature. At such points Oroonoko is almost a prototype for later heroes of black consciousness like Martin Luther King, his eloquence foregrounding the iniquity of differential treatment on the grounds of race alone. This is undercut, however, by the hero's acceptance of slavery as a consequence of defeat in battle (hence his possession of the slaves he gifts to Imoinda). His main objection to his condition in Surinam is that it has been achieved by deceit rather than by martial valour on the part of the English: 'Have they vanquished us nobly in fight? Have they won us in honourable battle? And are we by the chance of war become their slaves?'[22] The revolt that Oroonoko leads is as much a matter of personal honour as it is of humanitarian considerations, although the mere fact of stating the former raises the possibility of the latter. The colonists are not likely to make such fine distinctions, however, and for them Oroonoko has become a dangerous role model for discontented slaves.

It requires duplicity on the part of the English rulers of the colony before the slave revolt is put down, with false promises being made to Oroonoko yet again. Despite his belief that 'there was no faith in the white men or the gods they adored', Oroonoko is prevailed upon to surrender, whereupon his fears are confirmed and he is subjected to brutal torture.[23] The governor's council, consisting 'of such notorious villains as Newgate never transported', decide to make an example of Oroonoko in order to frighten the slave population into submission, and he is sentenced to death.[24] His supporters amongst the settlers rush to his aid and are successful in obtaining sanctuary for him, but the upshot is that in his despair he kills Imoinda and their unborn child to protect her from the risk of sexual assault at the hands of the

governor's men. Oroonoko is subsequently hacked to pieces by an exe-
cutioner, which simply goes to show the depths of cruelty to which his
captors are capable of descending. Despite the impression he has made
on much of the white population, Oroonoko is sacrificed to uphold the
system of slavery by which the colony thrives. The colonial enterprise
in general is made to look sordid and inhuman by his fate, and there is
no question as to where the moral victory lies at the end of the narrative. That colonialism can bring out the very worst in human nature
registers with great clarity.

Questions have been raised, however, as to whether the narrative
really makes an explicitly anti-racist point. Oroonoko after all is not
very representative of his race. S. J. Wiseman, for example, refers to
'the paradox of Oroonoko's different and ambivalent status – as royal
and slave, educated noble and rebel, European and African, reader's
erotic object and dangerous other, economic unit and tale-teller'.[25]
Oroonoko is not one of the masses, and it is his fate, rather than that
of the slave population as a whole, that attracts the narrator, and quite
probably most of the text's early readers. Ros Ballaster emphasises the
metaphorical side of Oroonoko's character, arguing that he 'serves less
as a symbol of ethnic superiority than as a model of absolute virtue isolated in a politically and socially corrupt environment'.[26] *Oroonoko* in
this sense is very much of the romance tradition, with both the hero
and Imoinda aspiring to mythic status, and the more that happens the
more we are diverted from the horrors of the colonial system to their
personal circumstances. It is with those two, rather than with the slave
trade, that the narrator takes her leave of us:

> Thus died this great man; worthy of a better fate, and a more
> sublime wit than mine to write his praise; yet I hope the reputa-
> tion of my pen is considerable enough to make his glorious name
> to survive to all ages, with that of the brave, the beautiful, and the
> constant Imoinda.[27]

The not so brave and not so beautiful other African slaves, now bereft
of their charismatic and resourceful leader and with him any real hope
of return to their native country, merit no closing mention.

We might just wonder too about the message that Oroonoko's
death sends to its audience. Behn is to be applauded for insisting on her

hero's humanity and intelligence, and thus calling into question white views on the inferiority of other races, views still only too prevalent in the West today. But his death suggests that any concerted challenge to these prejudices will be unwelcome. If Oroonoko demonstrates that blacks do not conform to white stereotypes, then he must be destroyed: the myth of white supremacy has to be upheld, as it would not long survive if others began to emulate him. It is that possibility as much as anything that disturbs the colonial rulers: that other Oroonokos may start to come through the ranks of the subjugated. Despite being abandoned by all except Imoinda and his compatriot Tuscan as the revolt loses momentum, Oroonoko still projects a powerful image of what black slaves are capable of if they choose to stand up to their masters. (Anyone who can kill a tiger single-handed surely has to be feared.) The fact that the sympathetic narrator and all of Oroonoko's white supporters in the colony, can only stand by powerless as he is executed in the most savage of fashions by being dismembered, able to do no more than mourn his fate and promise to keep his deeds alive in memory, is very telling (although at least one critic, Jane Spencer, has excused the narrator on the grounds of her gender rendering her a 'helpless' spectator to the proceedings).[28] Even if they would not go so far in cruelty themselves, the system itself is tacitly accepted: the colony will survive. There is an unspoken recognition that Oroonoko can only be a divisive force amongst them and that his death is probably inevitable: gallant slaves and colonies are mutually exclusive.

We could say that Oroonoko is executed both for his blackness and for his Europeanness, neither of which is acceptable to the colonial powers. The more of the latter he displays, the shakier the assumptions underlying slavery are made to appear: if he can develop a European sensibility, then it is not unique to whites. Such a talent notwithstanding, he leaves the slave system intact, indicating a degree of ambivalence on the author's part as to what the best way forward is on this question. When Oroonoko's slaughtered body is cut into quarters and circulated amongst some of the main plantations of the colony, the response of Colonel Martin, a staunch supporter of Oroonoko in the past, is very instructive: he

> refused it, and swore, he had rather see the quarters of Banister
> [the instigator of Oronooko's execution] and the governor himself,
> than those of Caesar, on his plantations, and that he could govern

his Negroes without terrifying and grieving them with frightful spectacles of a mangled king.[29]

Neither Oroonoko's personality nor his grisly fate has led Martin to reconsider the ethics of slavery itself, and his humanitarian feelings go no further than the issue of treatment. Freeing the slaves is not an option for a plantation owner; the 'Negroes' are 'his' to dispose of and he sees no contradiction in this. Oroonoko may have been exempted from slave treatment, but he must remain an exception; his experience cannot be generalised.

In S. J. Wiseman's assessment, 'the text lays bare some of the irreconcilable paradoxes of Eurocentric perceptions of difference and similarity, only to erase them'.[30] I think this is a bit harsh and that we must not underestimate the critical side of the author's portrait of colonial life, but one can see how the text's many contradictions could inspire such a judgement. The author makes Oroonoko more than a black slave, but it is as a black slave that he has to be treated. He is a noble savage, but exceptional in being so, only Imoinda being remotely comparable to him in character. As far as the plantation owners are concerned, their slaves are in a different category from such figures as Oroonoko, and as we know, they would continue to be thought so for well over century before slavery was finally abolished in British territories worldwide – and much later than that in other areas, such as America. We all know, too, that the abolition of slavery did not lead to the abolition of racial prejudice. Many would also argue that the trading relationship that obtains between the West and the Third World, where much of the West's consumer goods are now manufactured, amounts to a form of modern slavery, with wages often barely meeting subsistence levels and workers having almost no legal protection at all against job-related illness or injury. The anti-globalisation movement, which has created such a fuss in recent years, is a prime source of such arguments and is dedicated to bringing these to the widest possible public attention.[31]

The narrative's handling of the slavery issue, except in Oroonoko's case, is very matter of fact. Oroonoko himself, as already noted, has traded in slaves with the English. It is the practice in Africa for captives taken in battle to be sold into slavery, and this goes unquestioned by the narrator, who, as a resident in the colony of Surinam, well knows the benefits to be gained from slaves: in effect, the colony would not exist without them (which is no doubt why Indian slaves are being drafted in too). Since the narrator is so complimentary about Oroonoko's military prowess, this being part of his larger-than-life personality and general superiority, it is almost as if he is being absolved of any blame in the enterprise. Slaves are simply spoils of war (even slaves Oroonoko himself has sold into slavery express 'veneration' for him as their conqueror), but whether Europeans should take advantage of such cultural traditions is left unaddressed.[32] Only when the 'gallant' Oroonoko is enslaved, 'an indignity to his class rather than his race' as Ros Ballaster puts it, does any ethical consideration seem to arise, which indicates a narrow perspective on the issue in general[33] – slaves are fully acceptable, but gallant slaves are not. The narrator's implication in the colonial system means that her sympathy can only be extended very selectively.

For all that Behn is drawing on her own experience of a stay in Surinam however, the narrator cannot necessarily be identified with the author. This is an argument pursued by Jacqueline Pearson, for whom the narrator is engaged in an 'elaborate process of guilt and self-justification' which the careful reader can identify.[34] In Pearson's view, the narrator becomes 'a highly effective part of Behn's critique of subordination, of slaves and of women', suggesting that something other than an erasure of 'irreconcilable paradoxes' occurs at the narrative's end.[35] The fact that the narrator is so 'divided between sympathy and fear for the royal slaves and doubt and complacency about her own female powers and abilities, between criticism of European colonialism and her desire to earn the approval of the colonists' means that those paradoxes are only too apparent when the narrator signs off:[36] the reader can see through the narrator's tactics. Simple though the tale may be, there is from this perspective a high degree of sophistication in its unfolding, with the author being more aware of the ideological contradictions involved than some critics may be willing to give her credit for – even if she is unable, either directly or through her narrator, to resolve them entirely. But then racism continues to generate such contradictions through into our twenty-first-century experience.

CONCLUSION

It is still a widely held view amongst the white population worldwide that the black population is culturally inferior, and arguments have even been tendered that this is a genetic difference between the races.[37] Some blacks do manage to break through this stereotype, and are regarded somewhat in the manner of Oroonoko as larger-than-life personalities who merit a different response from the norm. Sports stars, for example, are very often held up as role models and do manage to inspire a certain amount of respect, even amongst racially prejudiced sports fans. The French football team that won the World Cup and the European Championship in recent years (1998, 2000) was felt to have made a very significant contribution towards improving race relations in France in the aftermath of those triumphs, as many of the team were either black or of Arab descent. Events since then have indicated this was only a brief reaction, however, and the incidence of racial prejudice in the country has not necessarily changed all that much. Le Pen continues to be a figure of some considerable note in French political life, his appeal based largely on his ability to stir up racial prejudice amongst the white electorate. Even the Left in France is culpable on this issue, with a leading politician in the Socialist Party complaining about the racial composition of the French team: 'I am ashamed for this country. soon there will be eleven blacks.'[38]

Rather as with Oroonoko, sports stars are mentally placed in a different category by most supporters rather than generalised on, and the same phenomenon can be seen at work in other European countries and North America. The fact that racial abuse of players is still so common throughout European football and the subject of frequent official complaints (which are quite often glossed over by the authorities, embarrassed at the bad publicity it brings) suggests that the exploits of black heroes are not on their own sufficient to overcome entrenched cultural prejudices. Spectators are quite capable of supporting black players on their own side while simultaneously racially abusing those on the other: 'the irreconcilable paradoxes of European perceptions' of race are still very much in evidence at such times.

Eventually that is the benefit of a text like *Oroonoko* for us: that it reveals some of the major ideological contradictions that lie at the heart of race relations and continue to create problems in our culture. We are still capable of differential treatment of individuals on the basis of their race and still capable of prejudice in the face of evidence to the contrary – generalising on bad traits displayed by individuals, refusing to generalise on good ones. *Oroonoko* demonstrates the quagmire we can get ourselves into over such issues, identifying the blind spots, or evasions, that keep prejudice alive. We can idolise black sportsmen, but discriminate against their racial compatriots, failing to recognise the contradiction that this entails, or the injustice. Laura Brown has observed that 'the treatment of slavery in *Oroonoko* is neither coherent nor fully critical', but much the same can be said about the white attitude to other races in general.[39] The *Celebrity Big Brother* episode (discussed earlier) suggests that incoherence is only too likely to surface when race enters the scene, and Behn is to be applauded for having caught this so faithfully in the English novel's first major analysis of the racial issue.

CHAPTER 2

The Life and Strange Surprizing Adventures of Robinson Crusoe, Born-Again Theology and Intelligent Design

THE ISSUE

Evangelical Christianity has been an important factor in American life over the last few decades, both socially and politically.[1] It has been estimated that 35 per cent of the population there attends an evangelical church.[2] One of the key elements of evangelicalism is the notion that individuals can be 'born again', experiencing a dramatic renewal of their faith, leading to a belief in a very direct personal relationship with God and Christ. This can have the effect of convincing individuals that they are doing God's bidding in their daily lives, making them feel immune to criticism. President George W. Bush, for example, believes that he was called upon by God to resolve the political crisis in the Middle East by such actions as the invasion of Iraq in 2003. Such views tend to be held very dogmatically and are not open to negotiation – the individual just *knows* God is on his or her side and acts accordingly. Since negotiation lies at the very heart of the democratic process, the combination of evangelical religion and politics is not a particularly happy one – certainly not for secularists, in whose opinion religion and politics ought to be kept scrupulously separate. Although strongest in America, evangelical Christianity is increasingly active in missionary work around the globe and its ranks are steadily growing (by an estimated 3 per cent a year in the US), rendering it a force to be reckoned with in contemporary life. Secularism as a cultural ideal is increasingly under strain in the West in consequence, a development that the non-religious can only look on with dismay.

The roots of the evangelical movement can be traced back to radical Protestant sectarianism in the seventeenth and eighteenth centuries, which encouraged a similar sense of a very personal relationship between the believer and God. In Britain in the period the nonconformist movement, heavily influenced by Calvinist theology, espoused the belief that humanity was divided into the elect and the reprobate (the saved and the damned) and that unless individuals went through a 'conversion experience' – essentially an intense spiritual epiphany – they had no proof of their fitness for election. Spiritual autobiographies, the spiritual diaries that became so popular in the period, particularly amongst nonconformists, traded on such notions, portraying the believer's life as a series of trials and tribulations until he or she underwent the defining conversion experience. John Bunyan's spiritual autobiography, *Grace Abounding to the Chief of Sinners* (1666), is a classic example, with the author representing himself as a lost soul prey to psychologically destabilising fears and anxieties until God gives him unmistakable evidence of his grace being extended:

> But one day, as I was passing in the field, and that too with some dashes on my conscience, fearing lest yet all was not right, suddenly this sentence fell upon my soul, *Thy righteousness is in heaven*; and methought withal, I saw with the eyes of my soul Jesus Christ at God's right hand, there, I say, as my righteousness[.] . . . Now did my chains fall off my legs indeed, I was loosed from my afflictions and irons, my temptations also fled away: so that from that time those dreadful scriptures of God left off to trouble me; now went I also home rejoicing, for the grace and love of God[.][3]

The outcome of such an intense commitment to a personal, salvation-based theology was an unshakeable confidence in the rightness of one's actions as an instrument of God's will, which easily could harden into fundamentalism.[4] It is a process which is only too evident in our own age in evangelical circles: doubt is not a characteristic feature of such believers' outlook. While this is not an issue to secularists as long as it remains personal, it most certainly is when it comes to inform political policy-making. As the novelist Martin Amis has observed of contemporary American politics: 'All US presidents – and all US presidential candidates – have to be religious or have to pretend to be religious. More specifically, they have to subscribe to "born again" Christianity.'[5]

Such a theology also encourages belief in intelligent design, which has become a very powerful theory in evangelical circles, particularly in America, although its influence is beginning to spread globally. Intelligent design bases its view of the creation of the universe firmly in the Old Testament, specifically the Book of Genesis, which relates that God created the world in six days.[6] For the believer in intelligent design there are no accidents, and everything about the state of the universe has been precisely engineered – by God – to be that way. Both at the micro level of the individual's life and the macro level of the entire universe everything is deemed to fit together too neatly for it to be anything other than deliberate.[7] Such ideas, again particularly in the US, have a significant political resonance. They affect the educational system (where intelligent design is now widely taught), and even more crucially, the teaching and practice of science, with scientists increasingly finding themselves under attack from evangelical zealots. The impact of born-again theology has to concern us all.

THE TEXT

Daniel Defoe, *The Life and Strange Surprizing Adventures of Robinson Crusoe*

Daniel Defoe's *Robinson Crusoe* (1719) is structured on the pattern of spiritual autobiography, and the hero's own conversion experience, while stranded on an uninhabited desert island, effectively turns him into a born-again Christian with the deeply personal relationship to God that is so characteristic of the evangelical ethos. Being born again means that he feels a sense of security that was never there previously in his life (until then a series of fairly hair-raising adventures), and he comes to believe that God is watching over him closely and directing his career. When Crusoe reads the Bible it is as though God were speaking directly to him, guiding him towards those passages most appropriate to his condition so that he can reflect on God's likely purposes for him – and God will do so on a regular basis throughout his stay on the island. At a later stage in the narrative, when other marooned European sailors are offered sanctuary on the island, Crusoe claims governorship of the territory with all the assurance of a born-again politician convinced he is implementing God's will. Whether he is justified in this assumption is another question, as it is also in the case of all latter-day born-again claimants, such as President George W. Bush. That is why secularists have to be on their guard about what such figures do: inner conviction can be carried to extremes, as many consider has happened with Bush in Iraq.

Crusoe offers an intriguing insight into the workings of born-again theology on the individual psyche that can help us to understand what drives its present-day adherents and where they gain their inner conviction from, particularly their acute sense of being guided by God and of being an instrument of His will. It can also indicate how justified they really are in claiming that conviction. Given evangelical Christianity's influence in America, and thus by extension global politics, these are issues of some note for all of us.

The imprint of spiritual autobiography on the narrative of *Robinson Crusoe* is clear to see. As the classic study on this topic puts it: 'the hero's vicissitudes, highly individual and complex as they appear to be, actually follow a conventional and regular pattern of spiritual evolution.'[8] Crusoe describes a sinning youth, significantly involving a rejection of his father's advice to settle down into a middle-class lifestyle, and a run of adventures that tests his character severely – storms at sea, slavery at the hands of Barbary pirates and ultimately shipwreck on a remote island off the coast of South America where his survival is dependent on his ingenuity and strength of will. That strength and ingenuity are felt to be derived from God, however, with Crusoe undergoing the characteristic conversion experience that rescues him from a state of personal despair (Despair being his only too apt name for his island):[9]

> I was earnestly begging of God to give me Repentance, when it happen'd providentially the very Day that reading the Scripture, I came to these Words, *He is exalted a Prince and a Saviour, to give Repentance, and to give Remission*: I threw down the Book, and with my Heart as well as my Hands lifted up to Heaven, in a Kind of Extasy of Joy, I cry'd out aloud, *Jesus, thou Son of David, Jesus, thou exalted Prince and Saviour, give me Repentance!*[10]

Once his study of the Bible begins to reveals comforting messages such as this, Crusoe's life improves markedly, in terms of both his psychological and physical condition. He ceases to wallow in self-pity, now convinced that God is on his side and his survival guaranteed: 'My Condition began now to be, tho' not less miserable as to my Way of living, yet much easier to my Mind.'[11]

The assumption has to be that he has been chosen by God to be one of the elect to whom salvation will be granted, and the upturn in his fortunes from that point onwards is unmistakable. Crusoe certainly feels as if he has undergone a dramatic change of consciousness that signals a new beginning in his life:

> This was the first Time that I could say, in the true Sense of the Words, that I pray'd in all my Life; for now I pray'd with a Sense of my Condition, and with a true Scripture View of Hope founded on the Encouragement of the Word of God; and from this Time, I may say, I began to have Hope that God would hear me.[12]

The notion of one's life having changed utterly, of having taken on a new personality and sloughed off the old, sinful one, is the defining feature of born-again theology, and that is what Crusoe is going through at this point: rebirth into his faith, with all the psychological benefits that this brings. He can now recognise there was a reason for his being singled out from the rest of his shipmates to survive the shipwreck: the event is not to be put down to mere luck.

The relationship to God is notably personal, there being no clergy around to mediate between Crusoe and the divine in his isolated condition (a characteristically Protestant 'dream', as John Allen Stevenson puts it).[13] The metaphor is particularly strong, with Crusoe having to find God on his own in what is an intensely personal quest: Calvinist Protestantism would expect no less of him. In the best evangelical tradition, Crusoe communes with God through the Bible, accepting what his readings of the text appear to tell him about his fate as if they were divinely sanctioned. For such a character the Bible is literal truth, and its words carry an immense weight of authority that goes beyond any possible challenge. When an understandable sense of anguish over his protracted isolation descends on Crusoe on occasion, Scripture is always available to come to the rescue:

> One Morning being very sad, I open'd the Bible upon these Words, *I will never, never leave thee, nor forsake thee*; immediately it occurr'd, That these Words were to me, Why else should they be directed in such a Manner, just at the Moment when I was mourning over my Condition, as one forsaken of God and Man?[14]

Such scriptural literalness continues to mark out the born-again in our own time, with the Bible being taken as an infallible guide on how to conduct oneself and interpret one's experience.

The impact of being born again is to give one's life a narrative structure, with the individual coming to realise that he has progressed from sin to salvation according to God's preordained plan: his very own intelligent design, as it were, prepared for him alone. To have followed that narrative line is to have joined the ranks of the elect, and as a member of the elect individuals are automatically part of the universal struggle being waged against evil, which means that their actions have a much wider significance than merely the personal. Everything the individual does counts, for it is a direct expression of God's will; everything that happens is a sign from God and demands to be interpreted. Any upturn in fortune is thus to be read as an example of divine grace being extended towards the individual: for the born-again, providence is everywhere, and in modern terms equates to intelligent design. When his crops of barley, rice and corn flourish despite the concerted efforts of the local wildlife to consume them before they ripen, Crusoe detects God's hand at work, despite the fact that he has shown great determination and ingenuity in protecting the crops himself. All human effort is to be subsumed under the divine will, which must be awarded the full credit for whatever good fortune occurs. If God had not wanted Crusoe to survive, then none of the precautions he took against the local wildlife, such as shooting some birds and hanging them up amongst his crops to act as a deterrent to the others, would have been successful. God, after all, has dominion over all species.

The period differentiated between particular and general providence, the former involving direct divine intervention into human affairs, the latter underpinning the operation of the universe as a whole. By guaranteeing Crusoe's harvest, the particular makes its presence felt, much to Crusoe's relief and the reinforcement of his faith (although it is worth noting that belief was soon to decline in eighteenth-century English culture at the expense of the general).

The belief in providentialism can sustain the individual through the dark days that will continue to inflict even those apparently picked out for salvation. When Crusoe famously stumbles upon 'the Print of a Man's naked Foot on the Shore' after several years of isolation on the island, he is thrown into a state of panic that sends him scurrying back to his fortified lair thinking his life is in imminent danger.[15] His faith is temporarily shaken by this discovery, and he admits that 'my Fear banish'd all my religious Hope'.[16] Once the initial shock wears off, however, and he manages to persuade himself that the footprint is not likely to be the work of the devil, Crusoe's belief in being part of a providential plan gradually reasserts itself. He can even resign himself to the possibility that God may after all eventually consign him to damnation rather than salvation, meekly noting that ''twas my unquestion'd Duty to resign my self absolutely and entirely to his Will'.[17] But his doubts about his spiritual state are finally dispelled when the words of Scripture that first suggested God was protecting him on the island recur in his mind: '*Call upon me in the Day of Trouble, and I will deliver, and thou shalt glorify me*'.[18] The comforting memory inspires him to turn to the Bible again, and the first words that come to his attention on opening it are '*Wait on the Lord, and be of good Cheer, and he shall strengthen thy Heart; wait, I say, on the Lord*'.[19] From Crusoe's theological perspective it can be no accident that those words in particular present themselves to him at this critical juncture in his life: providence is plainly reiterating its support and reminding him of its power to intervene when and where necessary. We can see how ideas like intelligent design could develop from such a perspective, with providence demonstrating its awareness of even the smallest details of life in the universe.

Crusoe firmly believes that he is fulfilling the role of God's agent on the island, and one of the tasks this bestows on him is to evangelise on God's behalf if and when the opportunity occurs. Friday is his first convert, with Crusoe convinced that he is bringing him into the only true faith by eradicating Friday's savage past. Crusoe accepts it as his duty to act out a missionary role:

> During the long Time that *Friday* has now been with me, and that he began to speak to me, and understand me, I was not wanting to lay a Foundation of religious Knowledge in his Mind; . . . I began to instruct him in the Knowledge of the true God.[20]

Despite Crusoe's efforts, Friday manages to pinpoint some of the major weaknesses in Christian theology (which no doubt must have exercised the author as well, to be able to put them as provocatively as he does), querying, for example, how an omnipotent God could find himself locked in a protracted conflict with the forces of evil: '*But . . . if God much strong, much might as the Devil, why God no kill the Devil, so make him no more do wicked?*'[21] Crusoe's answer that God will prevail '*at last*' merely provokes Friday to ask, quite reasonably, '*Why not kill the Devil now, not kill great ago?*'[22] Confronted by one of the major paradoxes of his theological system, Crusoe is forced to dissemble and eventually to ask for God's help on the matter through prayer. The issue is, not surprisingly, fudged, with Crusoe taking delight in being appointed 'an Instrument under Providence to save the Life, and *for ought I knew*, the Soul of a poor Savage, and bring him to the true Knowledge of Religion, and of the Christian Doctrine', rather than engaging any further with the troubling theological dilemma, which is thereafter quietly dropped.[23]

While such a move may have satisfied readers at the time, it is far less persuasive now (except to the most committed of evangelicals), since it merely sidesteps the issue of omnipotence on which any monotheistic theology is dependent. If this is cast in doubt, then so is the entire religion, which loses its main source of appeal. All we are told by Crusoe in this instance is that after another 'long Discourse with him upon the Subject of the Redemption of Man by the Saviour of the World', Friday is won over and transformed into 'a good Christian' from then onwards – and good Christians cease asking awkward questions.[24] Despite both the character's and the author's sleight of hand, we are made aware that there are gaps in the theology, which can only be covered over by faith. To the secular that is never going to be a satisfactory resolution. Again, this poses no problem if it remains at the level of the personal, but it does when it becomes a basis for political action.

When Crusoe finally encounters another European on his island, a Spaniard whom he rescues from natives from the mainland intending to engage in a ritual of human sacrifice, he is not slow to adopt a proprietorial air towards him. Having freed Friday's father at the same time, he can now claim the existence of a proper community on the island, a community Crusoe proceeds to regard as his subjects:

My Island was now peopled, and I thought my self very rich in Subjects; and it was a merry Reflection which I frequently made, How like a King I look'd. First of all, the whole Country was my own meer Property; so that I had an undoubted Right of Dominion. 2*dly*, My People were perfectly subjected: I was absolute Lord and Law-giver; they all owed their Lives to me, and were ready to lay down their Lives, *if there had been Occasion of it*, for me.[25]

Crusoe even goes to the extent of granting 'Liberty of Conscience' to these subjects, although we know this has not been so in the case of Friday (presumably it extends to Catholics only, although it is worth noting that this is a very liberal position for the time).[26] Discovering from the Spaniard that there are another sixteen marooned European sailors on the nearby mainland, Crusoe authorises him to bring them to the island to escape the hostile natives, but only on condition that on arrival they too come under his command. The island's population is soon swelled further by a ship whose crew have mutinied and cast away the captain and two others on the island to perish. In conjunction with the captain and his other 'subjects', Crusoe succeeds in quelling the mutiny, thus paving the way for his eventual release.

Overruling the captain, Crusoe decrees that the mutineers can remain on the island as settlers while he returns to England with the ship, and it is noticeable how forcefully he asserts his authority over this issue. The captain is informed that 'they were my Prisoners, not his', with Crusoe declaring himself angry that the captain is refusing to acknowledge his governing power while on the island itself. He leaves behind what is in effect a colony, still considering himself to be its lawful ruler and everyone there – shortly to be joined by the Spanish and Portuguese contingent – to be his subjects. When he returns to the island several years later in the *The Farther Adventures of Robinson Crusoe* (1719) that is how he conceives of himself, as its homecoming governor whose inhabitants are expected to submit to his will and follow his governing dictates. For David Trotter, however, the hero 'demonstrates his unfitness for the positions of authority' that he claims over his island and its inhabitants by indulging his restlessly wandering spirit.[27] We are left with a picture of the character somewhat at odds with his vision of himself as a channel of the divine will: an unfinished individual rather than one with a completely worked-out narrative line. It is one of the drawbacks of providentialism and intelligent design, of course, that they make sense in retrospect only.

Born-again theology is not without its contradictions, therefore, and Crusoe certainly displays these in his thought and behaviour. He does not always heed God's warning signs as closely as he should, for instance, and the narrative of the first volume of his adventures ends with the hero embarking on yet another extended sea voyage, despite having been notably unfortunate at sea in his youth, culminating in his shipwreck on his island, Despair. Crusoe has already been told by a ship's captain after his first, very stormy, voyage, that this experience has been a warning from God (particular providence in action yet again):

> *Young Man*, says he, *you ought never to go to Sea any more, you ought to take this for a plain and visible Token that you are not to be a Seafaring Man. . . . [A]s you made this Voyage for a Trial, you see what a Taste Heaven has given you of what you are to expect if you persist.*[28]

But persist he does, with fairly drastic consequences; and persist he is still doing at the end of his first book of adventures. One can only assume that he is now confident that providence will always protect him, no matter what action he may take. This proves to be true in the longer term, but it takes twelve more years of frequently life-threatening escapades around the world, as outlined in *The Farther Adventures*, before Crusoe returns to England and security.[29] It could be argued that his sense of election has made him foolhardy; even that it has led him to challenge providence and God's will.[30] As Maximilian E. Novak points out, Crusoe is someone who 'sins in spite of his religious faith', which does raise some questions as to its depth – questions we would never ask about the faith of John Bunyan, for example, or Bunyan's main fictional protagonist, Christian, in *The Pilgrim's Progress*.[31]

The erratic quality of Crusoe's adventures might also make us question the notion of intelligent design. We might be moved to ask first why such design would require Crusoe to disregard the wishes of his father, who has the privileged position of being God's representative in the family and therefore the right to expect obedience from his children. Spiritual autobiography demands such a sinning youth, it is part of its standard narrative form which moves from sin to redemption (and back again various times before ultimate resolution), but it seems a long-winded way of bringing about a recognition of God's power over our lives. Then we might wonder why Crusoe's personal salvation can only be engineered at the expense of the death of all his unfortunate shipmates, drowned in the storm that shipwrecks him on the island. Presumably they are to be considered part of the reprobate and therefore expendable, but this seems extremely harsh (just as the modern reader is troubled at the fate of the meek and mild Ignorance in *The Pilgrim's Progress*, summarily thrown into hell from the gates of heaven). Defoe's contemporaries had fewer problems with this notion, with the Anglican Bishop Simon Patrick asserting in a sermon that '[n]o ship is cast away upon the Sea . . . but God is perfectly pleased with it, and it is impossible that any should judge so well as he, what is most convenient', but for anyone outside the born-again constituency this is an abhorrent argument which seems to mock human misery.[32] The resignation to God's will that Bishop Patrick is calling for feels more like collusion with a deeply unfair ideology. Why Crusoe needs a further set of adventures after having gone through the conversion experience and being rescued is also somewhat mystifying. He appears to learn nothing of real note in volume 2, and there is little sense of significant character development or deepening of his faith in his subsequent, somewhat aimless wanderings around the globe.

A providential pattern is harder and harder to discern as Crusoe's career unfolds, and one would have to say that he often gives the impression of taking providence for granted. It is just such a peripatetic lifestyle that leads at least one critic, Ian A. Bell, to question whether the narrative can 'be wholly assimilated to the world of spiritual autobiography'.[33] Certainly, the sense of intense religious belief that characterises a figure like Bunyan in the post-conversion phase of his spiritual autobiography is there only episodically in Crusoe's case, especially once he leaves the island and return to his old, footloose lifestyle. Bell questions theologically inspired readings of Defoe's work in general, arguing that God is simply a 'narrative assumption' on the author's part,[34] although I would rather see it, as I indicate above, as a case of the hero wrestling with the contradictions and inconsistencies of his belief system.

The get-out clause of the intelligent design lobby is always that, echoing Bishop Patrick, we are mere humans who can only ever guess at God's ways, which, as John Milton too was forced to concede in *Paradise Lost* (1667), can test our intellectual abilities quite severely.[35] Much as we try to understand these ways (and Milton tried harder than most of his contemporaries), they will lie forever beyond our comprehension, so we cannot criticise apparent contradictions since they will not be such to God (it would be all but heretical to think they could be). To say the least, this makes it difficult to debate with evangelicals, who will continue to assume design is present even in the most chaotic sequence of events – which is what Crusoe's life will appear to most non-religious readers. Providence's intelligent design is a given for the born-again, however, who cannot conceive of there being such things as chance happenings or accidents. Their lives are to be viewed as having a predetermined conclusion, which, paradoxically enough as it may seem to many of us now, they find a source of great comfort. For such believers God is manifestly not just a 'narrative assumption', but rather a narrative creator of great skill, and they are the raw material of the narrative, patiently recording its predetermined progress as a tribute to divine omnipotence. Which is to say that belief in both particular and general providence still exists: the particular in the life of the individual, generating the born-again experience; the general in the working out of God's master plan in the universe from the creation onwards. The difference in terminology notwithstanding, Crusoe's world and that of modern-day evangelicals are linked across the centuries.

CONCLUSION

Crusoe's career helps us to appreciate the mind-set and outlook of the born-again, but, even more interestingly, it reveals some of the glaring gaps in the theology, not least in its assumption of a providential intelligent design lying behind all human affairs. This has to be taken entirely on trust, even though the evidence for it is often scanty: Crusoe's life, for example, features far more bad fortune than good (Ian Bell's reading of the text continues to deserve consideration in this respect). One has to be very selective, and the born-again do tend to be, picking out what fits their scheme and discarding or ignoring what does not (or treating the latter as part of a divine master-plan that goes beyond human comprehension, and therefore just has to be accepted).

Those of us worried about what the born-again in positions of power may do (how many Iraq-style invasions do we want?) need to keep drawing attention to this selectivity and the gaps and contradictions it is attempting to cover up. It does come to mind to wonder just how many times Crusoe has to consult the Bible to find an appropriate message; most of us opening it at random tend to find far less pointed references.

It is the loose ends of Crusoe's story above all that we should keep returning to, because even here in what looks on the surface to be a born-again success story, rebellious youth brought back into the faith and an understanding of his place in the divine scheme of things to live happily ever after, there are inconsistencies which should cast doubt on the overall theology, not least in its claim of intelligent design. The scientific status of the latter is highly questionable, despite some scientists espousing it of late, and it can have a damaging effect not just on the practice of science, which has to jettison all notions of chance (not to mention evolution), but also on our personal psychology.[36] Intelligent design goes against our idea of free will, and that is not a particularly healthy development for democracy, which depends heavily on the notion of personal responsibility for our actions. This is not some esoteric metaphysical debate, but an issue that potentially affects all our lives quite dramatically. Intelligent design now has a very vocal lobby, and behind it lies the born-again ethos with its closed mind-set. Crusoe remains an intriguing character in this respect: someone who desperately wants to believe in divine control and a planned structure to his existence, but who is forced repeatedly to dig deep within his own internal resources in order to survive in a hostile environment. To most readers he appears to be more of an advertisement for individualism and self-development than for an omnipotent God carefully tending his universe and its inhabitants (Karl Marx being one of the first to point out this 'bourgeois' side of Crusoe's character),[37] although evangelicals would no doubt object to such a reading.

Perhaps what Crusoe really succeeds in showing us through his adventures are the flaws in born-again theology and the theory of intelligent design it entails. So much of the latter has to be taken on trust – that the Bible is literal truth, etc. – that it says more about our personal psychology, our need for security and fixed meaning in our lives, than it does about the nature of the universe. Neither is a theology very persuasive when it has to take refuge in evasions – as with awkward quesions like '*why God no kill the Devil?*' – to maintain its equilibrium. Crusoe has the grace to be embarrassed about the latter, but no modern-day evangelical has any more satisfactory a solution to one of the great paradoxes at the heart of not just Christian, but religious belief in general. Monotheisms are far better at explaining why there is good than evil in the world. At the very least Defoe's narrative provides the basis for a spirited debate between the evangelical and the secular reader, tapping in as it does to some of the most critical sociopolitical debates of our time.

CHAPTER 3

Gulliver's Travels, Multiculturalism and Cultural Difference

THE ISSUE

At least in theory all major Western countries are committed to multiculturalism: the belief that various cultures can coexist happily in one nation, with each respecting the values and lifestyles of all the others while acknowledging themselves to be fellow citizens under one national government. Cultural difference is not just to be allowed, but fostered and protected under such a system, with religious freedom guaranteed for all. Contemporary cultural theory is very much in favour of multiculturalism, with its implicit assumption that no one culture or way of life is superior to any other and that cultural difference need not lead to conflict, that in fact it can be mutually inspiring and help to engender a more tolerant world order. The West has led the way in this in a conscious attempt to address its own recent history. To adopt such a perspective, it is thought, is to distance oneself from the bad old days of cultural imperialism, where the West assumed it was its destiny to impose its own value system across the globe, trampling over all others in the name of progress. The key requirement now, however, is to refrain from making value judgements about other cultures and to accept that they are as valid as one's own. Diversity is to be celebrated.

In practice, multiculturalism has proved to be harder to uphold in its idealised form, despite official government approval throughout Western Europe. Immigrant groups, especially those from the Third World living in Europe, feel under constant threat from the dominant indigenous population, which often has a very different, and frequently irreconcilable, concept of human rights from theirs, creating considerable social tension when these clash. Islamic societies segregate the sexes in most public activities, for example (even including hospital care), which breaches Western notions of gender equality, which are held to be unchallengeable. To go against such notions is to undermine what the West understands by the concept of modernity. Rows have broken out in several countries of late, most notably France, about Moslem women's right to wear the veil, which again has become a complicated argument about the nature of gender equality. Is wearing it a proud assertion of gender identity or an imposition by a patriarchal cultural system concerned to keep women subordinate? Many political commentators have become deeply pessimistic about the multicultural ideal, arguing that it is more likely to lead to confrontation between competing cultures than harmonious coexistence.

Some commentators go as far as to regard multiculturalism as encouraging cultural separatism, with ethnic groups keeping to themselves and resisting any pressure to integrate into the wider society of which they are a part. The consequence is a series of parallel societies which have little contact with each other, and this hardly fosters cultural exchange. As one critic of this system, the French philosopher Pascal Bruckner, has remarked, the effect is to keep everyone 'imprisoned in their history', locking them into a particular tradition and preventing them from developing outside the conventions that involves.[1] As Bruckner goes on to argue, the inhabitants of each culture 'are refused what has always been our privilege: passing from one world to another, from tradition to modernity, from blind obedience to rational decision making'.[2] While this is admittedly a very Western-centric viewpoint, and somewhat emotively expressed, it does draw attention to what is arguably the most critical issue in this entire debate – the extent of individual rights. The West has put this concept at the centre of its cultural ethos, whereas other, generally more traditional, cultures have either resisted it or simply see no need for it. Overcoming such obstacles is one of the most pressing problems facing the multiculturalist cause.

THE TEXT

Jonathan Swift, *Gulliver's Travels*

In Jonathan Swift's *Gulliver's Travels* (1726) the hero undertakes a series of voyages across the globe, to arrive by accident in lands completely unknown to Europeans, where cultural clashes are generally the norm – not least between the hero and the native inhabitants – with human nature seemingly highly resistant to the virtues of multiculturalism and unable to overcome cultural difference. The Big-endians and Little-endians in Lilliput, for example, are embroiled in a series of wars because of a minor difference in their eating habits. Gulliver himself is treated with deep suspicion by the Lilliputians on their first encounter, and proves to be a disruptive force within a society containing various opposed factions; someone who, in a quite literal sense, just cannot fit in to the existing system. The Yahoos are about as far removed from the multicultural ideal as one could be, despite the model of sober and rational conduct provided by the ruling class in Houyhnhnm land. Yahooism represents the dark side of human nature that gives birth to unthinking prejudice against almost all others, and is a searing indictment of humanity by an author with a notoriously low opinion of his species ('But principally I hate and detest that animal called man').[3]

Swift very successfully portrays the barriers that exist to multiculturalism in what Frances D. Louis has called his 'anatomy of misunderstanding', and many contemporary commentators are in agreement with his essentially pessimistic view of human nature, seeing cultural difference as a divisive rather than unifying force in the world.[4] Whether we are really as self-interested and culturally chauvinistic as Swift seems to believe we are is a point still well worth pondering. At the very least the amount of conflict that currently exists between nations and cultures globally, and which shows little sign of dissipating, provides food for thought as to the validity of Swift's negative assessment. Suspicion of the other gives every impression of being hard-wired into the human character, as is a capacity for disagreement.

Gulliver is a trained surgeon whose wanderlust leads him to sign on for several long voyages as a ship's surgeon, sometimes only a few months after returning from the last, invariably danger-ridden, one. Curiosity about the world continues to motivate him, although what he finds on his travels does little to dispose him towards the rest of humankind. Each journey involves him being cast away on his own in a strange land, inhabited by even stranger races and species, conforming to none of the known characteristics of humanity: smaller than life-size, larger than life-size, distorted in feature, and then, to cap it all, horses endowed with speech and rationality. Each journey tests Gulliver's abilities quite severely – in effect, he is given a crash course in cultural difference. It is a course from which he emerges almost totally alienated from the rest of the human race, considering each member of it a mere 'Lump of Deformity' puffed up by entirely unjustifiable pride.[5]

Lilliput and Brobdignag place Gulliver in the position of the colonial oppressor and colonial oppressed respectively, because of the power imbalance that obtains between him and the inhabitants in each case. This gives him the opportunity to experience multiculturalism from two very contrasting perspectives. In Lilliput Gulliver swamps the culture by virtue of his size, becoming a factor in Lilliputian life that the inhabitants cannot ignore. His power of action is so superior to the Lilliputians as to render him a threat to their entire culture, as he is duly informed: 'it is certain, that an hundred Mortals of your Bulk, would, in a short Time, destroy all the Fruits and Cattle of his Majesty's Dominions'.[6] Quite simply, Gulliver looms over everything: 'the *Great Man Mountain*' as he is dubbed, who requires a daily provision of food and drink equal to that consumed by 1,728 Lilliputians.[7] The Lilliputians' attempts to keep him subdued prove futile, and they are thrown back on trusting to his goodwill, which luckily for them Gulliver does feel towards them. As Kathleen Williams observes, it is in Lilliput that Gulliver 'is at his most attractive' as a character.[8] He agrees to be bound by a contract as to his future behaviour, but the Lilliputians would be hard pressed to enforce this if Gulliver chose to breach any of its clauses.

The inability of nations to live in harmony with one another is revealed in the long-running conflict between Lilliput and its neighbouring island empire, Blefuscu. It is the disagreement between the Big-Endians and the Little-Endians over which end of an egg to break before eating it that lies behind this. When the monarchy throws its authority behind the Little-Endian cause after one of the royal family accidentally cuts his finger while breaking the big end, as custom has dictated, the result is full-scale civil war. The Blefuscudian empire is quick to take advantage by giving its support to the traditionalist Big-Endians, who are granted exile within their kingdom from where to continue opposition. The absurdity of the struggle is evident when considering their holy book's verdict on egg-breaking: '*That all true Believers shall break their Eggs at the convenient End*'.[9] The interpretation of this passage by Reldresal, a leading figure in the Lilliputian government, seems eminently sensible: 'which is the convenient End, seems, in my humble Opinion, to be left to every Man's Conscience, or at least in the Power of the chief Magistrate to determine'.[10] Yet for the parties in question such a compromise is unthinkable, and each is driven by a desire to prevail over the other, no matter how much bloodshed this may cause.[11] Even Gulliver cannot avoid becoming caught up in this conflict, and while still in favour with the Lilliputian court contrives to capture a large part of Blefuscu's fleet by shackling the ships together and pulling them ashore, much to the king's pleasure.

As well as this external threat to Lilliputian culture, there are significant 'intestine Disquiets' to record.[12] Lilliputian politics is blighted by a struggle between its two main parties: those who advocate the wearing of high and low heels respectively (*Tramecksan* and *Slamecksan*). So seriously is this issue taken to be that supporters of each side 'will neither eat nor drink, nor talk with each other'.[13] Swift deliberately makes the controversy ridiculous, but it is not so much more ridiculous than the religious divisions of his own day, as he is only too well aware, and just in case we are moved to feel at all superior, many of our contemporary religious disputes too. Seen from a future perspective, the current disputes in the Anglican and Catholic Churches over gay priests may appear just as ridiculous, as if sexual orientation was of any greater importance in the overall scheme of things than the height of one's heels. It is the ability of human beings to keep manufacturing such divisions that makes social existence so unstable, and, we might add, multiculturalism so hard to establish as a viable system. Humanity seems to have an infinite talent for creating division, particularly in the realms of politics and religion, and Swift's satirical eye is quite merciless in spotting this. One would have to say this talent is no less in evidence in the twenty-first century.

If anything symbolises the extent of the cultural difference between Gulliver and the Lilliputians it is the episode of the royal palace fire. Gulliver feels he has performed a great service to the nation in putting this out, but his hosts are appalled at his method: urinating copiously on the building from above. Since it is forbidden to urinate anywhere within the palace grounds Gulliver is technically guilty of treason, and although the emperor promises to obtain a pardon for him, the empress is so incensed that she vows never to enter the buildings again and swears revenge for the outrage to her royal dignity. Gulliver cannot really understand how much his coarseness has offended his hosts, nor does he put himself in their position to wonder what it would feel like to have one's surroundings drowned in urine cascading from a great height. Yet he is horrified when the situation is reversed in Brobdignag, where the Maids of Honour treat him as if he were no more than a pet whose presence can be disregarded: 'Neither did they at all scruple while I was by, to discharge what they had drunk, to the Quantity of at least two Hogsheads, in a Vessel that held above three Tuns.'[14] Eventually, the palace episode returns to haunt Gulliver. He is privately warned that he is about to be charged with treason for breaking the law against urination, and he finds it expedient to flee the country for Blefuscu to prevent the officially prescribed punishment of blinding being carried out on him.

It is court politics that leads to Gulliver's fall from grace, and political intrigues sour his stay in Lilliput:

> I had been hitherto all my Life a Stranger to Courts, for which I was unqualified by the Meanness of my Condition. I had indeed heard and read enough of the Dispositions of great Princes and Ministers; but never expected to have found such terrible Effects of them in so remote a Country, governed, as I thought, by very different Maxims from those in *Europe*.[15]

He has early evidence of court intrigue after his success in putting so much of the Blefuscudian fleet out of service. This exploit merely spurs the king on to ask for even more damage to be exacted, in the hope that Blefuscu can be brought under control as a mere province of Lilliput. Gulliver's refusal to comply with the king's wishes, the 'unmeasurable . . . Ambition' he shares with most other princes, means that he has made a very dangerous enemy, and the king immediately starts conspiring against him with some members of his Council.[16] From then onwards Gulliver is a marked man, who has to be extremely careful whom he trusts or confides in.

The mean-spiritedness of courts is a recurrent theme of Gulliver, and when the Emperor of Blefuscu also tries to press him into service Gulliver declares himself 'resolved never more to put any Confidence in Princes or Ministers, where I could possibly avoid it.' Instead he takes the opportunity offered by the discovery of a small boat washed up on the island's shore to make arrangements for his departure.[17] What he has learned from his stay in Lilliput is that court life promotes scheming and the development of factions, and that the impulse towards political division and civil discord is extremely powerful in human affairs. Politicians in general are disposed to harbour 'unmeasurable ambitions' in their breast and to treat such as Gulliver as mere resources to be exploited for their own sectarian interests.

In Brobdignag Gulliver discovers what it feels like to be in the position of the Lilliputians and forced to rely on the goodwill of others physically far superior to oneself. This leaves him perpetually fearful for his physical well-being, and he is often in a state of considerable anxiety about his safety during his stay there amongst a nation of lumbering giants, for whom he is no more than a curiosity. He is at the mercy of whoever is keeping him, as he discovers when his original keeper turns him into the equivalent of a circus novelty act in order to make money out of him, travelling from town to town to put him on display. In what is almost a parody of multiculturalism Gulliver is made to perform while being observed by the Brobdignagians as if he were a museum exhibit rather than a living being. To the Brobdignagians his ways are quaint and laughable, and they are unable to relate to him on a personal level as a creature like themselves. The discrepancy in size merely magnifies the cultural difference between them, which neither can overcome.

Gulliver is brought close to a complete breakdown because of the physical demands made on him by his keeper and the customers he attracts. His keeper's reaction to his declining health is to work Gulliver even harder, exploiting him to the full while he can on the assumption that he will soon die. There are a few exceptions to this somewhat callous attitude amongst the Brobdignagians, in particular his minder, Glumdalclitch, the daughter of the family where he first finds refuge. She remains caring and affectionate towards Gulliver all the while he is in her charge, but this does not save him from maltreatment from jealous individuals while they are both resident at court. The queen's dwarf, for example, takes a strong dislike to Gulliver, seeing him as a rival for royal attention, and at one point tries to drown him by dropping him into a large bowl of cream on the dining table.

The lack of generosity towards others different from oneself, which Swift regards as so characteristic of human nature, is graphically illustrated by the reaction of the King of Brobdignag to Gulliver's tales of the culture of his homeland:

> Then turning to his first Minister . . . he observed how contemptible a Thing was human Grandeur, which could be mimicked by such diminutive Insects as I; And yet, said he, I dare engage, these Creatures have their Titles and Distinctions of Honour; they contrive little Nests and Burrows, that they call Houses and Cities; they make a Figure in Dress and Equipage; they love, they fight, they dispute, they cheat, they betray.[18]

Gulliver bridles at the patronising air with which this is delivered, although it is not all that different from his own attitude towards the Lilliputians, amongst whom he wanders inspecting their customs almost as if they were a laboratory experiment set up for his benefit. The idea that each society might actually learn from the other is signally missing: other races are no more than objects of curiosity.

It is to the Brobdignagians' credit, however, that their king is so horrified at Gulliver's description of gunpowder, indignantly refusing Gulliver's offer to introduce it into his kingdom as a weapon to be used against his majesty's enemies. Swift's satire is at least as much at Gulliver's expense at such points, with his 'Indignation to hear our noble Country . . . contemptuously treated', revealing his own sense of clearly misplaced cultural superiority,[19] but the underlying point about the pretensions of human beings strikes home forcefully nevertheless. Such pretensions make it all but impossible that different cultures can ever live together in harmony and mutual respect, and indeed the only beings with which Gulliver feels such an idyllic existence would be possible turn out to be the non-human Houyhnhnms, who hardly treat Gulliver as their equal. (As one critic has put it, what distinguishes the Houyhnhnms is their 'unpleasant coldness [and] self-satisfaction', and Gulliver is to be criticised for his 'exaggerated devotion to them'.)[20] Human beings, of whatever shape or size, are not well disposed towards each other, particularly when cultural difference comes on the scene. In fact, they have the greatest difficulty making the leap of imagination required to see life from another cultural perspective than their own. They betray a distinct tendency to patronise each other, and assume their own cultural superiority when faced with radically different lifestyles. Multiculturalism in its more positive sense offers little appeal to such self-absorbed individuals.

Even within Europe we cannot rely on respect for cultural difference, however, with the author's characteristically caustic irony coming through in Gulliver's reflections on the lack of worldly knowledge of the Brobdignagian king: 'The want of which Knowledge will ever produce many *Prejudices*, and a certain *Narrowness of Thinking*; from which we and the politer Countries of *Europe* are wholly exempted.'[21] Gulliver's cultural chauvinism stands revealed for all to see. Prejudice and narrowness of thinking are what mark out human nature in general, and although Brobdignagian society has much to commend it, there are still elements of those traits in the king's dismissal of Gulliver and his fellows as 'diminutive Insects' ('impotent and groveling' too, as he arrogantly asserts).[22] Brobdignagians find it almost impossible to take someone like Gulliver seriously, and to that extent they too can be said to be 'imprisoned in their history'.

Gulliver's sense of cultural superiority is probably at its most marked during his stay on the flying island of Laputa, where he finds himself among a race of individuals absorbed in their own peculiar obsessions: 'the Minds of these People are so taken up with intense Speculations, that they neither can speak, nor attend to the Discourses of others, without being roused by some external Taction upon the Organs of Speech and Hearing.'[23] This obliviousness to their surroundings can only be overcome by their being gently struck on the mouth, ears or eyes at regular intervals by a bladder wielded by a servant called a Flapper. The most dramatic effect of these intense speculations is to be found in their Academy at Lagado, where Gulliver comes across a series of increasingly bizarre experiments while being shown round: for example, an attempt to extract sunbeams from cucumbers or to return excrement to its original state of edible food. Gulliver is predictably scathing about the entire operation. Indeed, everything about Laputa and its inhabitants proves to be skewed:

Their Houses are very ill built, the Walls bevil without one right Angle in any Apartment; and this Defect ariseth from the Contempt they bear to practical Geometry; which they despise as vulgar and mechanick[.] . . . I have not seen a more clumsy, awkward, and unhandy People[.] . . . They are very bad Reasoners, and vehemently given to Opposition, unless when they happen to be of the right Opinion, which is seldom their Case.[24]

Gulliver is dismissive about Laputa and its odd ways, remarking that 'I saw nothing in this Country that could invite me to a longer Continuance'.[25] Multicultural coexistence with the Laputans would not seem to be a very desirable objective: as far as Gulliver is concerned they have little to contribute to humankind's stock of learning. As a critique of cultural insularity, the Laputa episode is quite devastating. Here is a society which is unable to establish any firm relationship with the rest of the world, their floating condition neatly symbolising their detachment from everyday reality.

Laputa has its civil discords too, manifested in its uneasy relationship with the continent of Balnibarbi over which it hovers as the putatively ruling force. There has already been a major rebellion in the city of Lindalino, which had almost succeeded in disabling Laputa's mechanism for floating in the air, the intention being to kill the king and install a new government. Balnibarbi itself is in a state of considerable social disarray because of the passion for 'projecting', such as is being carried out at academies like that in Lagado. Because none of the many projecting schemes has been 'yet brought to Perfection . . . the whole Country lies miserably waste, the Houses in Ruins, and the People without Food or Cloaths'.[26] None of this has deterred the inhabitants, however, who remain as committed as ever to wildly experimental projecting, considering this the only way to improve their lot, their faith in its eventual success being unaffected by its present failure to deliver anything at all of value.

The impression of a culture which is incapable of governing itself correctly because of what we would now probably call an obsession with technology is very strong. It may seem mad to act this way, 'not only ludicrous but evil' in Kathleen Williams's assessment of the Laputan lifestyle, but there are various Third World countries which are expending vast sums on weapons or the pursuit of nuclear power, despite widespread poverty amongst their populations[27]. North Korea

and Iran spring readily to mind. The relationship between such countries and the West is fraught, and the cultural divide seemingly
unbridgeable. As Gulliver's host in Balnibarbi gently chides him, he
has to recognise 'that the different Nations of the World had different
Customs', but if these are as diverse as Gulliver's travels are revealing,
then there seems little hope for any beneficial cultural exchange.[28]
Gulliver cannot understand why they behave the way they do; they
cannot understand his objections. A society that contained citizens of
all the lands that Gulliver visits would be unworkable, defeating the
best efforts of even the most committed of multiculturalists. Cultural
diversity as Gulliver experiences it is more like cultural anarchy, with
cultures so far apart in their customs as to make any meaningful *rap-
prochement* between them all but impossible. If there is a common
feature, it is the inability to appreciate the perspective of others:
even the Houyhnhnms are baffled by the Yahoos, although as ultra-
rationalists faced by sheer brutes this is hardly surprising. But one does
not sense much of a basis for multiculturalism in any of the societies
Gulliver visits.

One possible exception to this anti-multiculturalist outlook is the
island of Luggnagg, one of the stops Gulliver makes on his journey
from Laputa to Japan. Here he finds a trading nation, in contact with
its neighbours, and 'a polite and generous People' who 'shew themselves courteous to Strangers'.[29] But even in this ostensibly happy
dominion Gulliver is to encounter a darker side to existence – the
Struldbruggs. These creatures are immortal, yet far from turning out
to be the 'superiour Beings' Gulliver expects, they prove to be pathetic
individuals cut off from their peers and totally lacking in the wisdom
that age is supposed to bring.[30] They eventually lose their memory, rendering them almost useless to the rest of society. It is as if they are
another race (Struldbruggs are even marked out from the mass by
having a large spot over their left eyebrow which changes colour several
times over the course of their lives), and the fact that the state declares
them legally dead after the age of eighty indicates that their fellow citizens hardly know how to deal with them. Being legally dead carries
with it the penalty of their estates passing to their heirs and the
Struldbruggs being left to survive on a meagre allowance. They are as
close to being classified as non-persons as it is possible to be. The
Luggnagians would rather they were not there, and do their best to
marginalise and ignore the Struldbrugg community in their midst.

This hardly looks like the multicultural ideal in operation either, with the Struldbruggs being barely tolerated. Once again we get the impression that human beings find it very difficult to deal with the different.

The Luggnagians may be courteous to those like themselves, but even here the court is to be treated with the utmost caution. It is one of its customs that those being presented to the king must '*lick the Dust before his Footstool*';[31] in other words, crawl up to the king on their belly while licking the floor in front of them. If the king turns against anyone, then the floor is sprinkled with poison which kills the unfortunate individual being presented within a day. When a maliciously inclined page deliberately neglects to clean the floor after one such episode, it causes the death of a blameless young noble. Gulliver is left to wonder again at the dangers of court life with its many intrigues. He has already discovered, while on the island of Glubbdubbdrib near Luggnagg, where he is enabled by magic to converse with the dead, that those who have done good service at such courts throughout history are omitted from the public record and go unknown to future ages.

Gulliver's sojourn amongst the Houyhnhnms turns out to be his most dramatic experience of culture shock, and his encounter with the Yahoos has a profound effect on his character. The Yahoos turn out to be Gulliver's worst nightmare: human beings devoid of reason and without a trace of fellow feeling for each other. The contrast with the calm and well-adjusted – if admittedly cold and somewhat self-satisfied – Houyhnhnms is stark. Gulliver's Houyhnhnm master informs him that 'the *Yahoos* were known to hate one another more than they did any different Species of Animals', which hardly suggests a future for multiculturalism there either.[32] The Yahoos represent a throwback to the state of nature, with Gulliver's Houyhnhnm master going on to observe that 'if . . . you throw among five *Yahoos* as much Food as would be sufficient for fifty, they will, instead of eating peaceably, fall together by the Ears, each single one impatient to *have all to it self*'.[33] This is humanity reduced to its most brutish, and the example of the Yahoos is enough to alienate Gulliver himself from the human race, to the extent that he can barely stand the company of his own wife and family when he finally returns to England:

> I must freely confess, the Sight of them filled me only with Hatred, Disgust and Contempt; . . . And when I began to consider, that by

copulating with one of the *Yahoo*-Species, I had become a Parent of more; it struck me with the utmost Shame, Confusion and Horror.[34]

Gulliver now finds it all but impossible to cope with the rest of humanity and does his best to live a parallel life to them, spending much of his time in the stables communing with his horses instead.

Gulliver's travels reveal a very odd world populated by some very strange races and species. But it is noticeable that he is just as much in danger from his own kind while on his travels; pirates cast him adrift at one point, and his own crew mutinies against him. Overall, humanity is not a very trustworthy group and little reliance can be placed on its innate goodwill. Civil discord seems to be endemic wherever Gulliver journeys, and even the Houyhnhnms, who appear to have abolished discord completely within their own species, have to deal with the Yahoos, who represent a rogue element in their society. Gulliver's attraction to non-human species becomes all the more understandable after his run of experience at the hands of humankind, and his closing judgement on the entire species is damning:

> I am not in the least provoked at the Sight of a Lawyer, a Pickpocket, a Colonel, a Fool, a Lord, a Gamester, a Politician, a Whoremunger, a Physician, an Evidence, a Suborner, an Attorney, a Traytor, or the like: This is all according to the due Course of Things: But, when I behold a Lump of Deformity, and Diseases both in Body and Mind, smitten with *Pride*, it immediately breaks all the Measures of my Patience; neither shall I be ever able to comprehend how such an Animal and such a Vice could tally together.[35]

At this point one suspects that the character's and the author's misanthropy come into alignment, with humanity being rejected out of hand;[36] the rich, the powerful and the learned being no less 'lumps of deformity' than criminals are, and no section of society seemingly being worthy of praise. The human race would appear to be beyond redemption, with Gulliver wishing to keep contact with it to a minimum in consequence.

CONCLUSION

Swift's is a particularly pessimistic vision of humanity, and he dwells at length on our many weaknesses and foibles: as Frances D. Louis sums it up, '[t]he dominant figure in Swift's satiric universe is man fumbling his way towards knowledge; the dominant event in that pilgrimage is man falling on his face'.[37] Extreme though Swift's assessment of his fellows is, it has a ring of truth when we consider the attitudes to cultural difference in our world. For all the talk of multiculturalism, cultural difference presents a significant obstacle to its implementation. One of the results of this is that, as various commentators have complained, multiculturalism is in danger of becoming a byword for cultural separatism, where there is minimal contact between cultures who instead lead parallel lives, thereby protecting their assumed cultural 'purity'. At the other end of the spectrum of debate are those who insist that all immigrants should seek to integrate fully into the society they have joined and to efface their differences with the host culture, arguing that multiculturalism runs the risk of undermining the ideals of liberal democracy.[38] To such thinkers, multiculturalism is a regressive step. Arguments against the use of the Islamic veil, which surface with great regularity in Western Europe these days, tend to see it as an expression of otherness and as such deeply symbolic of the threat an authoritarian theocratic culture could pose to a secular one like our own.

It is a positive step that multiculturalism is being explored as much as it is, because the West has proved such a magnet for other cultures, its prosperity and opportunities for economic advancement far outstripping the rest of the globe, and therefore being extremely attractive to citizens of impoverished Third World nations. This is unlikely to change in the foreseeable future. The social tensions that immigration has caused will only be eased once there is a recognition that all cultures have the right to exist and to express themselves in their own particular ways; but the issue of just how far that expression should be allowed to go remains. Undoubtedly there has to be some degree of integration, but that does raise the fear of complete assimilation, and cultures as a rule, particularly traditional ones, find that very threatening. It is a prospect that often has the unhelpful effect of making such groups retreat further into their own cultural system. Even if full assimilation is not demanded, there is still the barrier of suspicion of cultural difference to be overcome – no less a problem on the part of the host nation than its immigrant communities, it has to be emphasised. We may not share Swift's extreme pessimism about human nature, but, like Gulliver, we live in a world rife with feelings of cultural superiority, where far too many of us are in practice imprisoned in our history. Unless we overcome the attitudes involved in our imprisonment then a truly multicultural society is unlikely to emerge, but it will need a significant commitment to compromise on all sides that is only intermittently visible at present. Misunderstanding of each other is still, unfortunately, very much the rule in human affairs.

CHAPTER 4

Pamela; or, Virtue Rewarded and Sexual Abstinence

THE ISSUE

A move towards greater sexual freedom was a characteristic of Western societies over the course of the twentieth century. This was particularly encouraged by the feminist movement and gay rights campaigners, and there is no doubt that we live in a sexually much more open society than hitherto. Most of us in the West regard this as an entirely healthy development and appreciate the fact that there is now far less hypocrisy surrounding the issue than historically has tended to be the case. If there are social benefits that accrue from this changed cultural climate, then there are drawbacks too, such as the greater availability of pornography, which has created a great deal of controversy and opposition (even from feminists who are broadly supportive of more openness about sexuality). The fear of HIV/AIDS has also led to a reassessment of the value of this greater freedom, and conservative-minded campaigners on both sides of the Atlantic increasingly argue for sexual abstinence before marriage as the most effective method of reducing the incidence of the disease. The 'Silver Ring Thing' in America is a prime example of the backlash against sexual freedom. Describing itself as a 'para-church youth ministry', it is a movement inspired as much by religious belief (fundamentalist Christianity) as by fears of HIV/AIDS itself. In certain circles, therefore, chastity is back in vogue – or at least is being strongly touted by figures of authority – even if the failure rate in the 'Silver Ring' movement is so high as to make one question at the point of the whole enterprise.[1] Nevertheless, it does indicate that the ideal is an inspiration to some, even if upholding it in practice is proving to be far more problematic for the young adults at whom it is targeted.

The campaign for sexual abstinence before marriage goes much further than the 'Silver Ring Thing', however, and there have been several other campaigners on its behalf in both Britain and the US. American women have been advised to adopt 'the rules' for dating, and one of its main recommendations is the curtailment of sexual activity before marriage, the assumption being that if sex were available outside marriage – as it generally is in the West these days – then men would feel no need to marry.[2] Female sexual abstinence, it was felt by proponents, would coerce men into marriage, which of course was always a woman's ultimate goal. 'Mr Right' would come to respect a woman more if she kept herself pure, even if his own nature were oriented towards seduction for its own sake. Some recent writers have even tried to put a feminist spin on their campaign for female chastity, arguing that being what one critical voice, the journalist Zoe Williams, has called the 'gatekeepers of sex', empowers women.[3] Once again, the assumption is that men are predators and women their prey, both sexes being biologically conditioned that way, and that unless they are extremely careful, women will be taken advantage of by unscrupulous males looking for sex 'without strings' and leaving them in the emotional lurch afterwards. It may be a 'most unwelcome comeback' for such as Williams, but it has to be conceded there is once again a significant lobby for chastity as a specifically female virtue.[4]

THE TEXT

Samuel Richardson, *Pamela; or, Virtue Rewarded*

The heroine of Samuel Richardson's *Pamela* (1740) well understands the perils of pre-marital sex and the virtue of virginity. In her case, the fear is not just of sexual disease (which meant syphilis in the main in an eighteenth-century context), but more immediately of unwanted pregnancy in a society with no reliable means of contraception and a very unforgiving attitude towards unmarried mothers. Unmarried fathers, on the other hand, attracted far less blame, and indeed were often celebrated by their peers for their exploits – especially if they were members of the upper classes. From the Restoration period onwards the rake was a figure more often admired than criticised (as is often still so nowadays). The pursuit of Pamela by her master, Mister B, whose designs on her are, at least initially, purely lecherous has many humorous aspects, and Richardson plays up that side of the narrative with some success; but the underlying issues are very serious indeed to a vulnerable young woman such as the heroine. Virginity is her only protection against, at best, a lost reputation (with the distinct possibility of a slide into prostitution at some later date once she is cast off as a mistress), or ruined health and even death from an untreatable sexual disease. In a society in which brothels were commonplace, rakes such as Mister B were only too likely to have become infected through their various sexual adventures and in turn to infect their unsuspecting partners. When Mister B speaks of having 'pursued' sexual pleasure 'even to sateity' in the aftermath of an unhappy love affair, his meaning is clear.[5] The double-standard is fully in operation in this world, and Pamela has to be aware of this at all times and seen to be above suspicion. If they amend their conduct in later life, then reformed rakes can become respectable pillars of society, as Mister B does eventually, but reformed female sexual adventurers are another matter entirely: generally speaking there is no way back for them.

Pamela might be seen as a prototype of the 'Silver Ring Thing' ideal: a young woman whose moral identity is inextricably tied up with her sexual behaviour, and who is concerned to protect it at all costs. The heroine has her own version of 'the rules' which she sticks to with admirable tenacity, despite the severe pressure exerted on her to yield. She also reveals many of the less savoury aspects of the 'Silver Ring' notion, however, with sexual promise being used as a means of gaining power over others and of reinforcing traditional gender stereotypes: sex as a commodity to catch a man and ensure the security of marriage (which Pamela eventually achieves).[6] Pamela's marriage to Mister B raises her considerably in the social scale, and it could be said that her virginity has been deployed for economic gain – virtue in her case is amply rewarded. While 'Silver Ring Thing' enthusiasts would probably be shocked at such an idea, claiming that sex is first and foremost a moral issue, there is no doubt that their overall vision of sexual identity reinforces gender stereotypes, with men cast as predators and women as prey: biology dictates conduct in this group's opinion. Pamela's situation is much more extreme, and the threat of rape is very real to one of her social class. Chastity is therefore an eminently defensible tactic to adopt, but it does raise provocative questions about the relationship between sexual identity and morality that persist into our own day.

Pamela is an interesting individual in being far more cultured than one would expect of someone in service at the time. She has more the air of a lady than a servant, but cannot expect any of the social respect conventionally accorded the latter because of the poverty of her background. Her parents are only too aware of the dangers this poses, with her father pointing out that, as far as he and her mother are concerned,

> our chief trouble is, and indeed a very great one, for fear you should be brought to any thing dishonest or wicked, *by being set so above yourself*. Every body talks how you are come on, and what a genteel girl you are; and some say, you are very pretty. . . . But what avails all this, if you are to be ruined and undone![7]

As an impecunious young woman her prospects are very limited, which makes her a vulnerable target for a scheming male such as Mister B, who becomes her master when his mother, Pamela's original employer, dies. Mister B wastes little time to make his move, and obviously considers Pamela both fair game and a very likely conquest: her ruin is precisely what he sets out to engineer – and in a quite calculating and cold-blooded fashion. His gift to Pamela of four guineas and some coins which were on his mother's person when she died (something of a tradition in upper-class families at the time) carries with it what in retrospect is a very loaded statement on his part: 'if I was a good girl, and faithful and diligent, he would be a friend to me, for his mother's sake'.[8] What Mister B means by 'good' and 'friend' are a world away from Pamela's understanding of the terms, and her unexpectedly determined resistance to his sexual overtures merely inspires him all the more. Pamela becomes a challenge to his male pride, and he undertakes the project with relish, pursuing her relentlessly.

Her parents see through Mister B immediately, 'I hope the good 'squire has no design' as her father writes to her; but it is clear he suspects that her master does and expresses himself 'very fearful for your virtue'.[9] The scene is set for an epic struggle over that virtue, with Pamela forced to defend it against an overbearing male with all the considerable power that gender and superior class endow him in a society with a strict sense of hierarchy. Chastity becomes a weapon in the sex war; in effect, the only weapon that Pamela has at her disposal. If that is breached, then her social position is highly precarious. Her father states it in the plainest terms: 'we *fear* – Yes, my dear child, we *fear* – you should be *too* grateful, and reward him with that jewel, your virtue, which no riches, nor favour, nor any thing in this life, can make up to you.'[10] She is even advised later that she should 'resolve to lose your life rather than your virtue'.[11] As she is only in her mid-teens and unprotected while working in Mister B's house, they have ample reason to worry about her ability to withstand the pressures placed on her by such a socially powerful male as her new master. Pamela is adamant that she will never do anything to bring dishonour to her parents and she proves true to her word, but she is put through severe trials that test her resolve to the utmost before she reaches the safe haven of marriage.

Mister B strives mightily to relieve Pamela of her 'jewel', and deploys a wide range of tactics, some very underhand indeed. He showers her with gifts of clothes from his mother's wardrobe, including intimate apparel such as stockings, clearly sounding out her reaction to this intrusion into feminine territory. Pamela quickly finds her parents' fears realised when he makes an attempt on her, kissing her 'two or three times, with frightful eagerness' while they are in the summer house, calling her a 'hussy' when she objects, and then trying to bribe her with gold to keep quiet about the incident.[12] From that point onwards there is a battle of wills between them, with Mister B having by far the greater resources with which to prosecute it. He becomes a deeply symbolic figure, displaying all that is most deplorable in male sexual conduct; a bully with no thought for the feelings of his intended victim, who as far as he is concerned is merely there to be used and abused (although some argue that Mister B is perhaps more of a blusterer than an expert seducer or sexual menace).[13]

Richardson is capable of injecting an element of humour into the sexual chase that develops. Undressing for bed one night, Pamela hears a rustling in the clothes closet, and when she goes to investigate 'out rushed my master, in a rich silk morning gown'.[14] A tussle ensues during which the housekeeper, Mrs Jervis, steps in to protect Pamela and the heroine herself faints, thus saving herself from further harm. The scene has something of the air of a stage farce, with Pamela's later enquiries of those sitting either side of her bed when she awakes from her fainting fit, 'Mrs Jervis, can I be *sure* it is you? Rachel, can I be *sure* it is you?', being at once piteous and comical.[15] But humorous as the incident might seem, it has a more sinister side in indicating that nowhere in the house is safe for Pamela, and that Mister B has no respect for the concept of personal space or privacy. Pamela is forced to be on her guard at all times and in all places, becoming an extreme example of female vulnerability in the face of the predatory male. It is as if she is existing in a state of nature rather than a civilised society, likely to be assaulted at any time and having no higher authority to appeal to for help.

Pamela is eventually driven to such a state of despair by Mister B's pursuit, that she even contemplates suicide as the only way of protecting her purity, remembering her father's injunction that it would be better to lose her life than her honour. Her unavailing efforts to escape from the house where Mister B has imprisoned her finally seem to have broken her spirit and 'the sad thought' comes into her mind 'to throw myself into the pond, and so put a period to all my terrors in this world!'[16] At this stage, the spiritual autobiographical element of the narrative becomes most apparent, with Pamela experiencing an epiphany that makes her draw back from the act of suicide:

> How do I know but that the Almighty may have permitted these sufferings as trials of my fortitude, and to make me, who perhaps have too much prided myself in a vain dependence on my own foolish connivances, rely wholly on his grace and assistance?[17]

Pamela firmly believes that she has been the recipient of divine help at this low ebb in her life, and feels encouraged to resume her battle against Mister B almost as if it has now become a divine mission for her to carry out on God's behalf. The scene, 'the turning-point of the whole novel' in Mark Kinkead-Weekes's view, equates to the 'conversion experience' in spiritual autobiography, when the individual comes to realise that she has been singled out by God and is not alone in her trials.[18] A powerful sense of inner security soon develops. Pamela's conduct in protecting her virtue has been vindicated, and to reject Mister B's advances is in her view to follow the divine will.

Post-epiphany, she becomes an even tougher challenge for Mister B's seduction attempts, despite the superior resources he has at his command. The sex war has turned into a paradigmatic instance of the universal struggle between good and evil, and no matter how comical the narrative may be at times, that underlying seriousness of purpose remains. There is more at stake than Pamela's virtue: a high-level morality tale is being enacted. If Mister B is not thwarted, then mankind – specifically *man*kind – has regressed almost to an animal state, and is probably beyond saving.

Mister B is driven by Pamela's obduracy to make a written proposal to her to be his mistress, promising to treat her 'as if you were my wife' and assuring her that she will 'be mistress of my person and fortune as if the foolish ceremony had passed'.[19] To back up his claims, he offers her 500 guineas, a property in Kent, fine clothes, assorted jewellery including diamond rings, and a vague promise of marriage after a year if he is still pleased with her. Pamela's spirited reply demonstrates how much she has grown in confidence since stepping back from the brink of suicide, as many a serving maid in her condition would have been sorely tempted by such an offer (as Mister B's Lincolnshire housekeeper, Mrs Jewkes, is quick to remind her): 'What, sir, would the world say, were you to marry your harlot? That a man of your rank, should stoop, not only to marry the low-born Pamela, but to marry a low-born prostitute?'[20] Sex is merely an adventure to Mister B, and he is perfectly willing to pay the expense involved, as we learn he has done in past exploits; but to Pamela it is, and will remain, a moral issue that reflects fundamentally on her integrity. Her first sexual encounter will dictate the shape of her life from then onwards and she cannot treat it casually.

Mister B's matter-of-fact attitude towards sex is one that will never be shared by Pamela, therefore, and if recent campaigners for female chastity are to be believed, by the vast majority of women either. As one such commentator, Dawn Eden, has put it, 'Whatever Germaine Greer and her ilk may say, I've tried their philosophy – that a woman can shag like a man – and it doesn't work. Women are built for bonding. We are vessels and we seek to be filled.'[21] Pamela has a similar need for bonding which Mister B's clumsy attempts to seduce her never recognise. What to him is merely a 'foolish ceremony' is to her a crucial mark of personal respect, without which no relationship is possible. It is not just Pamela's virtue that is on trial, but Mister B's ideology also, his assumption that sex can be reduced to an economic transaction with minimal emotional commitment.

As we shall find later with Ann Radcliffe's fiction, the threat of rape hangs heavily over the narrative, and Mister B continually places Pamela in situations where she must fear that event will happen (in Richardson's next novel, the monumental *Clarissa* (1748–9), rape actually does occur).[22] Erupting from her clothes closet was one such incident to give considerable cause for concern, and one can only speculate what might have occurred had not Mrs Jervis been present. But Pamela's escape in this instance merely spurs Mister B on to take more drastic measures. Far from letting her return to her parents, as he had promised he would in the aftermath of the closet encounter, Mister B has her abducted to his Lincolnshire estate, thus leaving her even more at his mercy, since she is shorn of the protection offered by her fellow servants such as Mrs Jervis. There she finds herself under the control of the vile Mrs Jewkes, who does her utmost to persuade Pamela to submit to Mister B, while keeping her a virtual prisoner.

When Mister B arrives it is to present his proposal to Pamela that she become his mistress, and her rejection of this merely increases his desire to force himself on her physically, with Pamela fleeing in terror from his grasp yet again. Overhearing Mrs Jewkes recommend rape as a solution to Mister B's frustration with her is hardly calculated to put Pamela's mind at rest either. Mrs Jewkes proceeds to aid and abet Mister B in actually getting into bed with Pamela while he is dressed up as the servant-girl Nan, urging him on to commit rape in front of her: 'Don't stand dilly-dallying, sir. She cannot exclaim worse than she has done; and she will be quieter when she knows the worst.'[23] Fainting comes to Pamela's rescue yet again, but her vulnerability is never more apparent than in this scene, and her distress when she regains consciousness, 'I was on the point of abstraction', is only too understandable.[24] For a defenceless adolescent this can only be a deeply shocking experience.

Holding on to her virtue while under such intense psychological and physical pressure requires all of Pamela's resolve, although the more desperate Mister B becomes in his chase the more Pamela must see is to be gained from resisting him. His offers of money keep increasing as he vainly pursues her: 'I cannot bear denial. If the terms I have offered are not sufficient, I will augment them to two thirds of my estate.'[25] Such wild declarations can only increase Pamela's sense of self-worth, and even a naive sixteen-year-old might begin to realise that her purity has significant market value that could be to her advantage at some future date – if she is careful. All unsuspecting as well, Mister B is being led to regard Pamela less and less as a casual sexual adventure, bringing his own ideology into question. He is forced to realise that male power has its limitations and that money is not always enough to establish control over others.

Mister B eventually succumbs and agrees to marry Pamela as the only way of possessing her: a secret marriage in the first instance, then publicly acknowledged. Her campaign of resistance has been spectacularly successful and she has avoided the fate of so many other girls in her situation. She has maintained her virginity and forced Mister B to treat her as a respectable woman for whom nothing less than marriage is an acceptable outcome: he is forced to submit to 'the rules' with as good a grace as he can (and to be fair, he does seem to have been impressed by Pamela's resolve). Mister B is apparently a reformed character, Margaret A. Doody arguing that '[e]ventually, it is the force of femininity which defeats Mr B., or alternatively, brings him to victory by making him acknowledge the softer side of his nature'.[26] One might wonder cynically how long this reform will last once the novelty of marriage wears off (rakes being notorious for such recidivism), but even if this happens Pamela's position will be fairly secure as a wife and mother – even if her sexual health might be more at risk. Whether calculatingly or not, she has deployed her physical assets to the maximum and scored a considerable social victory for her class: 'the rules' have triumphed, and Pamela has been strikingly effective in playing the role of 'gatekeeper of sex'.

Pamela's attitude towards Mister B changes completely once marriage is proposed and his former transgressions are instantly forgiven. From being her persecutor he turns into a 'superlatively generous man' whom she dotes on and considers as her protector.[27] After a lecture from her husband-to-be, who now reveals a very moralistic streak to his character (at least where wives rather than mistresses are concerned), Pamela even compiles a list of forty-eight 'rules' by which to conduct herself in married life, including that a wife should 'draw a kind veil over her husband's faults'.[28] Now that Mister B has been transformed into 'Mr Right', Pamela is only too happy to comply with his wishes: 'I must think his displeasure the heaviest thing that can befal me', as another of her 'rules' has it.[29] With marriage in the frame, resistance is to be exchanged for obedience; Pamela happily embracing the norms of her society as regards gender relations. Margaret A.

Doody has claimed that '[t]he virtue that is rewarded is in large measure the virtue of rebellion', in Pamela having refused to give in to the power of Mister B;[30] but it is instructive how rapidly this turns into subordination to the will of the male. There may be, as Rita Goldberg has argued, a defence of 'spiritual egilitarianism' in the narrative, but the gender variety is another issue entirely.[31] As Patricia Meyer Spacks astutely remarks, Pamela's ' "victory" remains psychologically ambiguous'.[32]

Pamela's reward is not just respectability but economic security, even if Mister B dies before they have had any children: 'I have, therefore, as human life is uncertain, made such a disposition of my affairs, as will render you absolutely independent; as will secure to you the means of doing a great deal of good, and living as my relict ought to do.'[33] Pamela's parents are to share in their daughter's reward for keeping her virtue intact: Mister B's will provides for them for the rest of their days. Pamela's divinely ordained mission to reform Mister B, and in a symbolic sense male sexuality, has been brought to a thoroughly satisfactory conclusion.

The heroine has won security through adhering to the 'Silver Ring Thing' method, and Mister B has been brought back within the fold of Christian respectability – a reformed rake, to the extent of agreeing eventually to take an illegitimate child of his by a former mistress into the family unit to be brought up by Pamela. The wisdom of having protected her virtue is made strikingly apparent by her ability to do this – she could so easily have been in the position of the mistress in question, as she reflects:

> I cannot help being grieved for the poor mother of this sweet babe, to think, if she be living, that she must call her chiefest delight her shame[.] . . . And I have a twofold cause of joy. First, that I have had the grace to escape the misfortune of this poor lady; and next, that this discovery has given me an opportunity to shew the sincerity of my grateful affection for you, sir, in the love that I will always bear to this dear child.[34]

The sexual double-standard could hardly be more in evidence than it is at this point. The unfortunate mother, Sally Godfrey, is from a good family so the matter could be hushed up. But she felt it expedient to leave the country, effectively in disgrace, and has settled in Jamaica where she has since married. The child, meanwhile, has no knowledge of her parents and has been placed in a boarding school, where Mister B visits her periodically in the guise of her 'uncle'. Mister B is providing for Miss Goodwin, as she has been called to maintain the cover-up, but his conduct overall is very questionable. He has seduced the lady, and when her family try to force him into marriage he refuses to give in to their intimidation. The fact that he then proceeds to pursue Pamela with a similar motive in mind – hoping 'to prevail with her to be Sally Godfrey the second', as he candidly admits later[35] – does not say much for his moral sense. Yet it is Miss Godfrey who suffers the most, with Mister B's life continuing on much as always – he feels no need to hide himself away overseas to protect his reputation. Different rules apply for rakes.

While he does express a certain amount of regret about his treatment of his erstwhile lover – 'I am far from taking a pride in the affair[.] . . . I can truly abhor my past liberties, and pity poor Sally Godfrey'[36] – Mister B clearly does not think it should present any serious impediment to his becoming Pamela's husband. Her forgiveness is more or less expected – and quickly forthcoming. There seems to be a tacit agreement between them that male virtue is a matter of far less significance than female. Pamela would not be granted the same latitude: in fact, Richardson was mocked by some of his male readers for making the hero a male virgin in his later novel *Sir Charles Grandison* (1753–4).[37] Even by today's far laxer standards regarding sexual conduct, however, Pamela's reaction to this rather sordid episode in Mister B's life is incredibly generous: having one's partner spring an illegitimate child on one on the verge of marriage is a potentially traumatic experience, particularly for someone as young as Pamela. As far as Mister B is concerned he can redeem his lapse by meeting any financial responsibilities that arise as a consequence of it, and he gives the impression that his conscience is relatively at ease now that he has done so. Pamela seems to accept this at face value, even if she does express herself as 'sad' at hearing of the wild life Mister B led in the immediate aftermath of the Sally Godfrey affair.[38] He is certainly guilt-free enough, as we have just noted, to lecture Pamela on the moral conduct required of a wife. Neither does Pamela seem to consider there is anything hypocritical about his delivering a moral homily, despite the differences in their respective sexual histories: marriage has the effect of absolving all his past sins. The unfortunate Miss Godfrey is left with an altogether more problematic emotional legacy, separated from her child by several thousand miles, and with little prospect of ever seeing her again. Pamela can acknowledge this and feel sympathy, but nevertheless sees it as no bar to union with Mister B.

Part II of *Pamela* is little read these days, and as a description of the successful marriage between the heroine and Mister B it lacks the tension of Part I, consisting largely of scenes of happy family life as Pamela integrates herself into Mister B's social class. Without the sex war factor the narrative drags somewhat, but the reward of virtue is made very clear. Mister B appears to be sincere in his reformation, even if he does engage in an occasional bout of flirtation with the opposite sex. He supports Pamela in her various good deeds in the community (already being contemplated by her at the close of volume I), which enable her to take on an almost saint-like quality in the eyes of the local community. She employs an apothecary, Mr Barrow, and a surgeon, Mr Simmonds, to minister to the needy poor, and as the former puts it when she praises his work:

> O my good lady . . . who can forbear following such an example as you set? Mr Simmonds can testify as well as I (for now and then a case requires us to visit together) that we can hardly hear any complaints from our poor patients, let 'em be ever so ill, for the praises and blessings they bestow upon you.[39]

Pamela's efforts have borne fruit, and the value of keeping one's virginity intact until marriage is emphatically registered. She now has a secure position in society, the respect of all classes and the economic power to perform good works: purity pays.

CONCLUSION

It remains to be seen how successful the new campaign for female chastity will be in a general sense. To many it will simply seem reactionary, a 'most unwelcome comeback' of traditional notions as Zoe Williams had it. But it is clear that there is significant support for the concept from several quarters, inspired variously by religious belief and a backlash against radical feminism. If chastity is a genuine choice by an individual – whether male or female – there can be no argument with it, but if it becomes a weapon in the sex war, then its value is more dubious. The sexual abstinence movement tends to operate from a very fixed view of human nature, in which biological factors dominate: men are sexual predators who cannot be trusted; women are emotionally vulnerable creatures who must work out stratagems to protect themselves against rampant male sexuality. Sex is reduced to a reward for marriage.

The major difference between our time and *Pamela* regarding sexual mores is the wide availability of reliable contraception, which has removed some of the risk for today's Sally Godfreys, if not the emotional trauma of being badly treated by men. Whether the more open sexual climate makes such treatment more likely is a moot point however, and an argument can always be put that sexual experience before marriage can be a beneficial experience for both sexes, enabling them to test out their emotions and gain more knowledge of themselves and others. Marriage is still a very popular institution, and the existence of sexual relationships outside it does not seem to have affected it unduly. This alone would seem to disprove the notion that men are interested in sex alone, and that when this is freely available they will avoid marriage unless coerced into it in an underhand manner. Most people in a society like ours marry at some stage in their lives, and many men remain monogamous by choice. It does not require pre-marital chastity to achieve either state of affairs, nor is pre-marital chastity a guarantee of a successful relationship.

It is to be noted again too that it is female sexual abstinence that is insisted upon by campaigners, as if this was the only way that women could exert any control over the process ('the rules' position) or claim the moral high ground (the 'Silver Ring Thing' position). The notion that men might want something more from a relationship than sex, and that they might want to move on to that even after sexual contact has occurred, is largely discounted by such theories. Sex becomes the male's reward for doing the right thing, and that is not the most healthy basis for a relationship. Overall, it paints a rather depressing picture of gender relations, and that is probably the most questionable aspect of the whole campaign: its stereotyping of male and female nature. Those of us in favour of sexual freedom still have a debate on our hands therefore; one not all that far removed from that being conducted in *Pamela*.

CHAPTER 5

The History of Tom Jones, A Foundling and Anti-Social Behaviour

THE ISSUE

In the UK and many other Western countries increasing concern has been expressed in recent years about a decline in the standard of public behaviour. Many cultural commentators have claimed there has been a marked fall in respect for others, with Lynne Truss, for example, feeling herself moved 'to mourn . . . the apparent collapse of civility in all areas of our dealings with strangers', and sadly concluding in her book *Talk to the Hand* that rudeness is the new cultural norm.[1] Anyone who lives in the UK will be very aware of how much incivility and rudeness has come in the wake of the binge-drinking culture which is now such a feature of our night-time life. The unruly behaviour of night-time drinkers has become a national scandal. Incidents of violence and disorder are commonplace in British city centres, and the police and local casualty departments in hospitals struggle to cope, particularly at weekends. Many of the older generation consciously avoid downtown areas at night in consequence. Popular holiday resorts around the Mediterranean experience similar scenes throughout the summer season, largely fuelled by tourists from northern Europe, who tend to test the limits of the local population's tolerance quite severely.

Southern Europe has its own public order problems too, with the Italian football league being closed down entirely for a period in the 2006–7 season by the national government, because of the death of a policeman after a riot at a game in Sicily – the latest in a series of violent clashes involving hardcore fans of the country's leading clubs.

In the aftermath of the closure, many clubs were ordered to play in empty stadiums as a further drastic method of preventing crowd trouble. Italy is merely the current worst case of spectator-generated violence, however, and football hooliganism is a recurrent problem in the game throughout Europe, with international football being particularly susceptible to outbreaks.

The introduction of Anti-Social Banning Orders (ASBOs) is one example of how the authorities in the UK have reacted to this 'collapse of civility' towards others. Such orders are applied to persistently unruly individuals, who are then restricted in their movements, especially around areas where they have been known to cause trouble in the past. ASBOs have not been particularly successful, however, and have also been a source of much controversy as to whether they infringe human rights, but the government has felt the need to be seen to be doing something about the problem. Public order – or the lack of it – is clearly an issue which taxes the political class, with the media being only too ready to sermonise on the issue in the most sensational of language and images. Whether sensationalised or not, the phenomenon raises questions about human nature and the socialisation process. The general perception seems to be that the former is more volatile and the latter less assured than many have previously thought, and that there is a need for a significant reassessment of how our societies work. A prominent British politician has gone so far as to warn that the country is in danger of becoming 'decivilised'.[2]

The intensely individualistic, consumption-driven society of the West manifestly promotes selfishness as a cultural ideal. We are expected to compete against each other in the marketplace for jobs, status and economic power, and are actively encouraged to display that economic power at every opportunity by our purchase of consumer goods and services. As a result of a shift towards a less regulated market economy in most Western countries over the last few decades (the Thatcher years in the UK being the embodiment of this trend), there has been a growing disparity between rich and poor that has helped to generate resentment amongst those at the lower end of the socio-economic scale, who feel they are being left behind. The massive annual bonuses paid out to business executives, particularly in the financial services sector of the City of London, exacerbates the problem, involving sums beyond the wildest dreams of most of the population. For many commentators, the high level of petty crime in countries like Britain and America is a direct result of a more visible social inequality in an aggressively consumerist society, with the 'have-nots' taking their revenge on the 'haves' in a very direct manner.

Meanwhile, the movement in the US towards 'gated communities', in effect private towns permanently protected by a heavy security presence, indicates a fear amongst the affluent of those in the lower socio-economic brackets, who are considered to constitute a permanent threat to their wealth and possessions. This is not so much a case, as Lynne Truss has it in the subtitle of her book, of staying home and bolting the door as staying home and bolting the entire suburb. The decline into a drug-centred culture of many large American cities such as Detroit and Baltimore, which has led to a large-scale migration of the population from the inner city areas, can only encourage this trend towards the modern equivalent of walled cities.[3] It is a movement which is creeping into the UK and Western Europe too, with the same desire to keep the masses at bay. The phenomenon is based on the premise that humanity in general is not to be trusted, and that social order is a fragile condition that can breached at any time by envious individuals. We cannot rely on the goodwill of our fellow citizens. This is a belief which can be found throughout history ('the barbarians are at the gates'), but has become all the more problematic in modern times with the move towards a cut-throat free market economy – 'casino capitalism', as one disenchanted commentator has dubbed it[4] – and the subsequent decline of traditional constraints on behaviour that this provokes.

THE TEXT

Henry Fielding, *The History of Tom Jones, A Foundling*

Henry Fielding's *Tom Jones* (1749) pictures a society where almost everyone is motivated by self-interest. This works out as a drive to exploit and cheat others as much as circumstances will allow, generally under the guise of a hypocritical air of civility. This applies to servants no less than their masters and to the female sex as well as the male: the vast majority are on the lookout for personal advancement at the expense of others and have few scruples as to how they achieve their goal. Fielding's vision of society suggests that Thomas Hobbes was largely correct in his assessment of human nature: unless strictly policed, humanity in the mass will only too easily lapse into anarchy, a 'warre . . . of every man, against every man' in Hobbes's graphic summary, where no one is able to protect his or her person or possessions for any great length of time.[5] Even though he expressed a dislike of Hobbes's ideas, Fielding's view of human nature seems essentially pessimistic – a writer who 'frequently notes the natural malignity of man', as Claude Rawson insists.[6] Public order is continually threatened in this realm – strikingly symbolised by the appearance of the second Jacobite Rebellion on the fringes of the narrative, carrying with it the potential to generate full-scale civil war in the newly united nation (the union of England and Scotland having occurred in 1707). Only a few individuals, such as Tom, have the capacity to attain the wisdom and authority necessary to keep anarchy at bay. Prudence, which for Fielding is one of the most desirable of human qualities, is in short supply, and it is one of the greatest compliments he can pay his hero to note at the close of the story that '[h]e hath . . . by reflection on his past follies, acquired a discretion and prudence very uncommon in one of his lively parts'.[7] Society is desperately in need of such wise figures if it is not to collapse altogether, and Tom ends up being a role model for his fellows in this respect.

Whether or not one agrees with Fielding's conservative conclusions (as a practising magistrate in London he had ample opportunity to contemplate human venality in all its variety), it is clear that he sees social existence as a precarious construct, constantly bedevilled with the possibility of an outbreak of disorder. We must remember that this was a period when the mob was still a potent factor in social and political life, particularly in London where the authorities were very wary of its power. Politics to this author is largely a case of trying to keep that latent disorder at bay, with much of humanity displaying distinctly anti-social behaviour if given even the slightest hint that they might be able to profit from doing so. The social bond does not appear to be particularly strong in Fielding's world. The more pessimistic of our own current crop of cultural commentators would most likely agree with this assessment, and Fielding has identified a source of social conflict which is just as much of a concern to the political establishment now as it was then. A critical question that comes to mind in this context is: how much scope for self-interest can a society permit without adversely affecting the public good?

Hobbes believed that humankind was motivated almost solely by self-interest (the survival instinct lying at the heart of this) and that unless this trait was very tightly controlled then all were doomed to lead an insecure life, constantly at the mercy of the schemes of their fellows. Life in the state of nature, in his famous phrase, was 'nasty, brutish and short'.[8] His solution to this unhappy state of affairs was absolute monarchy, where all were deemed to have ceded personal sovereignty to an overall ruler when they entered into civil society, who would then keep order for the benefit of the whole of that society. The result would be an authoritarian system where all power resided in one individual (Hobbes was against rule by groups, such as Parliament, because of their potential to fragment into factions), but for the author this was far preferable to the threat of anarchy. And anarchy was precisely what Hobbes thought England had descended into in the 1640s, when civil war raged throughout the country between royalist and parliamentarian forces until the latter prevailed and abolished the monarchy – an outcome with which Hobbes was deeply unhappy. Although not as authoritarian in his outlook as Hobbes, Fielding had every reason to feel that the two Jacobite rebellions of 1715 and 1745 were proof of a similar tendency towards anarchy in his own time.[9] Neither man felt that civil society came naturally to humanity; in fact, in many ways it went against the grain of our basic, intensely competitive nature. It was the first duty of rulers to keep the latter suppressed as much as possible.

Tom Jones traces the career of its hero from birth, where he is passed off as a foundling to save his mother's embarrassment at having given birth to an illegitimate child, through his various adventures as an apparent outsider to polite society, until his eventual acceptance into the ranks of the ruling class, and the wealth and power that goes with that. This latter condition is sealed by his marriage to Sophia Western, the daughter of an important local landowner, who is openly hostile to the possibility of such a union until Tom is revealed to be of noble birth.

Although he is of 'lively parts' – for which read sexually promiscuous – we are supposed to regard Tom as lacking in the extremes of self-interest that motivate the mass of humankind. From a feminist standpoint this may be a more questionable assessment, however, and whether Tom's sexual behaviour is altogether free of the taint of self-interest is very much open to debate. Fielding suggests that it is the women who usually take the lead with Tom, who is a very handsome young man, and that he is not to blame for succumbing to the temptation; but he does not have to face the consequences of his promiscuity as they are fated to do. Molly Seagrim, for example, is publicly humiliated for her sexual conduct in a way that Tom never is, 'pelted . . . with dirt and rubbish' by her peers when her pregnancy becomes public knowledge and having to be saved from a mob by Tom's timely intervention.[10] Society is always likely to turn a kinder eye on a male sexual adventurer than a female, as Squire Western's reaction to the news that Tom is likely to be responsible for Molly's pregnancy clearly signals: 'where is the mighty matter o't?'[11] He treats it as a joke, to the extent of ribbing his daughter: 'You have not the worse opinion of a young fellow for getting a bastard, have you, girl? No, no, the women will like un the better for 't.'[12] Granted, when Tom shows an interest in Sophia his reaction changes sharply to one of anger, but as long as it is with a woman of a lower class the squire is quite blasé about a young man like Tom sowing his wild oats, and cheerfully admits that he did the same in his youth. As far as Squire Western is concerned, when it comes to sexual matters we cannot expect men to be anything but self-interested, driven as they are by their basic instincts.

Molly is rescued from the burden of a lost reputation at a later stage by the charitably inclined efforts of Tom and Sophia after their marriage:

> As for Partridge, Jones hath settled £50 a year on him; and he hath again set up a school, in which he meets with much better encouragement than formerly, and there is now a treaty of marriage on foot between him and Miss Molly Seagrim, which, through the mediation of Sophia, is likely to take effect.[13]

It is as if Sophia is concerned to erase all trace of Tom's past sins by making a respectable person of Molly (a degree of self-interest creeping in there perhaps); although whether marriage to Partridge is necessarily desirable for such a sprightly young woman is another matter. Being of 'lively parts' is more excusable in a man than a woman, especially now that the man is revealed to be of high, if illegitimate, birth, whereas the woman is from the lower orders of rural society. Molly is an embarrassment who has to be cleared away in order for Tom to become a model of 'discretion and prudence' for the local population to admire.

Travellers are fair game in Fielding's world, with landlords extorting what they can from them, most especially if they are from the upper reaches of society and travelling with a retinue. It seems to be a natural law that those lower down the social scale do their best to cheat those higher up. As the Man of the Hill puts it in describing his travels through Europe:

> In Italy the landlords are very silent. In France they are more talk-ative, but yet civil. In Germany and Holland they are generally very impertinent. And as for their honesty, I believe it is pretty equal in all those countries. The *laquais à louange* are sure to lose no opportunity of cheating you: and as for the postilions, I think they are pretty much alike the world over.[14]

The Man of the Hill is admittedly an embittered and cynical old man who has retreated from the world in disgust at what he perceives to be its evil ways; but his observations seem to ring true of what Tom and his circle generally find in their travels through the English country-side. Unscrupulous landlords and landladies tend to be the norm, and to stop at a wayside inn, as one cannot avoid doing on a long journey, is to offer oneself up to be fleeced. Meals are reheated after sitting for several days, but presented – and charged for – as if fresh; home-made drinks are passed off as more expensive liquors ('rum' being made from malt at one inn, for example); landlords are careful 'to inquire partic-ularly of all coachmen, footmen, post boys, and others, into the names of all . . . guests; what their estate was, and where it lay', in order to gauge what they might be able to charge; bills are shamelessly padded, especially when travellers are in a hurry to resume their journey and not paying attention to the details.[15] Coachmen typically treat their passengers 'as so much luggage', and strive to squeeze as many of them as they can into their vehicles between inns to increase their takings.[16] The traveller has to run this gamut of trials while on the road, only to find that the sharp practice moves to an even higher level of sophisti-cation once he or she arrives in London.

Servants invariably seem to be pursuing their own interest as well, and make the most of whatever chance arises to exploit their master or mistress. The classes are engaged in an elaborate game of deceit with each other, vying for power and influence, with servants using their positions as means of extracting money from guests and enquirers: 'The porter in his lodge answers exactly to Cerberus in his den, and, like him, must be appeased by a sop before access can be gained to his master.'[17] In other words, bribes are necessary to make any headway in the world of polite society, as Tom discovers when he attempts to gain an audience with Sophia in her London residence: a flat denial of any knowledge of the person in question changes rapidly to an escorted trip to her door once money has passed hands (sadly for Tom the expenditure proving useless, as Sophia has already left the premises).

The Man of the Hill provides an interesting case study of self-interest and how it can deflect the individual from the path of virtue. A promising scholar in his youth, he is led astray while at university in Oxford by a wealthy young nobleman, Sir George Gresham, whose spendthrift example succeeds only too well in bringing out the bad side of his fellow student's character:

> I had not long contracted an intimacy with Sir George before I became a partaker of all his pleasures; and when I was once entered on that scene, neither my inclination nor my spirit would suffer me to play an under-part. I was second to none of the company in any acts of debauchery; nay, I soon distinguished myself so notably in all riots and disorders, that my name generally stood first in the roll of delinquents.[18]

Growing debts force the Man of the Hill to obtain money under false pretences from his father, but when this source dries up he turns in desperation to theft from a fellow student and has to flee the university when a warrant is issued for his arrest. Escaping prison by good luck, he plunges into low life in London, consorting with gamblers and cheats, 'the whole fraternity of sharpers' who shamelessly use and abuse others for their own ends.[19] Eventually, he does manage to reform his ways, but his experience has convinced him that humanity in general is a bad lot: 'human nature is everywhere the same, everywhere the object of detestation and scorn.'[20] This is an extreme view and Tom tries to balance it by criticising the Man for 'taking the character of mankind from the worst and basest among them; whereas indeed, as an excellent writer observes, nothing should be esteemed as characteristical of a species but what is to be found among the best and most perfect individuals of that species'.[21] We could say that the Man of the Hill is too pessimistic and Tom too optimistic, and that the author wants to draw us into the debate at this point by posing such polarised views. Yet given the general pattern of human behaviour we find in the narrative, it certainly feels as if the author leans more towards the Man's end of the spectrum than Tom's. Unlike the Man of the Hill, Fielding does believe that there are some good individuals to be found – but not very many.[22]

Tom does his best to present human nature in a more positive light, but the Man's comment that 'you have lived, you confess, but a very short time in the world: I was somewhat older than you when I was of the same opinion' suggests that prolonged exposure to the human race will tend to reveal more evil than good and that ultimately this will test the patience of the best of natures.[23] Even one's friends and lovers cannot be trusted not to deceive, as the Man knows to his cost, and his own drastic solution is to withdraw into rural seclusion to avoid further disappointment at the hands of humanity.

As long as good-natured figures like Tom exist then the Man's ultra-Hobbesian views can be challenged: clearly, not everyone is driven by self-interest alone, no matter what the Man may think. But Tom does seem to be an exception to the general run of mankind, who are so often, as the Man complains, motivated by '[t]he same hypocrisy, the same fraud' in their dealings with others.[24] Keeping these negative character traits in check is no mean feat for the 'prudent' members of society. Even intrinsically well-meaning individuals like Mr Allworthy find it very difficult to restrain those around them, no matter how good an example they may set in their own conduct. Morality can easily give way to the dictates of self-interest, no matter how hard those like Allworthy may strive to set a contrary example. Mr Allworthy, in fact, is regularly taken advantage of because of his trusting nature, with the narrator describing him as being 'charitable to the poor, *i.e.*, to those who had rather beg than work'.[25] The sense of there being a moral vacuum at the heart of this society comes out strongly in the discrepancy between Allworthy and the majority of the community. Even his sister Bridget manages to deceive him by keeping her illegitimate child a secret, yet contriving to have Tom brought up by Allworthy as one of his family nevertheless. Allworthy's good nature is very much to his credit, but the narrator makes it clear that good nature alone is no protection from systematic deception on the part of one's fellows. Without prudence – not Allworthy's strong point – the good-natured individual is at the mercy of the schemes and machinations of the cynically self-interested, and these can be found even amongst one's closest associates.

That fear of 'riots and disorders' lying under the surface not just of each individual (as with the Man of the Hill), but of society at large, waiting to be activated, comes to a head with the outbreak of the 1745 Jacobite Rebellion, the latest news of which is filtering through to those on the road as Tom makes his journey to London. Fielding himself was fanatically anti-Jacobite, regarding the movement as one of the gravest threats to the well-being of the country, as he made clear in several published tracts; but as the near-success of the rebellion indicates, there was widespread support for the Jacobite cause. Squire Western is one such devotee with his diatribes against the monarchy ('the Hanover rats')[26] as is Partridge, although he is much less vehement about it. One of the landlords on the road to London is informed by 'a famous Jacobite squire' passing through his inn that 'All's our own, boy, ten thousand honest Frenchmen are landed in Suffolk. Old England forever! Ten thousand French, my brave lad! I am going to tap away directly.'[27] Misleading though these reports are, the sense of a nation in a state of considerable alarm is powerful, and with a record over the previous century of a civil war in the 1640s, a revolution in 1688–9 (the so-called 'Glorious' that drove the Stuart monarchy from the English throne for the second time that century), and the first Jacobite Rebellion of 1715, this is hardly surprising. From the perspective of the 1740s, Britain would not have looked the most stable of states, with civil disorder a fairly regular occurrence, well established in the folk memory.

London presents human nature at its most venal, social life there seeming to thrive on selfishness. Even Tom finds his character compromised in the city by being constrained into the position of a 'kept man' by Lady Bellaston (who makes him a 'present' of fifty pounds in the early stages of their relationship). The fact that he is so uncomfortable in this situation, on the verge of being 'a male prostitute' as one critic has put it, speaks well of his character, suggesting that he is not willing to take financial advantage of others as a way of life[28] – a highly unusual response in London, especially amongst impecunious young men with few prospects, contacts or marketable skills. Tom does spend the money, but nevertheless demonstrates his essential decency by breaking off with Lady Bellaston as soon as he can, having been advised by a friend well versed in the manners of London society life that the best method of turning her against him is to propose marriage. The ploy is successful, with Lady Bellaston accusing Tom in a letter of wanting to gain control of her fortune 'in order to enable you to support your pleasures at my expense' (the law of the time empowering husbands over wives in all family financial matters).[29] Soon she is calling him 'a villain' and barring him from her house, economic self-interest winning out conclusively over sexual desire.[30]

Tom is then made an offer of a relationship in a letter from a rich young widow, Mrs Hunt, which he finds very tempting; but he rejects that as well, despite admitting that the 'lady's fortune would have been exceeding convenient to him' now that he has finished with Lady Bellaston and is without any source of income.[31] In each case he has gone against his financial self-interest, thus revealing himself to be very different from the mass of his fellows, whose morality is largely financially driven. Man of 'lively parts' though he is, Tom has the kind of nature that society desperately needs in its ruling class, and his eventual ascendance to that rank finds him well equipped to take a leading role.

Everything is tied up very neatly at the end of the narrative, and for the time being social order appears to reign – at least within Tom and Sophia's sphere of influence in the West Country, where they have returned to live:

> Nor is their conduct towards their relations and friends less amiable than towards one another. And such is their condescension, their indulgence, and their beneficence to those below them, that there is not a neighbour, a tenant or a servant, who doth not most gratefully bless the day when Mr Jones was married to his Sophia.[32]

The history of Tom Jones is brought to a successful conclusion, yet one would have to say that this leaves unresolved issues in the rest of society: as Ian A. Bell has remarked, '[t]he fiction may be orderly and systematic, but the reality it encounters is most definitely not'.[33] Just to symbolise this, Tom's notorious half-brother Blifil, from his youth 'a sneaking rascal', is not only still at large, but living in the North and planning to purchase a seat in Parliament (a nicely barbed comment on the author's part about the standard of political morality in the country).[34] He also has designs on a rich widow and has even switched his religious allegiance to Methodism to expedite this, revealing himself to be the unrepentant spirit of self-interest. It is a spirit which is prevalent throughout society, particularly in London, with Blifil poised to add to the stock once he has entered Parliament.

The corruption and inhumanity of the capital will continue to fascinate, as well as to appal, novelists right through into the nineteenth century. One has only to look at the depressing account of the city given in the best-known novel of Fielding's sister Sarah, *The Adventures of David Simple* (1744), to see how alienating London's lifestyle could be to the sensitive.[35] The author has little good to say about the place, and her hero's rather pathetic quest to find a friend whose sincerity he can rely upon proves to be a largely fruitless exercise. In almost every encounter David has with others, surface civility masks inner deviousness. Lynne Truss may bemoan the disappearance of civility in public life in the twenty-first century, but as David Simple's experience proves, civility alone does not guarantee respect for others. The ending of the later added volume to the work (*Volume the Last*, 1753), with the hero driven to his death by a series of personal misfortunes brought on by the selfish actions of others, is one of the bleaker assessments of human nature that we are to find in the eighteenth-century novel. Henry Fielding himself could paint darker pictures of contemporary life than he does in *Tom Jones*, as witness such works as *Jonathan Wild* (1743) and *Amelia* (1751).[36] Clearly, there is a great deal of pessimism in the Fielding family regarding human nature; a feeling that there is a dramatic imbalance between its good and bad sides, with the latter far more in evidence in our everyday experience. The Blifils are always with us.

CONCLUSION

Fielding's society differs from our own in several critical ways, but it bears the mark of the modern world in the dominating influence of self-interest in human affairs. Selfishness is rife in Fielding's England, and he is deeply worried at the threat this poses to social order: traditional structures are no longer holding in the face of the rise of self-interested individualism, and in the author's view this urgently needs to be addressed. His is a very conservative social vision, but there are similar worries being expressed across the political spectrum today: a fear that selfishness is getting out of hand and that something needs to be done to protect the vulnerable, that civilisation is only a very thin veneer in many individuals. In both cases, anarchy is felt to be a real possibility unless the dark side of human nature is kept firmly in check. The authorities can achieve this up to a point, but it is really a change in consciousness that is required. ASBOs are a crude and ineffective way of tackling the problem (although one can understand the frustration that lies behind their imposition); essentially they deal with symptoms rather than causes. Legislation can only do so much – people have to want to follow its dictates and to create a safer society or it will not work. At the moment there are too many aspects in our culture working against that desire.

It is unlikely that we will eradicate the dark side of human nature entirely, human history would suggest that is a utopian dream; but we can encourage the expression of the good side as much as possible, and a move away from the worst excesses of consumer culture would be a step in the right direction. The eighteenth century saw various campaigns for the reform of manners, and these did work to some extent in improving public behaviour. Perhaps we need a twenty-first-century equivalent, appealing to the better side that exists in nearly everyone, even if there will always be exceptions to this rule. If we cannot persuade our fellow citizens to extend the maximum respect they can towards others, then our outlook is pretty grim. The social bond needs strengthening not loosening, and we shall all pay the penalty if self-interest is allowed to become even more dominant in our culture than it currently is. We cannot all live in gated communities (nor would we all want to), and the more of these that are constructed the more their presence signals a dysfunctional society which is heading for yet more problems: they have to be seen as symptoms, not cures for our social ills. It has to be worrying if there are no-go areas in major cities, as has happened in places such as Detroit and Baltimore; and it is instructive that this has happened in the very heartland of the free market system, where self-interest is routinely appealed to – although it has to be conceded that the phenomenon can be identified in many European cities also, if on a less dramatic scale.

Perhaps it is time to reconsider some of our cultural priorities and to emphasise the social over the personal, but hopefully without having to revert to the ultra-authoritarian solution proposed by Thomas Hobbes, or even the hierarchical society, with its selective prudent few in the upper class governing us, favoured by Henry Fielding. There is a delicate balance to be struck between self-interest and social order, and this constantly has to be renegotiated. Socialists among us would certainly want to believe that humankind can be changed for the better and that self-interest does not completely define our basic nature, that there are other aspects of our character that can be emphasised for the common good. Essentially that is what is at stake – the common good – and this can only suffer if self-interest is allowed too much latitude. Like Fielding, our political class is wrestling with this problem, unsure of how to keep our competitiveness within reasonable bounds.

CHAPTER 6

The Female Quixote; or, The Adventures of Arabella and Northanger Abbey: The Power of the Media and Popular Culture

THE ISSUE

The power of the media, particularly television and cinema, to affect audiences' behaviour has been much debated in recent times. Copy-cat crimes have been reported in the press based on television dramas and films (Oliver Stone's *Natural Born Killers* (1994) being one example), and the media have often been blamed for a general decline in moral standards in our society. For many commentators popular culture is a large part of the problem, with soap operas representing a classic instance of how the public can be emotionally manipulated. Song lyrics, too, are criticised for anti-social sentiments that might be taken at face value by their largely young audience, particularly if it is a case of violence being advocated or glorified. The reality is much more complex than that, and narrative, popular or otherwise, is just as likely to improve our behaviour as to have an adverse effect on it. It is nevertheless a topic which encourages much speculation, especially amongst the more moralistically inclined. Eighteenth-century society was just as wary of the power of narrative, with the new form of the novel attracting considerable attention and standing as the equivalent of film and the broadcast media now. The novel was regarded as popular culture at the time, and young readers, particularly young female readers, were often thought to be at risk.[1] Contemporary commentators feared that this audience would be unable to discriminate between fiction and everyday life, perhaps to the extent of imitating the actions of its favourite characters, to the likely detriment of their morals.[2]

There is a classical precedent for the fears that both the eighteenth century and our own have voiced about the effect of popular culture. Plato raised similar objections in *The Republic*, with the figure of Socrates arguing that poets who had the ability to inspire extreme emotional responses in their audience – through drama, say – should be banned from his proposed ideal commonwealth in order to promote social order:

> So if we are visited in our state by someone who has the skill to transform himself into all sorts of characters and represent all sorts of things, and he wants to show off himself and his poems to us, we shall treat him with all the reverence due to a priest and giver of rare pleasure, but shall tell him that he and his kind have no place in our city . . . and send him elsewhere.[3]

Instead, Plato recommended that only those willing to write in a didactic, propagandistic style should be allowed to present their works publicly. His greatest worry was that the young would be led from the path of virtue and social responsibility by the works of the more popular writers, whose ability to arouse emotions – always a problematic occurrence for this most rationalist of philosophers – could have socially damaging consequences. The young were very impressionable and only too likely to believe, or imitate, what they saw being performed on stage. On the Athenian stage, for example, the gods and ruling authorities were regularly mocked and satirised by the playwrights of the day, with Socrates himself being so treated in Aristophanes' *The Clouds*. In Plato's view the state was under an obligation to prevent any challenge to its system of values, and therefore justified in imposing censorship.

Neither the eighteenth century nor our own want to go as far as Plato in his treatment of creative artists (although censorship is still very common in countries such as China, where the authorities attempt to control access to the Internet), but a concern about the effect of popular culture on the young can be found in both societies. Actually proving beyond doubt that popular culture prompts individuals to copy the actions of fictional characters they identify with is always difficult, but there is equally no denying that we can be very profoundly affected by art. The fact that the novel has been so successful as a medium for social criticism is strong evidence of its impact on the general public, and one that is to be admired. As long as art does appeal to our emotions, however, there is going to be at least the possibility that it may have negative as well as positive consequences, so this debate will continue.

THE TEXTS

Charlotte Lennox, *The Female Quixote; or, The Adventures of Arabella*; Jane Austen, *Northanger Abbey*

Such concerns come together very interestingly in two novels of our period of study: Charlotte Lennox's *The Female Quixote* (1752) and Jane Austen's *Northanger Abbey* (sold to a publisher in 1803, but not published until 1818, after the author's death). Both novels feature impressionable young women on the threshold of adulthood, who immerse themselves in a world of popular fiction as an escape from the humdrum world they inhabit, developing a 'fiction-maddened imagination' in the process.[4] In each case parental neglect has allowed them to indulge their fantasies by avid reading of romances, seventeenth-century French heroic in Arabella's case (*Female Quixote*), Gothic in Catherine's (*Northanger Abbey*). The heroine's inability, or refusal, to distinguish between fiction and the real world leads to many humorous and often deeply embarrassing incidents, but each author has a serious underlying purpose – to explore the relationship between the imagination and reality. Lennox suggests the greater sympathy with her heroine, presenting her use of romance as a means of revealing the hypocrisy of male behaviour, while Austen's heroine is made to see that fiction can distort her view of reality to the detriment of her development as a responsible member of society. One could say that for Lennox popular narrative is potentially empowering, whereas Austen is more circumspect, even if we could note that, paradoxically, each novelist is using fiction to point up the dangers inherent in fiction.[5]

Arabella grows up in rural seclusion, where her father retreats after the early death of her mother. She is largely left to her own devices, and that includes raiding her father's library, 'in which, unfortunately for her, were great Store of Romances, and, what was still more unfortunate, not in the original *French*, but very bad Translations' (exactly how the bad translation affects the narrative line of the works is never explained, however).[6] She incorporates the values of those romances into her worldview, assuming that everyone she meets, particularly the men, will share those values and act in the way that her gallery of fictional characters do. Lovers are expected to follow the whims of their mistress to the letter, even if this involves waiting for years to hear a favourable word or engaging in duels to prove the depth of their commitment. Arabella proceeds to adopt both the extravagant language and ideas of this literary discourse, and to act as if nothing had changed from the older worlds they depict. In her case, fantasy equals reality. Not surprisingly, this leads to much confusion, with Arabella constructing an elaborate narrative out of her experiences which others fail to understand. The behaviour she expects of others is so foreign to the social ethos of her day ('I command him to live, if he can live without Hope', as one bemused suitor is instructed after making his addresses, unsuccessfully, to Arabella),[7] that she is in danger of turning into a figure of outright ridicule. This is suggested by those in her circle at more than one point, with her father declaring that, '[t]he Girl is certainly distracted . . . These foolish books my Nephew talks of have turned her Brain!' and her cousin, Miss Glanville, bemoaning the lack of 'Protestant Nunneries' in which to confine Arabella, 'by which Means she would avoid exposing herself in the Manner she did now'.[8] It is hinted at other times that she may actually be certifiably mad, so extreme does her behaviour become in terms of what polite society in eighteenth-century England expected.

Arabella's odd conduct rapidly becomes an embarrassment to everyone who knows her, although it also has the interesting side-effect of bringing out into the open much of the hypocrisy behind male treatment of women. Extravagant declarations of love and devotion are still part of the courtship ritual in this society, and their deferential tone disguises the patriarchal power that men in reality exercise over women. By taking these sentiments at face value, as her reading of romances encourages her to do, Arabella calls the bluff of her male admirers, whose lack of sincerity is swiftly revealed. They may be playing a game, but she is in deadly earnest. As a group, men are nonplussed by what she expects of them, with her peremptory commands, as in the following letter to one persistent suitor, to model their actions on those of her fictional favourites:

Remember I require no more of you, than *Parasitis* did of *Lysimachus*, in a more cruel and insupportable Misfortune: Imitate then the Obedience and Submission of that illustrious Prince; and, tho' you should be as unfortunate as he, let your Courage also be equal to his; and, like him, be contented with the Esteem that is offered you, since it is all that can be bestowed, by *Arabella*.[9]

The suitor in question is Sir George, who has decided that the best way to ingratiate himself with Arabella is to indulge her romantic fantasies. In modern terms of reference, we might say that he is engaged in grooming her, saying what she wants to hear in order to bring her under his influence – even to the extent of inventing adventures for himself in the style of the romances that Arabella is wholly engrossed by. To any third party Sir George's tale is ridiculous, but to Arabella it is entirely credible and she becomes very absorbed in it. As her letter indicates, however, this is a game Sir George can never really win, since Arabella will invariably respond in the character of a fictional heroine, making impossible demands on him. She cannot relate to him as an individual, only as a fictional ideal, and that means he can never be sure of his ground. The more plausible he is in spinning his narrative the less likely it is that he will succeed in his objective of winning her hand. The primary function of a romance hero for Arabella is to suffer uncomplainingly – and at inordinate length. Whether she has designed it that way or not, it is a particularly effective tactic for keeping unsuitable males at bay. The only problem is that it keeps suitable males, like Mr Glanville, at bay also. It is small wonder that Mr Glanville's father, Sir Charles (Arabella's guardian after the death of her father) takes such a dim view of his son's continuing infatuation with Arabella:

I am sorry, said he, to find you have set your Heart upon this fantastic Girl: if ever she be your Wife, which I very much doubt, she will make you very unhappy. . . . There is no making her hear Reason, or expecting Reason from her; I never knew so strange a Woman in my Life[.][10]

Perhaps it is this very strangeness, however, that is the source of Arabella's attractiveness to the opposite sex. At the very least her fantastic ways disrupt the standard pattern of gender relations, constraining men into a subsidiary role to her – which again has feminist implications. Arabella is never the submissive female of patriarchal expectation, and that intrigues, even as it baffles, her male admirers. What one critic has called 'the strained leaps' the character makes in the narrative she creates for herself have the effect of forcing her would-be suitors to reconsider their whole approach to the business of wooing.[11] Arabella proves hard work, which soon weeds out any but the most serious.

Arabella's romance-derived picture of the world causes her to act impetuously which can on occasion even be life-threatening. Out walking with friends one day, she decides on impulse that some horsemen approaching from a distance have villainous designs on the party and so throws herself into the River Thames, 'intending to swim over it, as *Clelia* did the *Tyber*', in order to escape being ravished.[12] If her fictional heroine is successful in her perilous endeavour, Arabella is not. She has to be rescued and falls into a fever from which she takes some time to recover.

It is after this episode that Arabella is finally brought to her senses by a 'Pious and Learned Doctor', who skilfully leads her to realise the eccentricity of her behaviour.[13] He emphasises strongly the dangers of being carried away by our emotions, in words that would have gained assent from Plato:

> It is of little Importance, Madam, replied the Doctor, to decide whether in the real or fictitious Life, most Wickedness is to be found. Books ought to supply an Antidote to Example, and if we retire to a Contemplation of Crimes, and continue in our Closets to inflame our Passions, at what time must we rectify our Words, or purify our Hearts?[14]

The point is forcefully made by the doctor that the romances Arabella has been entranced by are not true to life, and that they foster a distorted worldview. Their exaggerated notions of honour no longer have any place in the world: 'they teach Women to exact Vengeance, and Men to execute it; teach Women to expect not only Worship, but the dreadful Worship of human Sacrifices.'[15] It is just such discrepancies between the imagined and the real that signal a potential problem to moralists then and now. As William B. Warner has noted, 'Arabella's literal faith in the referent behind the text authorizes the dangerous acting out that had been the target of the antinovel discourse' that arose at the time.[16] Arabella is finally reduced to tears, recognising her foolishness in being taken in by these fantastic stories and promising to resist their influence in future. Predictably enough, marriage to her long-suffering admirer Mr Glanville follows soon afterwards, with Arabella now deemed to be mature enough to take her rightful place in society.

We might just wonder, however, whether something has been lost in the transition to maturity. One could say that Arabella has been made to conform (schooled into 'the ideology of femininity', as Janet Todd has it),[17] and that her imagination will now have to be curbed in line with what society expects of young married women. At the very least her life is about to become far more pedestrian, with the kind of excitement she has become addicted to having to be forfeited in favour of family and social duties. Arabella clearly has the potential to develop an interesting personality, and when given an opportunity to display her rhetorical talents in public shows herself to be more than capable of holding her own in debate. She makes the pompous Mr Selvin look a fool at a Bath assembly through the sheer profusion of examples she can draw on from her reading, where fact and fiction confusingly mix. Shamed 'at seeing himself [op]posed by a Girl, in a Matter which so immediately belonged to him', Selvin proceeds to bluster, but is out-manoeuvred by Arabella, who forces him into a series of blatant errors, thus striking a blow for her sex.[18] Even Sir Charles is moved to compliment her – 'I protest, Lady *Bella* . . . you speak like an Orator'[19] – high praise indeed in a society in which women are supposed to be demure, passive and submissive to the male sex at all times. Arabella stands up for her values, misguided though they may be. It is an act of considerable defiance to refuse to bow to pressure from a figure like Selvin, who has all the weight of patriarchal authority behind him. In this case, popular culture can be seen to have an empowering effect, enabling the heroine to assert herself in a context that most young women of her day probably would find very intimidating. Supporters of popular culture in the twenty-first century would want to make similar claims as to its beneficial effects, arguing that its appropriation can unlock the potential in individuals, giving them values to test out in real-life situations.

Her treatment of the vapid Mr Tinsel, another fixture of the Bath season, is equally dismissive, cutting to the heart of the superficiality of the season and those who frequent it, with considerable rhetorical expertise and moral disapproval:

> I will allow the Ladies to be sollicitous about their Habits, and dress with all the Care and Elegance they are capable of; but such Trifles are below the Consideration of a Man, who ought not to owe the Dignity of his Appearance to the Embroidery on his Coat, but to his high and noble Air, the Grandeur of his Courage, the Elevation of his Sentiments, and the many heroick Actions he has perform'd.[20]

As a put-down of a self-important society beau this would be hard to beat, and unrealistic as her conception of the past is, and manifestly founded on false data, Arabella's yearning for something more in her life than the tired social round of the upper classes certainly can elicit our support. One senses the author's sympathy shifting behind the character in this instance, too. Arabella's world, with its decidedly 'anti-romantic tenor', is not one in which the cultivation of imagination is going to be encouraged – particularly not the female imagination.[21] There is more to her than any of her contemporaries, and precious little scope for these talents to be developed in any meaningful way: hence her enthusiastic embrace of the heroic romance genre, which offers the excitement and thrills that her life and social position otherwise lack. Popular culture offers a lifeline to the heroine, and her belief in it, and imitation of its language and values, has a positive side, unsustainable though it may be in the longer term.

Catherine Morland has a similarly haphazard upbringing which leaves her unprepared for adult life. Although neither of her parents dies in her youth, as happens to the unfortunate Arabella, they take a very casual attitude towards their children, the younger engaging their attention at the expense of the elder. Catherine grows up to be first of all something of a tomboy, then a keen reader, without any substantial parental guidance: 'from fifteen to seventeen she was in training for a heroine; she read all such works as heroines must read to supply their memories with those quotations which are so serviceable and so soothing in the vicissitudes of their eventful lives'.[22] So far, so like Arabella, but Catherine meets no one onto whom she can project her romance-derived fantasies, no equivalent to Mr Glanville willing to put up with regular embarrassment in pursuit of his objective. She is a much more reticent figure than Arabella, with the author emphasising her sheer ordinariness. This is much in contrast to Arabella, who throws herself into the role of heroine with gusto, and in all respects is a much more spirited character than Catherine.

When she discovers Gothic romances Catherine is totally entranced. *The Mysteries of Udolpho* (1794) becomes her favourite reading and leaves a very deep impression upon her already overactive imagination.[23] Soon she is viewing the world through the eyes of a Radcliffe heroine, seeing danger, dark plots and conspiracies everywhere. Invited to the Tilney family home, Northanger Abbey, as a guest, Catherine allows her imagination to run riot, endowing the place with all the characteristics of the setting of a Gothic novel, complete with the air of menace and foreboding that they would have in her favourite authors. We then have what Peter Knox-Shaw has described as the 'Radcliffean shenanigans at the Abbey', despite its being a mundane house largely furnished in the modern style, quite unlike the gloomy Castle Udolpho that serves as a model for Catherine.[24] On discovering an old chest in her room, Catherine automatically assumes it must hold a mysterious secret, but it turns out to contain only bedclothes. A cabinet then yields up what seems like an old manuscript with several sheets wrapped up in it, but they prove to be nothing more interesting than a laundry list and some bills.

Persisting through such disappointments, Catherine continues to believe there must be dark secrets in the Tilney house, an attitude which is only strengthened when she hears of the death of the Tilneys' mother from a sudden illness nine years earlier. That is enough to suggest foul play to Catherine, especially since Mrs Tilney's room has been left untouched since the event. In true Gothic fashion, Catherine allows the wildest speculations to form in her mind. The fact that General Tilney is a rather forbidding figure, a petty tyrant within his own family, only prompts Catherine to push on and think the unthinkable. Eventually, she is brought to her senses by the sharp response Henry Tilney makes to her prying into the topic. On realising that Catherine has come to the conclusion that his father was to blame for his mother's death, as would so often be the case in the plot of a Gothic novel, Henry is deeply insulted:

> If I understand you rightly, you had formed a surmise of such horror as I have hardly words to – Dear Miss Morland, consider

the dreadful nature of the suspicions you have entertained. What have you been judging from? Remember the country and the age in which we live. Remember that we are English, that we are Christians. . . . Dearest Miss Morland, what ideas have you been admitting?[25]

As the opening sentence of the next chapter pithily puts it, '[t]he visions of romance were over'.[26] Henry's shocked reaction projects Catherine into adulthood, and she is made to realise that her infatuation with Gothic literature is childish and potentially damaging to her prospects in life.

Fortunately, things work out well for Catherine, with Henry forgiving her and eventually marrying her – despite some mildly Gothic tyranny on the part of his father in opposing his son's choice. But it could so easily have gone horribly wrong, and Catherine has been taught a lesson about the dangers of becoming too embroiled in fictional worlds. These must never be confused with real life, and it is a critical part of her rite of passage from adolescence to adulthood to come to this realisation. Catherine has to learn to read the world around her correctly and to make sober assessments of the people in it. Just as Northanger Abbey is far more ordinary than Castle Udolpho, so life in general is far more ordinary than any fantasy dreamed up by a Gothic author. 'Charming as were all Mrs. Radcliffe's works, and charming even as were the works of all her imitators, it was not in them perhaps that human nature, at least in the midland counties of England, was to be looked for', as the author puts it in her most pointed fashion.[27]

Catherine has to be humiliated to experience her fateful epiphany, but her friend Isabella Thorpe fails to make the same transition from childish behaviour into responsible adulthood within the course of the narrative. Catherine has soon made a solemn resolution 'of always judging and acting in future with the greatest good sense', but that is patently beyond Isabella, who continues to act with all the impetuosity of the heroine in a Gothic tale.[28] Suitors are treated with disdain, with Isabella revealing herself to be emotionally immature and only too likely to enter a bad marriage – no small matter in a society where marriage is almost the entire basis of a woman's existence. A 'mixture of sentimental claptrap and selfish ambition', as Mary Waldron has damningly described her, Isabella stands as a warning to Catherine of what can happen when one neglects to learn the rules of social conduct.[29] For women especially, reputation is crucial, and by switching her affections from Catherine's brother, James, to Henry's brother, Frederick, Isabella leaves her own reputation badly stained, drawing the disapproval of the social circles in which she moves. Henry for one believes that Isabella is fickle enough to go off with yet another, acidly remarking that Frederick might still escape his entanglement with her if 'a baronet should come in her way'.[30] Isabella is simply not to be trusted, and by implication Gothic literature has much to answer for in her case, exacerbating existing character failings. For those who follow Plato's line on the issue, that is always going to be the fear of what emotionally charged literary material can do to the impressionable.

The proper attitude to adopt towards literature is the one exhibited by Henry Tilney, who is more than happy to admit to finding enjoyment in reading Gothic romances:

> The person, be it gentleman or lady, who has not pleasure in a good novel, must be intolerably stupid. I have read all Mrs. Radcliffe's works, and most of them with great pleasure. The Mysteries of Udolpho, when I had once begun it, I could not lay down again; – I remember finishing it in two days – my hair standing on end the whole time.[31]

Henry goes on to say that he prizes 'invention' above all in his reading, but it is clear that he regards fiction as a form of entertainment, a pleasant diversion from the problems of everyday life rather than an accurate guide to it, as Catherine and Isabella are plainly taking it to be.[32] Neither of the latter seems able to recognise that the work of such as Radcliffe really is invention, and to be appreciated on that level alone; but then they live much more circumscribed lives than does Henry, who has already had the benefit of a university education to broaden his knowledge and understanding of the world. Opportunities of this kind are not open to Austen's heroines: women are still very much second-class citizens with very restricted horizons. Ultimately, that is one of the key points the author is making: that it is a lack of education and experience that leads women like Catherine and Isabella to escape so enthusiastically into literature, or what Peter Knox-Shaw has neatly termed 'gothic chic'.[33] Their need for an alternative reality is an indictment of the one in which they live, with its strict notions of decorum, particularly as regards women, and narrow social vision overall. What

Sandra Shulman notes of Arabella, that she is '[i]mprisoned as much by the conventions of her gender as by her delusions', is equally true of Catherine and Isabella.[34] Beyond finding a suitable marriage partner, there is little that the women of Catherine's class can aspire to; no career structure for them to take advantage of and thus exercise some degree of control over their lives. It is the sheer lack of opportunity for self-expression that makes Gothic romances, with all their lurid tales and narrative twists and turns, so appealing to young women of this class. One could argue that it is boredom more than anything that prompts imitation of popular culture, boredom with one's lack of acess to self-expression – an observation probably as true in our own day as it was in Austen's.

The overall aim of Austen's project in *Northanger Abbey*, therefore, is didactic (even if it has been suggested that she overdoes the irony in achieving her objective).[35] It is her intention to warn us against both an emotional overindulgence in art and the dangers of under-educating the young such that they fail to have a sense of proportion about art. Austen is well aware of literature's power to affect us – as an author she could hardly be otherwise – but she is aware as well of the necessity of not allowing this to get out of hand. If we let our emotions dominate us, then we must expect there to be unpleasant consequences. Isabella Thorpe is prone to just such behaviour, as a result of which she is fast becoming a social pariah by the end of the narrative, her 'insincere jargon' fooling no one.[36] At one point Catherine's mother delivers herself of the trite sentiment that 'we must live and learn', but it holds a moral for the tale none the less: Catherine does live and learn, Isabella fails to, and their respective fates are meant to convey a lesson to the reader.[37] The newly mature Catherine becomes painfully aware of Isabella's shallowness of character and comes to regret their friendship. Catherine has managed, in other words, to distance herself from her past, and with that the baleful influence of popular culture and the media; these will no longer be allowed to dominate her thoughts and form her worldview.

CONCLUSION

The differences between the two treatments of the theme are indicative of the wide range of response that the topic evokes. How, and to what extent, the media and popular culture affect our behaviour is very much an open question and one that still vexes parents and our political guardians alike. There are many who favour greater censorship of material for the young than is currently in place, and they point to apparent copy-cat crimes as evidence for the need to be stricter in controlling the output of popular culture and the media. The issue becomes particularly controversial when it involves violence and pornography, which still tend to polarise opinion. The latter hardly figures in the novels that are being read by either Arabella or Catherine (although it does in other eighteenth-century productions such as John Cleland's *Memoirs of a Woman of Pleasure* (1748–9; better known as *Fanny Hill*) and Matthew Lewis's *The Monk* (1796)),[38] but violence is certainly present. Arabella's rather casual attitude towards duels indicates a certain amount of desensitisation has taken place through her reading, and it is precisely such desensitisation that campaigners for censorship are most worried about. Arabella has come to regard violence as a standard part of her world picture, without ever having to deal with it in reality. Rather like children exposed to cartoons nowadays, she cannot appreciate that real suffering and pain lie behind the reality: a cartoon character may bounce back to life after being the subject of extreme violence; human beings do not.

There is little explicit violence in Radcliffe either, but it is certainly there in the world in which the villainous Montoni and his peers move, with its complex political intrigues and constant conflicts between states and rival factions. As pictured by Radcliffe, Italy is a land bordering on anarchy. Again, there is a danger of desensitisation on the assumption that this is simply the way the masculine world operates, and that women must accommodate themselves to it as best they can, accepting a degree of violence as part of the normal run of affairs. Radcliffe provides an antidote to this masculinist ethos in her heroine's development of a sensibility that marks her out from the crude culture of Montoni and his ilk, but it is not this moralistic side of the author's approach to Gothic that seems to attract Catherine and Isabella; rather, it is the more shocking material that suggests evil is a very real presence in human affairs. While this is an important realisation to make as one grows up, it does depend on what effect it has on the individual. One suspects that neither Catherine nor Isabella draws the moral lessons from *The Mysteries of Udolpho* that the author wanted her audience, and her female audience above all, to do, and that is where the worry would lie for those concerned with the welfare of the young. Radcliffe's heroines are invariably models of moral probity, but their milieu leaves much to be desired in that respect. It requires careful reading to avoid the 'gothic chic' of the latter and recognise the virtue of the former.

Popular culture and the media will always exert an influence for good or bad, and the argument surrounding censorship is essentially over whether one outweighs the other: do we accept the bad effects because of the good, or decide that no amount of good will excuse the bad? It is the liberal position versus the conservative, freedom of speech versus the need for protection of the vulnerable (which is usually interpreted as meaning mainly the young). Neither of our authors argues for censorship, but both demonstrate a strong concern for guidance and education when it comes to the consumption of narrative. What is tantalising about both Lennox and Austen is that they suggest that women have untapped reserves of imagination which are largely going to waste. There is a culturally subversive quality to this aspect of their work that deserves to be highlighted, even if it is fair to say that Lennox seems to have more feeling for her heroine in this regard than Austen does for hers (hence the observation of Amanda Gilroy that 'Arabella's earliest readers write about her as though she were a familiar friend and absorb her into their lives').[39] We could imagine Arabella turning into a novelist in later life, but hardly Catherine. Nevertheless, both heroines succeed admirably in pointing up the ways in which their societies strive to 'imprison' young women within their gender, and in consequence their respective dialogues with popular culture take on layers of meaning that still have relevance to our own debates on the topic.

CHAPTER 7

The Life and Opinions of Tristram Shandy, Gentleman and Genetic Inheritance

THE ISSUE

The extent to which we are the products of our genetic inheritance is a matter of considerable interest to our society and has implications extending from our perception of ourselves as autonomous beings to such concerns as health care and personal insurance. Particular illnesses and physical conditions – or the disposition towards these – can run in families, and insurance companies have begun to investigate the possibility of restrictions being imposed on those with a family history of some diseases when it comes to issuing policies. A case in point is Huntingdon's disease: children have to decide whether to be tested to discover if this has been passed on to them from their parents (whose symptoms only become evident when they reach their forties or fifties). If their test is positive, they will be denied medical insurance. The Human Genome Project (HGP) has held out the prospect of being able to pin down what lies behind such genetic transmission with some accuracy, once the relevant DNA has been sequenced. Genetics may well lead to a whole new system of classifying people, which could have a significant effect on our lives, depending on where we find ourselves in the hierarchy that is accordingly assembled. There is a school of thought which suggests that conditions such as depression might be acquired genetically, and again, that has the capacity to affect both our own and others' perception of us. Whether we should be penalised or blamed for inherited characteristics over which we have no control is a question of some considerable ethical import and has the potential to become a major political issue in the near future.

Patterns of behaviour and personality also appear to be transmitted from generation to generation, raising interesting social questions about the relationship between nature and nurture, genes and environment, in the formation of individual character. How much we are the prisoners of our family past is a fascinating metaphysical question that many of us wrestle with throughout our lives, as we seek to establish our personal identity separate from those of our parents. Genetic determinists draw some politically contentious conclusions from the data about genetic inheritance, particularly concerning race, and overall these place a question mark over our assumption of free will, and hence responsibility for our individual actions. (Genetic determinism has been defined by one eminent molecular biologist as 'the biological theory that complex characteristics of human beings are caused by specific genes'.)[1] The psychologist Hans Eysenck, for example, notoriously claimed that research proves that the white races are intellectually superior to the black, although he disputes the charge that this will fuel racism within Western society or that disseminating his research findings proves he is a bigot: 'Nor am I a racist for seriously considering the possibility that the demonstrated inferiority of American negroes on tests of intelligence may, in part, be due to genetic causes.'[2] Needless to say, his protestations have failed to prevent him from becoming a target of the anti-racist lobby, which totally rejects all such claims.

It has been the work of the Human Genome Project above all which has led to the issue of genetic inheritance gaining such a high profile in recent years. HGP researchers set out to map the complete genetic make-up of the human organism, and the project's findings have been somewhat surprising. It discovered there were far fewer genes making up the human genome than had been expected – a mere 30,000 or so, rather than the 100,000 researchers thought were likely, which suggests we are less complex as a species than we had supposed. Further, of that 30,000 there were only 300 unique to human beings, differentiating us from such organisms as mice. Critics have suggested that this finding casts doubt on the entire project, which, they contend, is deterministic in claiming that the genetic code will provide the key, not just to the way that disease operates in human beings, but to human behaviour generally. It has been claimed that the HGP assumes a direct link between every genotype (section of the genetic sequence) and a specific phenotype (the physical manifestation of that section), and that having traced the one the other can be predicted.[3] For critics it is a far less straightforward process than that, as a host of intermediary factors need to be taken into account. The debate that is raging has far-reaching implications in terms of whether our conduct is susceptible to the kind of reductionism that the HGP seems to be proposing, where genotype unproblematically translates into phenotype. It has brought the age-old philosophical issue of free will versus determinism into the wider public arena, with opponents of the HGP approach seeing themselves in the position of defenders of the concept of free will.

Given the critical role played by free will in Western ideology this is an extremely important topic. Few of us will want to be told that we are not really autonomous beings able to make proper choices, or that our racial heritage is an impediment to our intellectual development, but those are amongst the inferences to be drawn from a strong interpretation of genetic inheritance. Regardless of whether that was its objective, the HGP is thought by determinists to bolster their case, and is regularly cited as evidence. Nature is assumed to trump nurture by such theorists, and none of us can have any say in how that nature comes about. It is not necessary to go to the other end of the spectrum, however, and argue that we are the products of nurture alone; no doubt the truth lies somewhere in between the extremes, although the relative percentages allotted to each side would still be a matter for extensive debate. But unless there is some kind of interplay between nature and nurture in which we are involved as active participants, able to affect some aspects of each by our own efforts, then we cannot really be said to have any meaningful role in our own development. Most of us would find that to be a deeply worrying conclusion.

THE TEXT

Laurence Sterne, *The Life and Opinions of Tristram Shandy, Gentleman*

Laurence Sterne's *Tristram Shandy* (1759–67) explores the murky topic of genetic inheritance and its role in the formation of the individual in some philosophical depth, exploring the protagonist's life story in terms of the larger picture of his family history. While the author may not have the language or concepts to deal with genetic inheritance in our modern understanding of the phenomenon – as James Swearingen has noted, the author's 'genetic approach to the self . . . hardly prevails in eighteenth-century thought'[4] – the book nevertheless proceeds to catalogue what look very much like the effects of it on his hero's existence. Tristram himself is made to suggest an intuitive awareness of the process involved when he observes of '*Nature*' that 'she thrusts us into this or that place, or posture of body, we know not why'.[5] The issue of free will, or our lack of it (our not knowing why we have come to be in a particular situation), is central to the narrative. Tristram's character is seen to be the outcome of a series of events in his parents' lives, many apparently due to chance, which presumably could be tracked back even further to previous generations of their respective families. There appears to be something in the character traits of the Shandy family that precipitates many of these events, for all that they present themselves as being the outcome of chance. Recognisably recurrent patterns do emerge. The males, for example, tend to have their obsessions, or 'HOBBY-HORSE' as the author mockingly dubs it;[6] and as Wolfgang Iser has commented, 'the various hobby-horses unerringly lead their riders into trouble'.[7] (D. W. Jefferson refers to the particular 'intensity' of Uncle Toby's hobby-horse, but in truth there is something of that trait in all of the Shandy obsessions.)[8]

Clearly, Tristram cannot be held responsible for anything outside his own lifetime, any more than his predecessors can either. The origins of the patterns of events or behaviour that dog the family are shrouded in obscurity: 'we live amongst riddles and mysteries', as Tristram reflects at one stage, 'and even the clearest and most exalted understandings amongst us find ourselves puzzled and at a loss in almost every cranny of nature's works'.[9] What unites Tristram, his father and his uncle, the leading figures in this narrative, is that they are unable to control their destiny: 'nature's works' appear to conspire against them at every turn. Whatever plans the Shandy family make tend to go awry, suggesting that their freedom of action is illusory; hence Walter's bitter complaint:

It is in vain longer . . . to struggle as I have done against this most uncomfortable of human persuasions – I see it plainly, that either for my own sins, brother *Toby*, or the sins and follies of the *Shandy*-family, heaven has thought fit to draw forth the heaviest of its artillery against me; and that the prosperity of my child is the point upon which the whole force of it is directed to play[.][10]

Walter can only continue to act as if he had this freedom (as most of us do, even when we harbour doubts ourselves about its reality), yet his suspicion that he is a victim of a malign fate brings out the notion of an adverse genetic inheritance working its way through the male line of the Shandy family. Tristram's various misadventures merely seem to confirm this, and the narrative concerns itself with the hero's attempts to construct some semblance of a coherent personality in the midst of a desperately chaotic world.

The Shandy family give every impression of systematically attracting bad luck, with Tristram being merely the latest in a line to be reduced to complaining of fortune that it 'has pelted me with a set of as pitiful misadventures and cross accidents as ever small HERO sustained'.[11] Anyone could be such a victim, however, and Sterne calls for us to be sympathetic towards those trapped in a situation not of their own choice or making. Sterne's contemporary David Hume's picture of the individual was of a passive recipient of a constantly changing stream of sense impressions from the outside world, which militated against us ever achieving a stable personal identity: 'I may venture to affirm of the rest of mankind, that they are nothing but a bundle or collection of different perceptions, which succeed each other with an inconceivable rapidity, and are in a perpetual flux and movement.'[12] This is a condition which implies we are largely at the mercy of circumstance, and Tristram's career would appear to bear this out. The novel's often notorious sentimentalism is in fact a plea for tolerance, which genetic determinists would do well to note: a recognition that any of us might be afflicted by the onset of 'pitiful misadventures and cross accidents' at any time in our lives. To quote the well-worn phrase, it is a case of 'there but for the grace of God go I'.[13]

Tristram himself tends to shy away from making harsh judgements of others on the basis that we are all at the mercy of a combination of fate and blind chance:[14] so at the very least a measure of sympathy should be extended towards the rest of humanity. Toby is similarly constitutionally inclined towards sympathy for others and disposed to shed tears on hearing of their various misfortunes. In Tristram's admiring words: 'Thou envied'st no man's comforts, – insulted'st no man's opinions. – Thou blackened'st no man's character, – devoured'st no man's bread: . . . for each one's service, thou hadst a tear, – for each man's need, thou hadst a shilling.'[15]

Tristram's problems begin from the most trivial of incidents: his mother's artless, although strikingly ill-timed, question to his father at the very second of Tristram's conception: *'Pray my dear . . . have you not forgot to wind up the clock?'*[16] As Tristram sadly observes, the effect of the query is that it distracted his father and 'scattered and dispersed the animal spirits, whose business it was to have escorted and gone hand-in-hand with the *HOMUNCULUS*, and conducted him safe to the place destined for his reception'.[17] From conception onwards, as Tristram perceives it, his life unfolds as a series of disordered events over which he struggles, unsuccessfully, to exercise any kind of effective agency. Tristram almost invariably seems to be in the wrong place at the wrong time – all because of that one innocent remark of his mother's, but an innocent remark that links back to the history of his parents' relationship (which registers as 'one of mutual vexation rather than mutual enrichment', as Manfred Pfister has observed).[18] His particular genetic coding has as its phenotype the disorder of both his thought processes and his relationship to his environment.

Tristram is to a significant extent not just the prisoner of his past in terms of his family history, but the prisoner of his family's fragmented and chaotic past, with the myriad association of ideas that this involves going off in a host of directions – as the narrative proceeds to chart (and provide bizarre diagrams for at the end of volume VI).[19] It is a condition to which we are all prey in what Tristram with some feeling, and not a little justification given his personal experience, refers to as 'this scurvy and disasterous world of ours', although his case does seem to be more extreme than most. That the book is, as one critic has put it, 'all extension and no meaning, all analogy and metonymy and no metaphor and plot', is a tribute to just how extreme.[20]

Association of ideas, the philosophical theory that Sterne takes over from John Locke and works up into a full-scale theory of human existence, has a profound effect on Tristram, therefore, through the particular association his mother makes at a critical juncture (*the* most critical juncture as Tristram's worldview has it).[21] Locke had observed how ideas could become connected in our minds by chance, just as

Tristram's mother links sexual intercourse and the winding of the family clock because of his father's habitual pattern of behaviour:

> he had made it a rule for many years of his life, – on the first *Sunday night* of every month throughout the whole year . . . to wind up a large house-clock which we had standing upon the back-stairs head, with his own hands: – And being somewhere between fifty and sixty years of age, at the same time I have been speaking of, – he had likewise gradually brought some other little family concernments to the same period, in order, as he would often say to my uncle *Toby*, to get them all out of the way at one time, and be no more plagued and pester'd with them the rest of the month.[22]

Although there is not what philosophers would call any 'necessary connexion' between these two activities, the one not causally dependent on the other, Tristram's mother has come to associate them in that way, bearing out Locke's description of a process in which there is a

> Connexion of *Ideas* wholly owing to Chance or Custom; *Ideas* that in themselves are not at all of kin, come to be so united in some Mens Minds, that 'tis very hard to separate them, they always keep in company, and the one no sooner at any time comes into the Understanding but its Associate appears with it; and if they are more than two which are thus united, the whole gang always inseparable shew themselves together.[23]

Chance and custom combine to determine the course of Tristram's life, rendering him forever afterwards 'the continual sport of what the world calls Fortune'.[24] Genetic inheritance, association of ideas and perpetual flux and movement in the world around us represent a formidable array of forces working against the individual's search for order and tranquillity, and Tristram has soon enough resigned himself to victim status.

Tristram's naming is an instructive example of how his fate consistently is shaped by the notions and actions of others. His father has a theory about naming, as he does about almost everything else in life for that matter (generally of a far-fetched nature). The theory is that the name affects our psychological development, hence his choice for his son of 'Trismegistus', whom he lauds as 'the greatest . . . of all earthly beings'.[25] His instructions go drastically wrong, however, as the maid, Susannah, garbles the name to the clergyman conducting the child's baptism, at which, as luck would have it, Walter is not present (the male Shandy talent for being in the wrong place at the wrong time declaring itself yet again), and it comes out as Tristram, the name his father loathes above all others. To Walter Shandy Tristram is a '[m]elancholy dissyllable of sound! which, to his ears, was unison to *Nicompoop*, and every name vituperative under heaven'.[26] One could argue that Walter has courted trouble by picking a name which starts with the same first four letters as his pet hate, but we do not generally proceed on the assumption that whatever we do is bound to turn out wrong. Unfortunately, that does seem to be the fate of the Shandy males, however, whose apparently freely made choices so often rebound on them to leave problems they could never have envisaged arising. When this happens as regularly as it does in the narrative, one has to begin to wonder about a genetically acquired predisposition to misread situations and thus set up the basis for misfortune. Neither Toby nor Tristram proves any more adept at making decisions that work to their advantage, and it does eventually come across as a characteristic family trait.

Tristram's career certainly suggests that he is very largely a prisoner of his family history and not the autonomous being he aspires to be. This is a cause for, at the very least, melancholy about one's state and quite possibly even a deep sense of fatalism: for all its celebrated humour, *Tristram Shandy* is at heart a serious book with a tragic view of human existence, regarding it as more likely to turn out badly than not. Tristram takes refuge from his seemingly endless succession of problems in sentimentalism, a wry recognition that the human condition is not what he would wish it to be, nor his individual situation within it. Circumstances are stacked against him and give a clear impression that they will remain so for the remainder of his days, almost as if male Shandys are the subject of their own version of the strange attractor phenomenon, whereby bad luck inexorably spirals in upon them, imposing a pattern on their lives they are powerless to resist.[27] But Tristram is not alone in his predicament; others have been even more unlucky in life's lottery on 'this vile, dirty planet of ours' than he has.[28] There is the case of Uncle Toby, whose life is blighted by a war wound that leaves him, most likely, impotent: 'owing to a blow from a stone, broke off by a ball from the parapet of a horn-work at the siege of *Namur*, which struck full upon my uncle *Toby's* groin':[29] a classic case of the 'pitiful misadventures and cross accidents' with which the family is plagued.

Discharged from the army, Toby returns to England and proceeds to spend much of his time and energy trying to recreate the battlefield in miniature in his backyard in a vain attempt to capture the essence of this defining moment and the causes underlying it. He decides that consulting a map of Namur and its surroundings 'might be a means of giving him ease', and the enterprise, his own particular 'HOBBY-HORSE', develops from there.[30] Soon, with the enthusiastic help of his valet, Trim, it has become 'an amiable obsession that grows by devouring every topic in view'.[31] The obsession has its effect on Tristram as well, because it is through Trim's appropriation of assorted household materials with which to build the model of the battlefield that the nursery window in the Shandy household is robbed of its lead weights. The direct result is that Tristram too suffers genital damage, with Susannah not realising when she is holding him up to the window that there is no longer anything to prevent it crashing down – which it promptly does. The reader is initially led to assume that castration has occurred, although Tristram hints later that it is only circumcision ('–'TWAS nothing, – I did not lose two drops of blood by it–'twas not worth calling in a surgeon, had he lived next door to us – thousands suffer by choice, what I did by accident'),[32] but it is one more genital mutilation in what is beginning to seem like an unfortunate family tradition. As Gabriel Josipovici has remarked, 'the theme of castration and impotence runs strongly through *Tristram Shandy*', and that has a wider metaphysical significance, of being impotent in determining how one's life will work out.[33]

Tristram's genital accident is merely an addition to an earlier physical mishap – the crushing of his nose during a forceps delivery by Doctor Slop. Yet again, chance appears to be targeting the Shandy family, which has an obsession with the length of the family males' noses: 'For three generations at least, this *tenet* in favour of long noses had gradually been taking root in our family.'[34] Walter's theory is that the family has been held back in their social rise by bad luck in this regard: 'He would often declare, in speaking his thoughts upon the subject, that he did not conceive how the greatest family in *England* could stand it out against an uninterrupted succession of six or seven short noses.'[35] Clearly, Tristram is not going to improve the family's position on this score, and what appears as chance might just as easily be interpreted as an extension of a well-entrenched sequence. His grandfather reports of his father (Tristram's great grandfather) that he had 'no more nose . . . than there is upon the back of my hand'.[36] When taxed with his small nose his great-grandfather claims that his father had an even shorter one (although Tristram's great-grandmother objects that he is thinking of an uncle instead). Short noses may have jumped a generation in Walter's case, only to reassert themselves with a vengeance when it comes to Tristram – albeit by an unusual method.

Nature and nurture are in a complicated dialectical relationship in the novel, therefore: 'If education planted the mistake', as Tristram notes of the process, then 'my father watered it, and ripened it to perfection'.[37] The net result is that all his father's attempts at creating the conditions for Tristram to develop go badly wrong – in the main because of Walter's character with its peculiar obsessions. The *Tristrapaedia* is a glaring example of this. It is designed by Walter to be a guide to Tristram's upbringing, but it takes him so long to compile that Tristram is growing up in the interim without any paternal guidance at all. In later life Tristram recalls,

> the slow progress my father made in his *Tristra-paedia*; at which . . . he was three years and something more, indefatigably at work, and at last, had scarce compleated, by his own reckoning, one half of his undertaking: the misfortune was, that I was all that time totally neglected and abandoned to my mother; and what was almost as bad, by the very delay, the first part of the work, upon which my father had spent the most of his pains, was rendered entirely useless, – every day a page or two became of no consequence.[38]

The guide comes to stand as a symbol of the lack of any direction or shape to the hero's life; always subject to digression depending on chance circumstances. Walter's only too practical demonstration of 'the inadequacy of the ultimately linear act of writing to inform the constant shiftings of plot time' is to be replicated on the much larger scale of his son's entire existence[39] – perhaps yet another character trait making its way down the Shandy male line? Tristram is ever at the mercy of the actions of others in his family circle, and cannot seem to break free from 'the sins and follies of the *Shandy*-family', bemoaning the fact that 'nothing ever wrought with our family after the ordinary way'.[40] Nature conspires to prevent nurture, with the obsessive character that is the inheritance of the male Shandys proving a real impediment to the latter. The *Tristra-paedia* proves only too accurate a reflection of Tristram's condition.

Carol Watts has argued that the novel's sentimentalism acts as a 'compensation for the shortcomings of society', but I would want to extend that to say that it constitutes an attempt to come to an accommodation with the effects of fate and chance on one's life (effects with which everyone in society has to deal).[41] Through his hero, Sterne suggests that he is committed to the doctrine of benevolism, whereby we are thought to be innately well disposed towards each other. One of the most eloquent defences of the doctrine in this period comes from David Hume, who bases his ethical theory on it. For Hume, benevolism is the highest human attribute, creating a feeling of community from which all will benefit:

> it seems undeniable *that* nothing can bestow more merit on any human creature than the sentiment of benevolence in an eminent degree; and *that a part*, at least, of its merit arises from its tendency to promote the interests of our species, and bestow happiness on human society. We carry our view into the salutary consequences of such a character and disposition; and whatever has so benign an influence, and forwards so desirable an end, is beheld with complacency and pleasure.[42]

Hume notes how in a theatre the audience is drawn into emotional identification with the play's characters by a common sense of benevolence:

> Every movement of the theatre, by a skilful poet, is communicated, as it were by magic, to the spectators, who weep, tremble, resent, rejoice, and are inflamed with all the variety of passions which actuate the several personages of the drama. Where any event crosses our wishes and interrupts the happiness of the favourite characters, we feel a sensible anxiety and concern. But where their sufferings proceed from the treachery, cruelty, or tyranny of an enemy, our breasts are affected with the liveliest resentment against the author of these calamities.[43]

Tristram is similarly empathetic towards his fellow men, particularly when they fall on hard times or are the victim of events outside their control. He certainly suggests a fellow feeling with Toby in this regard, no doubt intensified by being the subject of a genital accident himself. Toby becomes an ideal for Tristram of how to conduct oneself in the face of suffering and misfortune:

> my heart stops me to pay to thee, my dear uncle *Toby*, once for all, the tribute I owe thy goodness. Here let me thrust my chair aside, and kneel down upon the ground, whilst I am pouring forth the warmest sentiments of love for thee, and veneration for the excellency of thy character, that ever virtue and nature kindled in a nephew's bosom.[44]

If his father is less overtly benevolent in outlook, tending instead towards exasperation in his dealings with the many problems of life, Tristram could be said to have inherited similar character traits to his uncle's. But whether the Shandys react with annoyance or resignation, it is clear they are at the mercy of circumstances and are not the engineers of their own destiny.

Ultimately, the point to be made about Tristram is that he is unable to transcend his family heritage and has to face up to a life of powerlessness; impotence being one of the critical concerns of the narrative, a 'shadow' which 'hovers like a dubious halo over the head of every Shandy male, including the bull'.[45] Genotype dictates phenotype with monotonous regularity. The profusion of accidents and misadventures that go to make up the Shandy family history resound through the generations and Tristram is their hapless victim; the latest to find that events are almost entirely outside his ability to affect, and appearing to conspire against him. There is much humour in this for the reader, but overall it offers a fairly pessimistic view of human endeavour.

CONCLUSION

None of us is immune from genetic inheritance, and it is not unreasonable to describe us as being in some way prisoners of our family history. Whether this moulds our lives to the degree that it appears to do with someone like Tristram is another issue altogether, and our society does assume the existence of free will in every individual that enables us to rise above our genetic conditioning at least some of the time. If that were not so, then we could not have any concept of personal responsibility for our actions, and that would invalidate much of the basis of our social system. The arguments of genetic determinists hold out the possibility that we cannot escape our inheritance, and that has political implications as we have noted earlier – hence the controversy over the findings and methodology of the HGP. Again, the point needs to be made that the HGP may not have set out to make the case for genetic determinism, but that is what it is being used as evidence for by some commentators. It is all too easy for institutions to discriminate against those with a family history of certain diseases and for that to be enough to block access to life or medical insurance – even to blight individuals' employment prospects (it is likely that companies will rely ever more heavily on such data in future). When racial issues come on the scene, as in the work of Hans Eysenck, then the possibility of more widespread public discrimination arises.

One of Sterne's great virtues for us now lies in his exploration of the emotional landscape of this debate, genetic determinism versus free will, as it is experienced at individual level. Tristram has to negotiate a series of physical and emotional crises throughout the narrative and is left feeling that he has precious little room for manoeuvre in the planning of his life against the effect of 'nature's works' and their many mysterious 'crannies'. If not fatalism, there is an air of resignation to the book, and one suspects that genetic determinism often encourages such a response in those who take it seriously. It is not to society's benefit for that notion to achieve wide acceptance, and the more it can claim a scientific basis – hotly contested though this may be – then the more dangerous it becomes. We do not need yet more excuses for discriminating against each other, and genetic determinism offers those in abundance to anyone looking for such material. Hume notwithstanding, not everyone is motivated by benevolist principles at all times – especially in a competitive culture such as the West features nowadays. Genetic determinism is a gift to the prejudiced and has to be considered a dangerous notion for that reason.

It is worth noting too that where determinism in a general sense does take hold, as in many religions where devotees believe their lives are directed by God, the consequences can be very unpleasant for those outside the religion in question. Rather than resignation, what we find in such cases is an unshakeable belief in the rightness of one's actions in the furtherance of the divine cause. Fundamentalist terrorists, for example, are convinced they are carrying out God's will and they simply write off the rest of the human race as being of no consequence in any action they may undertake. Where this can lead is something we shall explore in Chapter 12, when we turn to James Hogg's *Confessions of a Justified Sinner* (1824) and relate it to contemporary developments in religious fundamentalism.[46] Determinism of any kind is not in society's best interests. If we want to keep prejudice at bay, then we should be resisting such reductionist theories of human existence as strongly as we can wherever they arise.

CHAPTER 8

The Mysteries of Udolpho, A Romance and Family Values

THE ISSUE

Politicians in the United States America and Britain are fond of promoting the virtue of the family unit as a way of reducing our dependence on the state and of establishing the right moral values in the individual. The assumption is that parents can always be relied upon to have the child's best interests at heart, and that intervention by the state is more likely to be detrimental than beneficial: the 'nanny state', so called, is a particular target of ridicule for the political Right, which argues that it destroys initiative and erodes our moral fibre. In many parts of the non-Western world the extended family is still a dominant factor in social life, often being more powerful collectively than the official political structures of some states – unsurprisingly, given the minimal welfare provision found in most of the Third World. Given this situation, the family has to take care of its own; therefore, the more extended the better. One might think the West has less need of the extended family, but for many Western conservatives the family is the answer to almost all our social problems and they are quick to attack anything that reduces its influence or its power to direct its own affairs. In extreme cases this can mean opposing any socially progressive legislation such as abortion, and even women's rights in general, since the male is traditionally the dominant figure in the family, with women being consigned to a caring and nurturing role. Conservatives see any alteration in these roles as symptomatic of moral decay and consider it their duty to campaign against this as champions of family life as traditionally understood.

Such appeals are based on an idealised vision of the family unit, which ignores many of the negative features to be found there in real life. They are often cloaked in a cloying sentimentalism too, which comes to a head at the Christmas time in the West and trades heavily on unrealistically nostalgic images of family life. Family units can, of course, be caring and nurturing, but they also can be personally stultifying, claustrophobic and inculcate values which are not always to the benefit of society at large. Parents do *not* always act in the best interests of their children; some are more concerned to mould them to their own image of what they think they should be than to let them develop in their own way. One thinks of young sports or music prodigies, for example, pushed into carrying out the dreams of their parents at the expense of their own emotional growth (with many reacting against this in later life). There is a large psychiatric and psychoanalytical literature cataloguing just how repressive the family can be and how hostile an environment to individual development, yet it remains a central concept of political life and of public policy throughout the world.[1] There are few politicians who would openly challenge family values; these are more or less sacrosanct in official circles, and many a political campaign is based on support for the family. Despite this, there is a sizeable constituency who find the sentimentalism surrounding the concept hard to accept: what case can be made for their views will now be explored in terms of the work of the Gothic novelist Ann Radcliffe.

THE TEXT

Ann Radcliffe, *The Mysteries of Udolpho, A Romance*

Ann Radcliffe's *The Mysteries of Udolpho* (1794) constitutes a thought-provoking case study of just how inimical the extended family unit can be to the individual's personal development and of how family authority can be abused by its dominant members. After the death of her parents, the young Emily St. Aubert finds herself under the guardianship of her aunt, Madame Cheron, and is drawn into the web of intrigue surrounding her aunt's new husband, the sinister Signor Montoni, a financially embarrassed Italian aristocrat. Emily is prevented from seeing her suitor Valancourt, and shortly thereafter is immured in Montoni's stronghold, the remote and gloomy Castle Udolpho deep in the Appenines, repository of various family secrets and scandals. Montoni's attempts to marry Emily to one of his acquaintances in order to restore his family's financial fortunes (in effect, Emily is being sold) are stoutly resisted by the heroine, but at the cost of her personal freedom – for long stretches of the narrative she is cut off from the outside world within an enclosed domestic environment where servants and retainers spy on her. Montoni's strongly patriarchal conception of the family unit means that Emily counts as no more than property to him, as her primary male guardian, and he reacts with considerable hostility to all efforts she makes at self-assertion. He considers his will to be sovereign and her individual desires and preferences not to matter when weighed against the needs of the Montoni family honour, as he interprets it. Montoni proves to be the patriarchal head of family writ large.

Although Emily manages ultimately to escape the clutches of her family and to achieve happiness with Valancourt, the narrative is a powerful argument against the oppressiveness of the patriarchal family unit, providing a catalogue of the latter's sins against the individual and her understandable wish for personal growth and emotional fulfilment. It is particularly women who suffer the greatest oppression in the traditional family, with both Emily and her aunt finding themselves almost completely under male control, their movements very carefully monitored, reported on by servants, most of whom go in great fear of their master. The family unit becomes a prison for the two women, with Montoni the equivalent of their jailer, stipulating their living conditions, deciding where they will reside and preventing them from having any meaningful connection with others outside his circle. Their interests are always seen to be secondary to his. As Montoni chastises Emily during a typically heated exchange between them, the virtues expected of womanhood are 'sincerity, uniformity of conduct and obedience'.[2]

At least implicitly there is a feminist agenda to be noted in Radcliffe's work, carefully calculated though this is to stay within the bounds of the social conventions of the time. Radcliffe is calling for women to be given fair treatment rather than for any more modern conception of women's rights, as contemporaries like Mary Wollstonecraft were beginning to do. Nevertheless, Radcliffe is very much concerned at how the patriarchal system, particularly as expressed through the extended family, oppresses women, and she deserves to be enrolled in the wider feminist movement that has come to prominence since her day. The situations that Radcliffe places her heroines in make gender inequality starkly evident, and in so doing she becomes a champion of what Ellen Moers has called 'heroinism':[3] creating a narrative structure where her heroines are given trials to test themselves against that are as character-building as those faced by their counterpart literary heroes. At the very least she is arguing that there are limits to what men should be allowed to do to women, and Radcliffe is clearly opposed to the notion that women are to be considered as mere property and used to further the family's interests at the expense of their own. Arranged marriages are manifestly not part of the Radcliffean worldview, and her heroines invariably marry for love not for social advantage. Emily proves to be one of her most representative heroines in this respect, someone determined to assert her rights within the limited space allowed her.[4] Her sphere of influence may be small, but she protects it with her own brand of firmness, refusing to be harried into any action that threatens her personal integrity. Merely to insist that she has an existence outside that of the family unit is in its own way subversive. To reach that stage Emily has to develop considerable inner resources, most often in the teeth of opposition from her guardians. The narrative charts that conflict between Emily's little narrative and the grand narrative of the patriarchal family system through to Emily's eventual hard-won triumph.

The Mysteries of Udolpho traces the course of Emily's life from childhood to young adulthood, and we observe her develop into a sensitive and eminently sensible young woman with the courage to resist the many pressures exerted on her by patriarchy. She faces a series of trials which strengthen her character and resolve, and by the novel's conclusion she is a notably self-possessed individual with a keen sense of moral virtue: a model of how one should conduct oneself socially in a world full of hypocrisy and corruption. Emily's relationship with her parents is very close, and in this instance the family unit is seen to be nurturing, although it proves to be uncharacteristically so compared to the lifestyle of her other relations. Her closest relatives, Madam Cheron and Monsieur Quesnel, are self-interested, socially ambitious individuals who give little thought to the needs of others. We might also note that the retired lifestyle her father has adopted is not necessarily the best way to teach his daughter about the wider world she will have to face after her parents' deaths; a world where everyone is not as trustworthy and guileless as those she meets around the romantically situated family estate in Gascony, La Vallée (a 'Crusoesque island' is Maggie Kilgour's description).[5] But there is no denying that this particular family unit is protective and that Emily feels quite content there.

Emily is very much her father's daughter, displaying the same pragmatic, rather melancholic attitude towards life that he does. Her father's character is on the depressive side in fact, and this becomes more marked after the death of his wife, an event which draws father and daughter ever closer in their mutual grief. Emily is soon exhibiting the same style of finely tuned sensibility that her father did, with a similar disdain for the world of fashionable society and its many hypocrisies. Like her father, Emily would rather live a retired existence far from the corruption of Paris where his arrogant brother-in-law, Monsieur Quesnel, resides. The steady growth of her sensibility is revealed over the course of the narrative by Emily's ability to commune with nature, expressed in Radcliffe's famous, and numerous, descriptions of the sublime landscapes of the mountainous regions of France and Italy. During their travels in the south of France after her mother's death, their shared love of the sublime landscape is very apparent, and forms a bond between the two as her father's health rapidly declines.[6]

Her father's subsequent death brings the rude shock for Emily of being taken into the care of her vain and unsympathetic aunt, Madame Cheron, who makes it clear that she regards her niece as a burden to be borne only for the sake of family duty. But Madame Cheron also takes more than a certain delight in bullying Emily and showing the extent of her power over her charge, forbidding her, for example, from having any say in who pays court to her – as the chevalier Valancourt, whom her father had both known and respected, proceeds to do. Valancourt only becomes acceptable as a suitor once his family connection to Madame Clairval comes to light, Madame Cheron being a notorious snob and social climber who defers to such socially important figures in Toulouse society. Given that Madame Clairval's 'establishment was such as to excite the general envy and partial imitation of the neighbourhood', a family connection is deemed to be desirable and is duly set in motion.[7] This idyll is brought to a close when Madame Cheron marries Montoni, a shadowy figure who has turned up in Toulouse and about whom little is known, although rumours are circulating that he is not a particularly salubrious character and that his affairs might not withstand much close scrutiny.

Montoni soon decides to move the entire family group to his home country of Italy, and Emily is forced to break off her engagement to Valancourt or even to see him again as this no longer fits in with the family's plans, as dictated now by Montoni. From this point onwards she becomes more and more a pawn in Montoni's devious schemes, her wishes never taken into account. With Montoni as the head of the family unit Emily finds herself having to struggle to maintain any sense of personal integrity, and once in the Castle of Udolpho her sense of being trapped is palpable:

> As she looked on the massy walls of the edifice, her melancholy spirits represented it to be her prison; and she started as at a new suggestion, when she considered how far distant she was from her native country, from her little peaceful home, and from her only friend – how remote was her hope of happiness, how feeble the expectation of again seeing him! Yet the idea of Valancourt, and her confidence in his faithful love, had hitherto been her only solace, and she struggled hard to retain them. A few tears of agony started to her eyes[.][8]

Udolpho is not just a prison; it is also the site of secrets and mysteries, which the gloomy surroundings – all dark passageways, hidden staircases, cheerless rooms and deserted wings – only intensify. Emily is never at ease while wandering round this forbidding edifice. There is, for example, the picture frame covered by a black veil, which causes Emily to faint when she looks behind it. It turns out to be a gap in the wall with a lifelike representation of a dead body behind it moulded in wax. The mystery of why it is there is eventually cleared up (it's a memento mori), but it indicates how chilling a place the castle is, designed to induce fear in those unfortunate enough to be compelled to stay there.

One of the primary ways in which Emily's character develops is through communion with the natural world, a talent she has displayed from childhood: 'It was one of Emily's earliest pleasures to ramble among the scenes of nature.'[9] She withdraws into profound personal contemplation at such points, landscape having, as Daniel Cottom has noted, 'a talismanic importance' for the Radcliffe heroine.[10] Although awed by the sheer power of nature, especially in the mountains, Emily is also given a sense of proportion about her struggles against the machinations of Montoni and the lack of help offered by her aunt to resist these. Powerful though Montoni may be, he is no match for brute nature, and Emily can take comfort from observing the landscape of the Appenines in all its fearful majesty, even as she is being carried off to be sequestered in the Castle of Udolpho:

> The immense pine-forests, which, at that period, overhung these mountains, and between which the road wound, excluded all view but of the cliffs aspiring above, except that, now and then, an opening through the dark woods allowed the eye a momentary glimpse of the country below. The gloom of these shades, their solitary silence, except when the breeze swept over their summits, the tremendous precipices of the mountains, that came partially to the eye, each assisted to raise the solemnity of Emily's feelings into awe[.][11]

The power of Montoni's 'masculine sublime' will never equate to that of the landscape sublime in which his ancestral home is situated, despite possessing a character that is 'unprincipled, dauntless, cruel and enterprising', and Emily can draw strength from this realisation.[12] No matter how much he tries, Montoni can never induce quite the same sense of awe in her that nature can, and Emily learns to stand up to him and refuses to do his bidding. This stands her in good stead in a world where male pressure is unrelenting. The unfortunate Madame Cheron, however, does succumb to Montoni's power, finding herself unable to negotiate the 'labyrinth of misfortune' into which he has led her by their hasty marriage.[13] It is a measure of Emily's growing maturity that she is so successful in blocking Montoni's schemes: ' "You may find, perhaps, Signor," said Emily, with mild dignity, "that the strength of my mind is equal to the justice of my cause; and that I can endure with fortitude, when it is in resistance of oppression" .'[14]

Emily engages in a protracted battle of wills with Montoni, and this emboldens her to reject the overtures of other males as well. When Count Morano tries to bully her into putting herself in his power to escape from Montoni's clutches in Udolpho (Montoni having fallen out with Morano in the interim), Emily proves just as obdurate as she has been with Montoni:

'This discourse, Count Morano, sufficiently proves, that my affections ought not to be yours,' said Emily, mildly, 'and this conduct, that I should not be placed beyond the reach of oppression, so long as I remained in your power. If you wish me to believe otherwise, cease to oppress me any longer by your presence. If you refuse this, you will compel me to expose you to the resentment of Signor Montoni.'[15]

Considering the parlous situation she is in, effectively imprisoned in a castle in a remote corner of a foreign land, these are brave words and indicative of a strength of will on Emily's part that not even her rather melodramatic tendency to faint when under severe stress can undermine. When put to the test Emily will prevail one way or another (fainting does have the effect of thwarting her male tormentors, if only temporarily). Even Valancourt has to learn not to press Emily too far, for she will not suffer her personal integrity to be eroded.

Emily's situation becomes even more critical when her aunt dies, a victim of Montoni's maltreatment and wrath, thus terminating what Maggie Kilgour has aptly described as their truly 'gothic marriage'.[16] The most immediate effect of this is that Montoni becomes Emily's principal guardian, which puts him in a position to exert even more pressure on her to do his bidding, which he proceeds to do, seeking to trick Emily into signing over to his control some disputed estates that have devolved to her on her aunt's death. Emily once again refuses, but her aunt's death raises the dread spectre of Montoni plotting to marry her against her will in order to break her resistance – a scheme of which he is entirely capable. In fact, the threat of rape hangs over much of the narrative, lending a very sombre tone to the proceedings.[17] By forcing her into marriage with Count Morano that is precisely what Montoni would be party to, since Emily makes it clear from the first encounter that she detests the count and will not change her mind about him. It is only when Montoni discovers that Morano's finances are as embarrassed as his own that he abandons the scheme; but that merely means that he sets about soliciting a replacement elsewhere in his circle of acquaintances. The secret passageway into her room in Udolpho that locks on the outside only signals the ever-present danger of sexual assault while Emily is under Montoni's guardianship. Montoni's frequent threats to exact vengeance on her for refusing to obey his commands carry that unspoken threat, especially in such an isolated spot

as Udolpho, and the unruly company the castle attracts can only exac-
erbate her sense of vulnerability: predatory males seem to be lurking
around every corner, with Emily feeling herself constantly 'exposed to
the rude gaze of Montoni's associates'.[18] Emily is patently an object of
male desire and in her unprotected state is always at risk, although
Radcliffe never discusses this explicitly. Unlike contemporaries such as
Matthew Lewis (*The Monk*, 1796) or Charlotte Dacre (*Zofloya*, 1806)
she will always stop short of such sexual sensationalism, leaving this to
the reader's imagination, but it forms a powerfully suggestive background to events throughout the narrative.[19] Emily's fear of Montoni
is only too well founded.[20]

Montoni turns into a parody of patriarchal power after his wife's
death, well aware of the air of menace he can exude and determined to
use this talent to the full to exact submission from the female sex. Even
though there is no blood relation between them, Emily is still caught
up in the web of the extended family: a victim of a social system that
allows women to be used as bargaining chips by unscrupulous males.
It is almost as if she can never really break free from the grasp of the
extended family, despite the death of her closest relatives. When she
escapes to France she finds that her only surviving relative, Monsieur
Quesnel, has little interest in her plight. Instead, he is 'cold and
formal . . . expressing neither concern for the evils she suffered, nor
pleasure, that she was now removed from them', and willing to offer
only the most minimal help in recovering the estates she has signed
away under duress to Montoni.[21] It is only with Montoni's death that
Emily is freed from her worst fears and able to reconstruct her life
according to her own wishes.

Emily may appear to be complicit in her victim status to some extent,
as she turns down various offers of help to flee capture – from both
Valancourt and Count Morano, for example – and often seems more
concerned with propriety than her personal safety. Modern readers
can find her conduct quite irritating in this respect. But we have to
remember it is a very different culture that she inhabits from our own –
although not necessarily so different from that of many non-Western
countries nowadays. With her acutely keen awareness of 'the delicacy
of female honour' Emily defers to convention, and convention dictates
that women have to observe a very strict moral code, as well as accept
a social hierarchy where men are the ultimate wielders of power.[22]

From her own perspective, Emily has to operate within such constraints, and those are constraints which would be recognised by women in various countries at present. The family unit and male authority over it hold sway around much of the world, with arranged marriages – Montoni's initial desire for Emily – a common feature in many cultures (India and Pakistan, for example).

Despite the examples offered by her father and Valancourt, the male sex in *Udolpho* does not appear to very good advantage, being only too willing to abuse the power over women that their social position endows them with. While it can provide a refuge, as it does in childhood and youth for Emily, the patriarchal family unit can be very oppressive to the individual, as Emily discovers when she is taken into the care of her extended family. Once this happens her wishes are never consulted, nor considered of any particular note, and she is treated as a mere bargaining counter in an elaborate dynastic game. Family honour always outranks individual honour, especially when it comes to the female sex. We could say that Emily strikes a blow for the latter and against the former, and in that sense there is a subversive undercurrent to Radcliffe's work. Emily's marriage to Valancourt at the end of the narrative signals the creation of yet another family unit, but it is of a different kind from that ruled over by Montoni, or even by Emily's father. The 'delicacy of female honour' notwithstanding, Emily is a far stronger, much more self-possessed individual than either her mother or Madame Cheron – or the status-obsessed Madame Quesnel for that matter.

Radcliffe summarises her intentions in *Udolpho* in the most conventional of terms:

> O! useful may it be to have shewn, that, though the vicious can sometimes pour affliction upon the good, their power is transient and their punishment certain; and that innocence, though oppressed by injustice, shall, supported by patience, finally triumph over misfortune![23]

While the novel is clearly concerned with the struggle between good and evil, the narrative has a much darker side to it than the author chooses to admit. The many trapped and mentally tortured females who feature in the story hint at a world where self-realisation is actively

frowned upon and where the individual is sacrificed to the needs of
the system. Emily and her aunt are not the only females to suffer in
the name of family honour: the unfortunate Marchioness de Villeroi,
St. Aubert's sister as she is eventually discovered to be, is forced by her
domineering father to marry against her will. In her own way even
Laurentini di Udolpho, mistress of the Castle of Udolpho before
Montoni comes on the scene, is a victim of the social order of her time,
with its strict rules about how women are expected to behave. A woman
driven by her passions, she is made to pay the price of giving in to these
by being forced into a convent after provoking her lover, the Marquis
de Villeroi, into murdering his wife. Since he has already gone back on
his promise to marry her, making her his mistress instead when he
learns of her 'depraved' character (a lack of sincerity, uniformity of
conduct and obedience presumably), one might think the guilt should
lie more heavily on him than on her. But whereas Laurentini is banished to the seclusion of convent life, to go mad over the years, the
marquis throws himself into a life of dissipation in Paris and adventures in the wars, holding his mistress mainly to blame for the murder
that has been committed. The author is contrasting Laurentini to
Emily, thus playing up the latter's 'delicacy of female honour' as an
ideal even more, but what also comes through is a strong impression of
the sexual double-standard. Radcliffe is always searching for a balance
of reason and emotion in her novels, and Emily shrinks from '[t]he
fierce and terrible passions' which drive figures such as Montoni,
'bearing down the barriers of reason'.[24] Unlike Emily, Laurentini does
not achieve the desired state of 'balanced self-government', but patriarchy must take at least some of the blame for this.[25]

Men can suffer at the hands of their family as well. Monsieur Du
Pont is warned by his father not to pay suit to Emily, a near neighbour
in Gascony, because she is 'inferior in point of fortune', the same argument deployed by the father of the Marchioness de Villeroi to prevent
her marriage to the man she loves.[26] The desire to improve the family
fortune is given precedence over any considerations of personal happiness, with the family unit exerting a malign influence on the vulnerable individual – all the more vulnerable if the individual is female. In
Emily's case, her grandfather's decision to go against his daughter's
choice is to have a profound impact on Emily's life a generation further
down the line. Emily's own decision to wed Valancourt, despite the fact
that he is penniless (a condition later rectified, in the convenient

manner of the fiction of the period, through a bequest from his brother), represents a clear break with the past. Emily marries for love, although her sense of propriety demands that Valancourt first clears his name of the slurs made against him alleging misconduct and loose living while with his regiment in Paris. Female honour has its own criteria that must be satisfied.

The repressive effect of the family on the individual is a theme that Radcliffe returns to in her next novel, *The Italian* (1797), where Ellena Rosalba and her suitor Vincentio di Vivaldi are kept apart by his family, notably his scheming and unscrupulous mother, the marchesa, because of Ellena's poverty. Again, the heroine is pursued by a larger-than-life male villain, this time the monk Schedoni, who in an interesting twist of the plot briefly thinks himself to be Ellena's father and moves from attempted murder of her at the marchesa's behest to using her as a pawn in his own devious schemes. The family unit, with its exaggerated notions of honour, is yet again seen to be inimical to the interests of the individual, and it is only when Ellena is discovered to be the daughter of a noble family 'no less respectable . . . in rank' to the Vivaldis that the lovers can be united.[27] If anything, Ellena undergoes even more severe trials than Emily, with Radcliffe being at pains to show how the concept of family honour clashes with the desire for self-realisation, and how a commitment to the former can severely distort one's moral sense. Emily lives in fear of being murdered, and Ellena finds herself seconds away from being so, illustrating the lengths to which families will go if they feel their honour requires it.

Although the narrative of *Udolpho* travels full circle to return us to La Vallée and the pleasant Gascon countryside to which the heroine is so attached, the overall atmosphere is gloomy and claustrophobic, the many grandly sublime landscape scenes through which Emily passes notwithstanding. This is Gothic at its most oppressive, with a strong sense of entrapment when it comes to Emily, who is shuttled between locations with little regard for her wishes. We get a sense of the family unit as a Gothic nightmare in which the individual is imprisoned, her development inhibited, her movements monitored at every turn. For all her conventional moral sentiments, Radcliffe does not paint a very attractive picture of the family or, for that matter, of the male sex in general. Tyrannous males are only too common in her fiction, and females more often at risk than not. Decorous and propriety-conscious though her heroines may be, they are nonetheless successful in calling into question many of the values traditionally associated with the patriarchal family system and in managing to establish their own in their place, despite the fierce opposition offered by villains such as Montoni and Schedoni.

CONCLUSION

The difficulty that individuals can have in wresting themselves away from family control and constructing their own personalities is well illustrated by Emily's experience in *Udolpho*. Emily eventually is successful in asserting her own identity, but it is a bitter struggle that she has to engage in and one that demonstrates the inequality between the sexes in her culture: an inequality that the patriarchal family unit serves to perpetuate. Family values are not always to the advantage of the individual, as Emily discovers to her cost: this is always likely to be the case where dynastic considerations are allowed to dominate. When they do, the female comes to be viewed as property to be used for the aggrandisement of the family. It could be argued that Emily is over-protected by her father and then shamelessly exploited by her guardians, and she has to work extremely hard to establish an identity of her own in such unpromising circumstances. Against the odds, and against the grain of social convention at the time, Emily becomes an individual separate from the family unit, able to make her own decisions as to how to conduct her life and determined not to be defined by others.

   Much of the defence of family values in our own time is deeply dubious, harking back to an assumed golden age when moral standards were higher and authority respected rather than challenged or mocked, as is deemed to be happening now. Patriarchal authority is the backbone of such a system for conservative thinkers, and the negative aspects of it rarely examined: it is simply taken to be the natural order of things, almost divinely ordained (and there is often a strong religious element to be noted in campaigns for family values). The rise of feminism has forced us into just such an examination, however, demonstrating how oppressive male power can be. Few feminists are going to make a fetish out of family values, regarding them instead as part of the mechanism of ideological control by which women are kept in an inferior position socially: in the family, rather than making a life for themselves in the wider world. The family values movement represents a backlash against feminism, and it should be seen for the reactionary force it is within our culture. Family values can mean inculcating fundamentalist religious beliefs in children (creationism or intelligent design, for example),[28] and in general opposing liberalising legislation. This is not to argue against families as such, they are likely to remain the reality for most of us in terms of our living arrangements, but only against a certain kind of family set-up – that is, the hierarchical one of tradition, in which parental authority (particularly male) goes unquestioned. Conservatives have little time for other kinds of family unit, with the one-parent family invariably drawing their ire as a symbol of our supposed steep moral decline in recent generations, not to mention any union based on gay couples. Family values is a synonym for conservative values: there is always a political agenda when they are brought into play, and this needs to be emphasised.

Radcliffe is writing at the point when the traditional system was beginning to be questioned, even as regards women, and in exploring the situation of such figures as Emily she reveals the fault-lines in the patriarchal family unit as far as the female sex is concerned. We become aware of where the ideology of the family can go wrong; where it can become unreasonable in terms of the demands it makes on its members; in a general sense, where it can inflict emotional damage on its members. Without making any explicit political statement on the issue, Radcliffe succeeds in showing how outmoded concepts such as family honour need to be reassessed. For Emily to uphold 'the delicacy of female honour' is to insist that the little narrative of the individual should take precedence over the grand narrative of the patriarchal family unit, and that is a point still very much worth making against those who claim that family values are the answer to all our social ills.

CHAPTER 9

Caleb Williams, or, Things As They Are and the Surveillance Society

THE ISSUE

The rise of fundamentalist terrorism in recent years, exemplified by the dramatic events of 9/11 and 7/7, has led a succession of Western governments to re-examine the issue of public security. In many cases this has involved debates about civil liberties that most of us consider part of our natural birthright and not up for renegotiation: freedom of movement and freedom of speech, for example. The Homeland Security Act has made travel in and out of the US considerably more difficult for visitors; in Britain, the government has been arguing for some time that we must learn to accept certain restrictions on our civil liberties in order to guarantee our safety. The length of time that suspects can be held by the police for questioning has become a particular area of contention. Although the government has succeeded in having this period extended, it has not been by as much as they claim is necessary to enable the police to carry out their various checks on the suspect exhaustively enough, and the debate rumbles on. In the US, government policy now condones the use of torture with terrorist suspects (Guantánamo Bay and Iraq being the most conspicuous examples), even if the practice itself is disguised by various euphemisms in public pronouncements. Critics have argued that such initiatives increase the power of the state and that this is inimical to the spirit of modern culture as it has developed since the Enlightenment. The climate of fear that terrorism engenders, however, makes it more and more difficult for politicians to speak out against the government line.

To do so is to risk condemnation, especially in the popular press, for providing support to the enemy.

The key issue here is civil liberties, and we are told by the ruling authorities that these will have to be curbed in order to cope with the continuing terrorist threat we face. Freedom of movement and speech are cornerstones of Western liberal democracy, but these are being chipped away steadily in countries like Britain. The introduction of identity cards is still on the political agenda, and there is legislation against the public expression of anti-religious sentiments in the Racial and Religious Hatred Act 2006. The furore over the Danish newspaper cartoon picturing the Prophet Mohammed as a religious terrorist in 2005 indicates just how high feelings can run on such issues, and the debate about freedom of the press has been reopened with a vengeance throughout Western Europe. Politicians in general seem to favour the implementation of further restrictions on most of our major freedoms, feeling the need to keep tighter control of their citizens. Such moves are for our own safety, it is argued; the only way to protect us against the very real threat of terrorism. Every terrorist outrage that occurs merely entrenches such views and drowns out the voices of critics.

Many of those critics see us sliding into what has been called a 'surveillance society'. In a surveillance society CCTV monitors almost our every move in the main public spaces – town centres, shops, public transport outlets, airports, work. Official documentation – an identity card or passport – is required to move around those public spaces, to be produced on demand by public officials on pain of detention and questioning. Security checks become ever more elaborate and time-consuming at airports and other transport centres, as well as in official buildings. The police are increasingly armed and increasingly visible. Official databases amass an ever greater amount of information about all of the state's citizens. As the journalist and cultural commentator George Monbiot has warned, this state of affairs can creep up on us by stealth until we discover it is too late to do anything very much about it:

> There will be no dramatic developments. We will not step out of our homes one morning to discover that the state, or our boss, or our insurance company, knows everything about us. But if the muted response to ID cards is anything to go by, we will gradually submit, in the name of our own protection, to the demands of the machine.[1]

The net effect of the application of such surveillance techniques is to extend the state's power considerably, and there will always be a fear in a democracy that this will lead to abuse by those in positions of authority promoting their own special interests. Knowledge really is power in this context – power over others. The greater the might of the state and its functionaries, the more vulnerable the individual becomes, especially if the safeguard of civil liberties is significantly weakened. The confrontation between civil liberties and terrorism, or more correctly the official response to terrorism, is set to become one of the major ideological battlegrounds of our time.

THE TEXT

William Godwin, *Caleb Williams, or, Things As They Are*

Fears about state power are nothing new and were certainly being voiced in the eighteenth century, an era largely lacking in the civil liberties we have come to expect in our own day, but in which demands were beginning to be made by radical thinkers for these to be introduced (as they would be to some extent in the aftermath of the American and French Revolutions at the century's end). William Godwin's *Caleb Williams* (1794), for example, provides an extended investigation of to the perils of increased state power as far as the vulnerable individual is concerned. The protagonist, Caleb, discovers a secret that his master, Falkland, has kept hidden for many years and that throws doubt on Falkland's integrity. The latter proves to be a murderer, having killed an opponent in cold blood in a dispute about personal honour. Falkland's authority would be severely undermined were his secret ever to come out, as would by extension the socio-political system, the *ancien régime*, of which he is considered to be such an illustrious representative. Caleb is falsely accused of a crime in order to silence him when he threatens to leave Falkland's employ, forcing him to become a fugitive from justice in order to survive.

The state machine set in motion by Falkland proceeds to track Caleb down wherever he goes, refusing to allow him to settle and live a normal life. Whenever he attempts to do so, news of his supposed crimes soon follows and few are willing to believe Caleb's side of the story when compared to the official version which has the full weight of state authority behind it. It becomes a case of Caleb's word against Falkland's, and the latter's reputation as a man of honour inevitably prevails in the public mind. It is inconceivable to the average citizen that Falkland could be guilty of duplicity, and it is he, not Caleb, who is taken to be the injured party. Much to Caleb's chagrin, some of the lower orders even contrive to cast him as a folk-hero for his supposed criminal activities, with their connotations of rebellion against the authorities. The contest is ridiculously unequal and, folk-hero status notwithstanding, Caleb in real terms has no one to turn to for aid in his struggle.

Caleb is clearly a victim of the surveillance society of his time, and as a dissident member he cannot be allowed to escape, his very existence representing a challenge to the authority of the ruling powers. It is almost as if he becomes a test case, with those powers determined to make an example of him. Caleb is continually hounded, and periodically imprisoned, until a final confrontation with Falkland unexpectedly, and perhaps not entirely convincingly, resolves the issue in his favour – although not in the author's original ending, which is far bleaker, with the character subsiding into madness, the state system having triumphed over him. The unfortunate Caleb's plight, the author contends, is the real state of affairs in terms of the relationship obtaining between the individual and the state in eighteenth-century England. The book's original title was 'THINGS AS THEY ARE', with Godwin setting out to present, as the Preface put it, 'a general review of the modes of domestic and unrecorded despotism, by which man becomes the destroyer of man'.[2] *Caleb Williams* constitutes a plea for a more open form of society, where state power is massively reduced and the individual need no longer fear the actions of the ruling class or its agents.

The context of the novel is worth emphasising: the 1790s, with a repressive British government headed by William Pitt the Younger cracking down hard on the spread of revolutionary ideas from France. A network of government spies is operating throughout the country and many radicals are being imprisoned as evidence of the government's resolve to maintain the status quo. Godwin's narrative is an intervention into the most critical political debate of the day – the old order versus the new. In Gary Kelly's reading, there is 'a provocative and complex contemporary historical allegory' being worked out in the text, in which Falkland 'could be seen to represent France of the Old Regime'.[3]

The reduction of state power lies at the heart of Godwin's political philosophy. In his famous treatise, the *Enquiry Concerning Political Justice* (1793), the case is put for political anarchism, with Godwin's main concern being to shift political power away from the state and onto its citizens. From this perspective the state as traditionally constructed is an impediment to all human progress and individual development, the root of most of humankind's problems. Godwin's enquiry is designed to prove 'that government is, in all cases, an evil', and 'that it ought to be introduced as sparingly as possible'; furthermore, that '[m]an is a species of being whose excellence depends upon his individuality; and who can be neither great nor wise but in proportion as he is independent'.[4] The author is a proponent of the minimal state, arguing for no more public institutions than are necessary to guarantee basic personal security. Godwin prefigures the postmodern in being an implacable opponent of what we now call 'grand narrative'.

Godwin's anarchism, as Isaac Kramnick has noted, reduces to three main principles: political simplicity, public inspection and positive sincerity.[5] Political simplicity will be achieved by a decentralisation of government into smaller units, or 'parishes', which will be more responsive to local needs. Within these parishes, the 'observant eye, of public judgement' would act as a check on the actions of all citizens, tempering any anti-social desires that may emerge.[6] Each of us would be expected to become 'the ingenuous censor' of our neighbour, prepared to 'tell him in person, and publish to the world, his virtues, his good deeds, his meannesses and his follies', all with perfect 'sincerity'.[7] These concepts are not without their problems, however, with public inspection sounding uncomfortably close to spying on one's neighbour. Citizens in totalitarian states are invariably asked to be similarly vigilant on the authorities' behalf, with Soviet Russia, Maoist China and Nazi Germany providing some nasty examples of where this can lead, with relatives and friends being encouraged to inform on each other – and even children on their parents. The line between sincerity and 'holier than thou' moralisation is hard to draw too, one suspects.

In *Caleb Williams* public inspection is put into play as a policy, with Caleb subjecting Falkland to it with drastic consequences for the both of them, culminating in Falkland's death.[8] It is by no means clear that public inspection is an attractive prospect at the end of the novel, Caleb himself expressing remorse at what he has done, and one commentator referring to 'misapplication of the energies that should have been devoted to altruism' on Caleb's part.[9] The author could always argue, however, that this is not the most propitious of circumstances in which to apply public inspection. Godwin's projected society would be almost the antithesis of the *ancien régime* that Caleb is born into, and would view such a practice in a very different light (although many of us would still remain sceptical of the virtue of yet another form of surveillance of our person, no matter how sincerely it was intended by our local 'ingenuous censors').

Falkland is presented to us in the first instance as a rather distant figure with a reserved, melancholic and often gloomy manner that casts a pall over his whole household. Although he takes Caleb into that household and offers him the chance of self-advancement as his secretary, he makes no real attempt to befriend the young man, remaining aloof from any such intimate human contact:

> His mode of living was in the utmost degree recluse and solitary. He had no inclination to scenes of revelry and mirth. He avoided the busy haunts of men; nor did he seem desirous to compensate for this privation by the confidence of friendship.[10]

Although Caleb is grateful for being raised up the social scale by Falkland, this does not stop him from wanting to pry into his master's business. Caleb's defence of this side of his character predictably seeks the best possible interpretation:

> The spring of action which perhaps more than any other, characterised the whole train of my life, was curiosity. It was this that gave me my mechanical turn; I was desirous of tracing the variety of effects which might be produced from given causes. It was this that made me a sort of natural philosopher; I could not rest till I had acquainted myself with the solutions that had been invented for the phenomena of the universe.[11]

It is a scientific curiosity that he is describing, and this is an admirable trait, representative of all that is most appealing in Enlightenment thought: a desire both to understand and to improve the world around us by penetrating nature's secrets. But when it is applied to the more mundane activity of discovering his master's secrets, the trait loses much of its appeal. Being a spy subtly alters Caleb's personality, making him more secretive himself and increasing his sense of self-importance as a leading player in the exciting drama he envisages himself caught up in.[12]

What Caleb's curiosity does succeed in doing, however, is revealing the huge gulf that separates the *ancien régime* from the new revolutionary spirit that is taking hold in continental Europe. Although Godwin disliked the methods employed in the French Revolution (he was in favour of 'a gradual but uninterrupted change' based on the use of reason, instead of the 'Terror' employed there),[13] he is nevertheless in agreement about the need for radical political change. At least initially Caleb's curiosity can seem to be part of this concerted challenge to tradition and received authority, 'the arbitrary power rooted in the institutions of society' which Godwin so detested, and thus defensible.[14]

It will prove to be this trait of curiosity that the old order feels compelled to suppress at all costs: public inspection of its operations is the last thing it wishes to happen. State power must preserve its mystique, otherwise its hold over the populace is in danger of being seriously weakened. In the wake of the French Revolution, the former is precisely what Pitt the Younger's government is concerned to uphold, the latter to avoid. Godwin's remarks in the *Enquiry Concerning Political Justice* about the political climate in which the work is being published are worth noting in this regard:

> The period in which it makes its appearance is singular. The people of England have assiduously been excited to declare their loyalty, and to mark every man as obnoxious who is not ready to sign the Shibboleth of the constitution. Money is raised by voluntary subscription to defray the expense of prosecuting men who shall dare to promulgate heretical opinions, and thus to oppress them at once with the authority of government, and the resentment of individuals.[15]

That loyalty will be only too apparent in *Caleb Williams*, rendering the hero obnoxious indeed to his fellow citizens: an enemy of the state to be silenced for the public good.

Falkland's depressive character and retired way of life stem from some unfortunate events in his earlier history, in particular from his rivalry with another local landowner, Barnabas Tyrrel, an uncouth figure who appears to considerable disadvantage when compared to the sophisticated and worldly Falkland. Tyrrel's brutal treatment of his niece Emily, whom he drives to her death by his thoughtless actions, brings the animosity between the two men to a head. After a quarrel at an assembly Tyrrel assaults Falkland, leaving him feeling publicly shamed: 'To Mr. Falkland disgrace was worse than death. The slightest breath of dishonour would have stung him to the very soul. What must it have been with this complication of ignominy, base, humiliating and public.'[16] Soon after leaving the assembly Tyrrel is murdered. When suspicion not surprisingly falls upon him, Falkland successfully pleads his innocence, and two disgruntled ex-tenants of Tyrrel, the Hawkinses, father and son, are subsequently charged and found guilty of the crime. The real culprit is Falkland, but he allows the Hawkinses to go to their deaths to save his honour, thereafter retiring from public life to become a recluse. Honour is put above justice, and it is this terrible secret that Falkland spends the rest of his life trying to keep hidden. Until Caleb arrives on the scene this objective is achieved and Falkland's reputation remains untarnished, even if living the lie exacts a heavy toll on his psychological well-being.

Caleb is unconvinced by the official line on Tyrrel's murder and decides to test its truth: 'I determined to set myself as a watch upon my patron.'[17] So successful is Caleb in his personal surveillance campaign that Falkland feels trapped into a confession: 'I am the blackest of villains. I am the murderer of Tyrrel. I am the assassin of the Hawkinses.'[18] The catch is that Caleb is sworn to secrecy, which effectively makes him a prisoner of Falkland:

Do you know what it is you have done? To gratify a foolishly inquisitive humour you have sold yourself. You shall continue in my service, but can never share in my affection. I will benefit you in respect of fortune, but I shall always hate you. If ever an unguarded word escape from your lips, if ever you excite my jealousy or suspicion, expect to pay for it by your death or worse. It is a dear bargain you have made.[19]

The truth is far more complex than that, and it is not simply a personal matter involving the two men. Caleb has discovered how unjust the code of personal honour is on which Falkland has based his life. In other words, he has discovered the corruption that lies at the heart of the old order's ideology: it is only interested in power, using the mystique of honour to keep the population in a state of awe and subjection. From that point onwards there is a rapid descent into the 'theatre of calamity' that becomes Caleb's post-confession existence, where he is transformed into 'a mark for the vigilance of tyranny'.[20] If, as Patricia Meyer Spacks has argued, Caleb and Falkland are engaged in a struggle 'for narrative dominance' over each other's lives (plot–counterplot, as it were), then the latter can call on far greater forces to impose his own story on events.[21]

That vigilance begins almost immediately Caleb is let into Falkland's dreadful secret. Caleb's subsequent attempt to detach himself from Falkland and all that he symbolises is met with the curt rejoinder from the latter: 'You write me here, that you are desirous to quit my service. To that I have a short answer. You shall never quit it with life. . . . Your innocence shall be of no service to you: I laugh at so feeble a defence.'[22] Falkland's chilling response, with its knowledge of just how much state power it can marshal to make good its threat, initiates a vigorous campaign against the dissident Caleb. He is accused of theft, pursued by Falkland's agents and soon imprisoned without trial. The travesty of his treatment at the hands of the authorities, for whom Falkland is a pillar of virtue whose word is not to be disputed, brings forth the following bitterly ironic sentiments from Caleb about the political settlement prevailing in eighteenth-century England:

> Thank God, exclaims the Englishman, we have no Bastille! Thank God, with us no man can be punished without a crime! Unthinking wretch! Is that a country of liberty where thousands languish in dungeons and fetters? Go, go, ignorant fool! and visit the scenes of our prisons! witness their unwholesomeness, their filth, the tyranny of their governors, the misery of their inmates! After that show me the man shameless enough to triumph, and say, England has no Bastille![23]

The message is clear: the authorities will be utterly ruthless with all those who transgress their code or threaten their power base; the status quo is not to be challenged. In essence, this is the political condition of England in the 1790s.

Caleb eventually escapes, but now finds himself condemned to life as a fugitive, required to cover his tracks wherever he goes and to engage in perpetual deception to stay one step ahead of his pursuers. His fame follows him remorselessly: eating in an alehouse, he is alarmed to overhear some workmen discussing the career of 'the notorious housebreaker, Kit Williams' who apparently now has a bounty of a hundred guineas on his head.[24] Caleb is soon reduced to disguise, dressing as a tramp and adopting an Irish accent. Even this fails to protect his person for very long and he is forced to keep altering his appearance and adopting new identities as the forces unleashed by Falkland relentlessly close in on him.

For all his ingenious efforts he never really escapes the reach of the surveillance system; as Falkland informs him at a later point in the narrative, when Caleb falls into his hands again: 'I had my eye upon you in all your wanderings. You have taken no material step through their whole course with which I have not been acquainted.'[25] The fact that a pamphlet is being hawked around London at this point ('The Wonderful and Surprising Adventures of Caleb Williams') while Caleb is still resident there, containing all the details of his case described in the most sensationalised way to the hero's disdavantage, merely confirms Falkland's claims. Caleb is a prisoner wherever he goes, with no real private space he can retreat into: in the words of Jacqueline T. Miller, 'Falkland has been the "author" of Caleb's life, and Caleb's own efforts to be the author of his own history and identity have been impotent'.[26] It is almost as if the system is toying with Caleb by allowing him to continue to exist at all, knowing it can move against him at any time, a point repeatedly made by Falkland: 'At least I have a power respecting you, and that power I will exercise; a power that shall grind you into atoms.'[27]

Even Caleb's most determined attempt to avoid surveillance, his removal to a small town in a remote part of Wales, cannot take him out of the clutches of the system. Falkland proves to be known to the family he befriends there, and when copies of 'The Wonderful and Surprising Adventures of Caleb Williams' reach the locality his friends turn against Caleb, leaving him isolated yet again. He finally has to acknowledge that he can never put himself beyond 'Mr. Falkland's menaces' and the political regime that licenses them; their persistence simply cannot be worn down.[28] Caleb is even forbidden by Falkland, on pain of being arrested and imprisoned if he ever tries to do so, from leaving the British Isles, so that his enemy may continue to monitor his progress without hindrance. As Falkland's agent Gines puts it, '[t]he squire is determined you shall never pass the reach of his disposal'.[29] Caleb's freedom of action is revealed to be an illusion: surveillance has achieved its object of keeping the individual under constant control.

Godwin's original ending is more consistent with the tone of the narrative's opening lines, where the hero's despairing cry is that,

> My life has for several years been a theatre of calamity. I have been a mark for the vigilance of tyranny, and I could not escape. My fairest prospects have been blasted. My enemy has shown himself inaccessible to intreaties and untired in persecution. . . . I have not deserved this treatment.[30]

Caleb in this first version of the ending is a broken man, rapidly declining into madness as a consequence of the highly efficient vigilance with which Falkland and the state have hunted him throughout England. What one commentator has described as the main theme of Godwin's fiction, 'the crushing of the individual by the forces of organised society', come across very strongly:[31]

> At present I by no means find myself satisfied with the state of my intellects. I am subject to wanderings in which the imagination seems to refuse to obey the curb of judgment. I dare not attempt to think long and strenuously on any one subject.[32]

The *ancien régime* has defeated him, and Caleb's sad story concludes with the character in a condition of extreme wretchedness, comparing himself to a gravestone, 'an obelisk to tell you, HERE LIES WHAT WAS ONCE A MAN!'[33] He has chosen to stand up to the power of the state and its surveillance society, and has lost. To the critics of current government moves to counter terrorism by restricting our civil liberties and increasing the power of the state and its police, this is the more likely of the two endings when the surveillance society is significantly enhanced. Uncovering the secrets of the authorities, or even attempting to do so, carries the strong risk of leading to a very bad end for the individual involved. There is every reason to fear state power and every reason also to oppose its extension in a culture based on Enlightenment ideals.

The narrative's published ending sees Falkland overcome by the tenacity (and 'sincerity' as Caleb sees it)[34] of his opponent. In a charged courtroom scene Falkland breaks down and publicly admits his guilt: 'Williams, said he, you have conquered! . . . I have spent a life of the basest cruelty to cover one act of momentary vice and to protect myself against the prejudices of my species. I stand now completely detected.'[35] His death three days later removes any possibility of punishment, however, and he is never held to account for his crime. Caleb's victory has not materially altered the character of the state that has made his life such a misery and cost the lives of the innocent Hawkinses.[36] Other Falklands, we are to assume, lie in wait for other unsuspecting Calebs if they allow their curiosity free rein and delve too deeply into their secrets, 'the imposture that would persuade us there is a mystery in government which uninitiated mortals must not presume to penetrate', as Godwin puts it in the *Enquiry Concerning Political Justice*.[37]

The hero himself seems unable to break free from Falkland's spell, and is distraught at his master's public disgrace:

> I thought that, if Falkland were dead, I should return once again to all that makes life worth possessing. I thought that, if the guilt of Falkland were established, fortune and the world would smile upon my efforts. Both these events are accomplished; and it is only now that I am truly miserable.[38]

Caleb blames 'the poison of chivalry' for distorting Falkland's character, but that chivalry is at the core of the political system Falkland unreservedly supports.[39] It is not just a personal concern, but the basis of how that system works and how its rulers exert their control over the populace. Falkland and his peers are to be looked up to and respected for the family honour they represent, and the code of honour itself is never to be questioned: to do so is to invite persecution by the powerful in the manner of Caleb.

While Caleb is right to speak of the code as a poison, especially given the fate of the unfortunate Hawkinses, his own misery at Falkland's death shows how difficult it can be to overcome the pull of the dominant ideology and just how complicit we can be as individuals in maintaining its historically sanctioned 'imposture'.[40] It must be remembered how much of a lone voice Caleb is in the narrative, and how willing almost everyone else is, even those in humble positions socially, to collude with the surveillance society the authorities have set up to protect their political ideals against any sustained challenge. It is those very authorities who are always given the benefit of the doubt, never Caleb. Changing 'THINGS AS THEY ARE' can look like a herculean task from the perspective of the mere individual, as long as the grand narrative can command such a high degree of loyalty.

CONCLUSION

The abuse of state power that Caleb is forced to suffer continues to have considerable resonance for our own time. If civil liberties are significantly curtailed, if the surveillance society is both extended and tacitly accepted by the bulk of the populace as so many Western governments appear to wish, then we run the risk of putting the clock back both socially and politically. It may not be the *ancien régime* that we resurrect, but it might well be a totalitarian society of the kind that caused so many of the horrors of the twentieth century: the communist or fascist models, for example, where individual rights were systematically overriden in the name of the greater good of the state, causing widespread misery and human suffering. The fear then would be that, like Caleb, we could never put ourselves beyond the reach of the ruling authorities, that they could say of any of us too: 'I had my eye upon you in all your wanderings. You have taken no material step through their whole course with which I have not been acquainted.' Given that the data on any of us have become so easy to amass, that spectre certainly beckons.

Godwin's answer to tyranny was to reduce significantly the power of the state, cutting back drastically on its institutions and opting for a parish-based model of government instead; the local being preferred over the central. Trust was to be placed in the ability of individuals to police themselves as much as possible (by means of public inspection and positive sincerity for example), without requiring the heavy hand of the state to keep transgressors in line – except in such extreme circumstances as war or invasion. We may not wish to go as far as Godwin in terms of the minimal state; paradoxically for such an anti-traditionalist thinker, he is closer to modern neo-conservatives than liberals on this issue (for both, the less government the better). But he provides a timely warning nevertheless of how easily the state can turn into a repressive mechanism acting against the best interests of most of its citizens. The need for public accountability as regards official authority also comes across very strongly in Godwin's work, although we might be wary of public inspection turning into yet another version of the surveillance system which threatens our civil liberties at present: not all censors are likely to be as 'ingenuous' as Godwin expects. The more the public realm encroaches into the private, the more the hard-won gains of the Enlightenment on freedom of movement and speech are eroded. Curiosity must have its limits, too; 'obsession and self-love', as one critic has pointed out, are traits that Caleb and Falkland share, and neither is really in the best interests of liberal democracy when pushed to extremes.[41]

That is the ground on which this battle must now be fought: over the degree of surveillance, and the curiosity – ingenuous or otherwise – that motivates it, that reasonably can be allowed. Most of us would agree that some surveillance is inescapable in an advanced society, and that this can operate for the public good (sometimes the CCTV *does* lead to the capture of the criminal), but only when it protects civil liberties, not, as so often seems to be proposed nowadays, when it severely curtails these in the name of public safety. The 'demands of the machine' alone must not be permitted to set the agenda. 'Safe but unfree' is hardly a suitable slogan for a liberal democracy – that way the despotism so despised by Godwin surely lies. The power of vigilance to turn into tyranny should never be underestimated.

CHAPTER 10

Waverley, or, 'Tis Sixty Years Since and Disputed Sovereignty

THE ISSUE

Sovereignty is a hotly debated issue in contemporary politics, the source of many disputes around the world, threatening global peace. In Northern Ireland, for example, there are competing visions of who should be in control, and one of the solutions that has been put forward by political theorists is dual sovereignty over the one territory.[1] Not surprisingly, this has been resisted by Unionists and Nationalists, both of whom would prefer to exercise total control; but each nevertheless manages to exercise a form of sovereignty over its followers, down to the level of unofficial courts and tax-gathering methods. In the Middle East, Israel and Palestine are locked in a similar struggle, with dual sovereignty again being mooted as a possible solution. The emotive nature of sovereignty, the question of who exercises it over a particular territory and whether their claim is accepted by all the territory's inhabitants, is well demonstrated by such cases. Whether that right is going to be respected, not just by those inside but by those outside one's national borders, is the next critical issue, and one that impacts directly on the lives of the whole populace. Lebanon is a current example of a state which finds itself unable to achieve either of these conditions consistently, with the Islamist Hamas group within, and Israel without, treating the central government with disdain, much to the distress of the mass of the population. When sovereignty is in open dispute, daily life tends to become less secure for all the citizens of a state. Not knowing where power lies can be a source of much anxiety in times of trouble: to whom does one appeal for help if there is no effective central government? (a problem the entire Iraqi nation is currently facing).

Most of the larger nations in the old world are unions of one kind or another, with different cultures, ethnic groups, languages and state-like regions within their boundaries. The United Kingdom, with four clearly defined national territories within its boundaries, is a prime instance. In the New World there is the conflict between colonisers and original inhabitants to be taken into account, and although in some cases this is resolved by a limited form of dual sovereignty (as in the case of the US and Native Americans with the reservation system), it is an issue with the potential to become divisive at any point: it never quite goes away and can always be accessed by activists. Dual sovereignty is the exception rather than the rule, however, and when disputes about sovereignty flare up the outcome is more likely to be national fragmentation than an amicable redistribution of power. We have the example of the former Yugoslavia to ponder, and also the Soviet Union, both of which have broken down into a myriad of smaller nations in the aftermath of major sovereignty crises in the late twentieth century. When political sovereignty is badly compromised, the result is generally a decline into chaos. Czechoslovakia has undergone a 'velvet divorce' into the Czech Republic and Slovakia, but it is rarely that peaceable or straightforward a process when sovereignty comes under severe strain. Russia has managed to maintain its national integrity despite losing vast swathes of its former empire, but Yugoslavia is now no more than a memory. Totalitarian communism kept a lid on sovereignty problems, but once this system collapsed, age-old disputes soon re-emerged. The sense of national sovereignty is notoriously hard to eradicate from the public mind.

THE TEXT

Sir Walter Scott, *Waverley, or, 'Tis Sixty Years Since*

Disputes over sovereignty lie at the heart of many of Sir Walter Scott's novels, with his first, *Waverley* (1814), establishing this as a major concern for the author. Here we have an actual historical conflict over sovereignty, the second Jacobite Rebellion of 1745, as the crux of the narrative. Various issues of sovereignty are at stake: sovereignty over Scotland (recently joined in union with England, despite considerable opposition to the loss of national identity this entailed); sovereignty over the entire British Isles (disputed by the banished Stuart royal family line, living in exile in France since the late seventeenth century); sovereignty over the border areas between Scotland and England, where it is not always clear where national allegiance lies (these having been disputed territories between the two nations for centuries, leaving it something of a no-man's land). In the figure of Edward Waverley all these issues are brought to a head, and he is drawn into a conflict the outlines of which are never completely clear-cut. Waverley's sympathies and emotions are pulled in various directions in what turns out to be a showdown between the old and new political orders, the Stuarts representing the former and the Hanoverians the latter, with individuals finding their loyalties becoming increasingly confused as the rebellion unfolds. An argument can be made for either royal line according to the customs of the time, which is not a particularly healthy state for the nation to be in since it leaves the threat of rebellion always open. After its turbulent history in the seventeenth century, including a civil war and various regime changes (succession being a recurrent problem throughout the period),[2] the prospect of further division is a distinctly worrying one for the British populace to have to contemplate.

Scott very convincingly brings out the confusion of such struggles (a civil war in all but name), while exhibiting a measure of sympathy for both sides.[3] Just how difficult it can be to overcome disputes of this nature can be seen in the fact that three centuries after the Act of Union (1707) Scotland has achieved devolution within the UK, which for the time being amounts to a form of dual sovereignty over Scottish territory, with parliaments sitting in both Edinburgh and London. The former has more limited powers than the latter, but even so some English MPs are unhappy with the situation, feeling that it erodes the power of the Parliament in London. For the more traditionally minded, such a division of sovereignty is anathema; a subversion of the very concept itself. To purists, sovereignty has to be indivisible to be effective. Whether the two-parliament system is a lasting solution to the clash between political and emotional sovereignty in this particular case remains to be seen. The Stuart royal family may no longer be part of the equation, but what they represented is still a potent factor in both Scottish and English politics, with the Union being an issue even now capable of stirring up heated debate: Scottish nationalism has considerable public support, although it can ebb and flow – an indication of just how complex the overall issue of sovereignty is. As in Scott's narrative, individuals can find themselves with divided loyalties and unclear as to which is the best course of action to take. Commitment can shift from one grand narrative to the other depending on circumstances, with a wide range of intellectual and emotional factors coming into play such that outcomes can be unpredictable: the brave new world of independence can appeal on one level, while hard-headed economic calculations might be a more powerful consideration on another. *Waverley* provides an in-depth study of that unpredictability against a background of major national crisis.

Edward Waverley is English, with a family history of allegiance to the Stuart monarchy. His father has turned against this tradition and entered politics under the Hanoverian monarchy, but the latter's elder brother, Sir Everard, now the master of the family estate, has maintained the Waverleys' 'hereditary faith . . . in high church and the house of Stuart' throughout his life.[4] The brothers are on opposite sides of the political divide therefore, but Sir Everard, who has no children of his own, develops an affection for Edward, who is brought up to be the heir of the family estate. In 1745 memories of the Stuart monarchy, banished from the English throne in the 'Glorious Revolution' of 1688–9, are still fresh, and there is significant support in the nation for their cause. Figures like Sir Everard are to be found around the country (as Henry Fielding was also communicating in *Tom Jones* with Squire Western and his boast at being 'a true Englishman, and not of your Hanover breed, that have eat up the nation').[5] The Jacobite Rebellion of 1715 (the backdrop to Scott's later novel *Rob Roy* (1817))[6] was an indication of the seriousness of Stuart intentions, and the fear of a new uprising is certainly present amongst the ruling classes from that event onwards. (Scott will go on to make particularly striking use of the recurrent Jacobite threat in *Redgauntlet* (1824), which postulates a third rebellion in the 1760s, although no more successful than the actual ones had proved to be.[7])

Against such a tense political background Edward Waverley takes a commission in the army and is posted to Scotland to join his regiment, stationed on the Angus coast, quite near to the Highlands, the least loyal part of the kingdom to the current English monarchy and the most likely source of trouble if it is to arise again. There is nothing to suggest that he is anything other than a patriotic subject at this stage, and he seems set fair for a career in the service of the British Crown, despite some misgivings on the part of Sir Everard, who still has difficulty reconciling himself to the new royal line (to the extent of pointedly having kept himself out of public life since the 1715 rebellion). Whether Waverley's convictions run very deep is another question, and he registers as a romantic, impressionable young man, who is led by his emotions much of the time, with sudden enthusiasms being a notable feature of his character. In other words, he is a figure who may not prove to be entirely reliable in politically turbulent times when loyalties are becoming very confused, with two sides claiming to be the only legitimate sovereign authority and demanding that a choice be made between them. Waverley's very impressionability mirrors that of the British nation, which suggests a similar capacity to be swayed by events at this point in its history: 'sentimental Jacobinism' can cast its spell over the unwary.[8]

The event that changes Waverley's life is his visit to Tully-Veolan, the Perthshire estate of the Baron of Bradwardine, an old friend of his family and a fellow Stuart sympathiser who had fought on the Jacobite side in 1715 but escaped punishment thanks to help from Sir Everard. Waverley is drawn into the Scottish lifestyle which suits his romantic temperament, and particularly so when he travels further into the wilds on a mission to retrieve some stolen cattle for his host. There he meets the Highland chieftain Fergus Mac-Ivor Vich Ian Vohr, infamous for exacting blackmail from Lowlanders as a means of subsidising his feudal lifestyle, replete with a retinue of armed retainers who act like a private army. Waverley becomes a guest on Vich Ian Vohr's estate, where he falls in love with the latter's sister, Flora. Both Vich Ian Vohr and Flora are ardent Jacobites, willing to go to the limit in their support for the Stuart monarchy and its new head, prince Charles Edward, whom they consider to be the lawful king of Scotland. When the prince lands on the west coast of Scotland, Vich Ian Vohr is one of the first to greet him and to join the uprising which soon follows, positively revelling in the excitement this creates and the opportunity it offers to demonstrate the depth of his loyalty to the Stuarts. The second Jacobite Rebellion has begun, catching Waverley unaware in its midst. Placed in this compromising position he is soon put under pressure by Vich Ian Vohr to join the uprising.

Waverley eventually agrees, having resigned his commission at what he perceives to be some high-handed treatment by his commanding officer and subsequently finding himself accused of treason by the authorities. He is spurred on by Fergus's rabble-rousing polemic, with his challenge to Waverley that he should take revenge 'upon the usurping house of Hanover, whom your grandfather would no more have served than he would have taken wages of red-hot gold from the great fiend of hell'.[9] For all Fergus's impassioned rhetoric, there is always a shadow of doubt in Waverley's mind as to whether he has made the right decision in throwing in his lot with the Stuarts, and although he can defend it in terms of the wrongs done to him and his family by the present government (his father has also fallen out of political favour in the interim), he recognises that this is not necessarily the strongest of grounds for changing sides – and, as it appears, countries too. He indulges in much heart-searching and finds it extremely difficult to be vengeful towards his English adversaries, until recently his army colleagues, going out of his way to aid them in battle and as prisoners of war. 'I have indeed acted towards you with thoughtless cruelty', as he feels himself prompted to declare to one of his tenants, whom he comes across dying on the field of battle after fighting on the English side:

> I shunned my own share of the burthen, and wandered from the duties I had undertaken, leaving alike those whom it was my business to protect, and my own reputation, to suffer under the artifices of villainy. O, indolence and indecision of mind! if not in yourselves vices, to how much exquisite misery do you frequently prepare the way!'[10]

Despite this epiphanic moment, Waverley continues in the service of the Stuart army as it sweeps down into England – a further indication of how his feelings, and sense of loyalty, can be swayed in such a volatile political climate. Clearly, he is torn as to where his duty lies; 'under which king', as one study has put it, to serve.[11]

Scott is careful not to go into detail about Waverley's battle exploits, as if to protect him from the charge of being a real rebel (authentic rebels kill their English enemies with gusto and exhibit little mercy to their foe), and overall he is not the most convincing of Jacobites, despite his family history. In John Sutherland's withering assessment, the hero 'wanders through the battlefield offering as little danger to his foe as a dormouse in a tiger's cage'.[12] As an English recruit, however, Waverley is particularly highly prized by the prince, for whom he has considerable propaganda worth, living proof that he has claims to the loyalty of the English as well as the Scots, that this is no mere nationalistic struggle that is being waged: 'The Prince detained him for some time, asking various questions about the great tory and catholic families of England, their connections, their influence, and the state of their affections towards the house of Brunswick.'[13] The presence of such a socially high-profile figure as Waverley helps to give a greater air of legitimacy to the Stuart cause, although Waverley's ambivalence about the whole enterprise also serves to undermine that by showing how shaky its foundations really are. 'Indecision of mind' really is the order of the day for much of the country and that can work against, as well as for, the Stuarts. Other than that offered by the Highlanders, support for the Stuarts is brittle. The Highlanders may be tenacious in their loyalty, but others are not necessarily to be relied upon for long. Waverley becomes a deeply symbolic character, a site on which the national dispute over sovereignty is played out in miniature, in all its confusion and complexity; someone whose commitment, only too appropriately, is often seen to waver.

When the Jacobite army finally turns back at Derby from its hitherto successful advance on London Waverley finds himself in an extremely parlous situation, stranded in England on what is now doomed to be the losing side. He is by this stage no more than a half-hearted rebel. In reality he has probably never been much more than that, never having felt himself to be properly on the inside of the cause, not being Scottish – the uprising has remained a predominantly nationalist affair. Waverley has also become alienated by all the political infighting around the prince. The mere promise of sovereign power has brought out the worst in the character of the Scottish landed nobility following the prince, with factions forming almost instantly before there is any real power to be shared out, Vich Ian Vohr being as guilty of this as anyone. Nevertheless, Waverley is now guilty of treason like all the rebels, and treason brings dire consequences in its wake. His grievance with the government is personal rather than political, but at least initially such fine distinctions are not being made by the authorities, whose concern is to ensure that Jacobite sympathy in the nation is wiped out and further rebellions avoided. (Their ruthlessness in doing so lingers on in the Scottish public consciousness, where Bonny Prince Charlie remains a popular hero to this day.) Waverley becomes a hunted man, his life constantly in danger as the army limps back towards Scotland harried by the resurgent English forces.

Eventually, Waverley has to seek refuge in the borderlands between England and Scotland, a territory where loyalties are particularly fluid after centuries of local conflict, border-raiding being a popular prac- tice on both sides. It is symptomatic of that fluidity that he is able to remain hidden there for some time, despite the general air of crisis infecting the area as the rebel soldiers are being rounded up and shown little mercy in the process. As his first protector, a border farmer, puts it when Waverley pleads for sanctuary: 'Be ho Scot or no . . . I wish thou hadst kept the other side of the hallan; but since thou art here, Jacob Jopson will betray no man's bluid; and the plaids were gay canny, and did not do so much mischief when they were here yesterday.'[14] He subsequently finds refuge with a Farmer Williams and his family, where he is allowed to pass himself off as a kinsman for some time, until family misfortunes draw him to London.

The personal rather than strictly political nature of Waverley's grievance with the government is ultimately his salvation, as Colonel Talbot, whom he had earlier rescued from captivity by the rebel forces, is able to sue for pardon for him on those grounds. This can all seem rather too convenient to the reader, but Waverley becomes an interest- ing symbol of the nation at the time, of its deeply divided loyalties that somehow will have to be reconciled, even if it requires a fair degree of compromise to do so (and possibly also wish-fulfilment in the author's case). The man for whom Charles Edward is at one point '[a] prince to live and die under' is brought back within the establishment fold grate- ful to be allowed to resume his privileged existence as a major landowner and pillar of his local community.[15] The zealous rebels such as Vich Ian Vohr are not as lucky, and are excluded from all govern- mental clemency: Fergus and his close associates are hanged at Carlisle and their heads put on public display in the town as a reminder of the fate awaiting traitors.

We can read Waverley's shifting allegiances as evidence of immatu- rity, a product of his romantic temperament and thus excusable as youthful indiscretions, or we can see them as signs of a deeper malaise in British culture, an inability to decide where its true loyalties actu- ally lie, and perhaps even a sense of guilt about its treatment of the

Stuart monarchy. Despite the fact that Stuart monarchs had twice been removed from the English throne, in 1649 and 1688 (Charles I and James II respectively), it is still a culture in the eighteenth century that considers such events as against the natural order of things, for all that political theorists such as John Locke are claiming a right to rebellion when monarchs fail to act in the best interests of their subjects.[16] Respect for traditional authority dies hard, and the Stuarts are able to exploit that, for all their well-documented failings as rulers.

Ultimately, Scott is trying to consign disputes over sovereignty to history and suggesting that the best way forward for Scotland is to embrace the new political order, the Union with England that is by then over a century old. He can express sympathy for the old order and is never dismissive of its values; rough and crude though the Highlanders can be, they are given a sense of dignity nevertheless. Yet Scott has no desire to turn the clock back: ''Tis Sixty Years Since', as the novel's sub-title puts it, and although we are made aware of the passions that claims to sovereignty could evoke in our ancestors, the clear intention is to show them as the product of a bygone era. For Scott, the Union has now proved its worth and removed any basis for opposition:

> There is no European nation which, within the course of half a century, or little more, has undergone so complete a change as this kingdom of Scotland. . . . The gradual influx of wealth, and extension of commerce, have since united to render the present people of Scotland a class of beings as different from their grandfathers, as the existing English are from those of Queen Elizabeth's time.[17]

In Scott's mind at least, the issue of sovereignty has been resolved and Scotland has entered a new phase in its history which it should embrace with enthusiasm (even if the Highlanders would demur at the loss of their culture this involved). As James Kerr has pointed out, '[t]he larger historical subtext of the novel is the anglicization of Scotland', and Waverley has been a test case to show how this could be achieved, his pardon having immense symbolic importance.[18] Nearly two centuries later, however, we can see that the issue has merely lain dormant and still has the power to provoke profound political reaction. National identities are not so easily dissolved, and where they linger sovereignty is always likely to be a critical factor in the political process – we need look no further than the former Yugoslavia for proof of this. Scott may have thought he was writing the obituary of old-style Scottish nationalism, albeit with a certain regret, but history has proved him wrong. Sovereignty is a matter that transcends even economics, although it is interesting to note that it is the economic arguments that tend to weigh most heavily with those against or ambivalent about breaking up the Union now. Scotland's economic situation after independence is a topic of much speculation, with a wide spectrum of opinion as to the likely consequences of the process.

Scott's genius, however, lies in making his protagonist English rather than Scottish: the novel is no mere nationalistic confrontation, where it is easy to see why sides have been chosen. What it demonstrates more than anything is the arbitrary nature of political power, although Scott would most likely have been surprised by such a conclusion. Waverley manages to serve two masters (two grand narratives we might also say), and ultimately to return to the one he first betrayed to be accepted back without punishment, presumably no longer perceived to be a threat to the ruling order. This does seem to suggest that political loyalty can be expedient: that it is a shifting and indeterminate rather than fixed entity, a product of sudden enthusiasms and emotional swings as much as of careful intellectual calculation (just as Waverley's affections can shift from Flora to the Baron of Bradwardine's daughter, Rose, by the close of the narrative). The hero's Englishness is, paradoxically enough, being expressed through Scottish nationalism for much of the book and that Scots nationalism is being used by the Stuarts as the basis for recovery of its English dominions. Equally paradoxically, the nationalistic taint attaching to Waverley can only be resolved by his political enemies, with Colonel Talbot engineering Waverley's pardon despite his rebel status. Some very pragmatic decisions are being made by the governing authorities, no doubt aware of just how complicated the entire loyalty issue is.

The treatment meted out to the Baron of Bradwardine is similarly lenient, again hinting at an element of wish-fulfilment on the author's part. As a result of his involvement in the uprising the baron loses his estate and is forced into hiding. Waverley finds him in these desperate straits when he returns to Scotland, travelling under a passport obtained for him by Colonel Talbot while awaiting news of the latter's plea for pardon on his behalf. This is soon forthcoming, although Waverley is still capable of joining the baron in the interim in expressing 'cordial hopes for the safety of the unfortunate Chevalier', despite the fact that the hero has in essence switched sides again.[19] It is noticeable throughout the narrative, in fact, that the prince is seen in a very favourable light, as if to acknowledge that his bid for power has a certain legitimacy: this is no mere political adventurer, but instead a 'prince to live and die under'. Once again, however, an accommodation is engineered between the English and the Scots that restores the social and political equilibrium. Not only is Waverley pardoned, but the baron is also, and when Waverley decides to marry the baron's daughter, there is an interlocking set of land deals by which Waverley sells part of his family estate to Colonel Talbot in order to raise money to buy back the baron's estate and reinstate him as its owner until his death. The fact that the estate has been undervalued only adds to the overall satisfaction of the parties concerned: 'look at the rental book', as the Baron's agent gleefully invites him.[20]

Again, this may seem all rather too neat to the reader nowadays, part of what James Kerr regards as the author's 'reemplotment' of history to make it fit a romance framework;[21] but it serves the author's objective of talking up the positive effects of Union. The marriage between Waverley and Rose symbolises how the two nations can become, not just reconciled to each other, but true partners with a happy and prosperous future to look forward to: as Claire Lamont has remarked, Scott 'had to force himself to beat the drum for progress'.[22] The benefits of their union are manifest and play their part in securing relations between their respective countries. But the contrast with the fate of Vich Ian Vohr is stark. In Colonel Talbot's assessment, the latter 'has studied and fully understood the desperate game he has played', and thus cannot expect to be treated as leniently as Waverley and Bradwardine.[23] The establishment has judged who has the ability to reform and who has not, and acted accordingly. Vich Ian Vohr becomes the scapegoat the state needs as a public demonstration of its power over its citizens, just in case some of the latter are tempted to interpret its treatment of such as Waverley and Bradwardine as a sign of weakness. The state's decision is final in such matters – that is what sovereignty means: 'When the guilty are so numerous, clemency must be extended to far the greater number', but, crucially, not to all.[24]

Scott's message overall would seem to be that even the most bitter of sovereignty disputes can be resolved; but we might equally conclude that any such resolution has an arbitrary quality to it. If it had gone the other way and the rebels had won in 1745, Waverley would have done even better for himself, and presumably the rest of the nation would have made an accommodation with the revived old order as best it could. There is little sense that one side has greater legitimacy than the other (again we should note the sympathetic portrayal of the prince), and although the Stuart cause is defeated, once and for all as we now know, strictly speaking its claims have not been. As we observed earlier, it is because those claims are so closely identified with Scottish nationalism that the sovereignty issue is still a live one in British politics. Bonny Prince Charlie remains a Scottish national hero, entrenched in the popular consciousness in various songs like 'The Skye Boat Song' and 'Charlie is My Darling':

> Charlie is my darling, my darling, my darling,
> Charlie is my darling,
> The young Chevalier.[25]

Given that the Stuarts never did return to the throne, such songs, romantic though they are, are an act of defiance against the established ruling order and its exercise of sovereignty. The Scots' attachment to the Stuarts is in various ways illogical – the latter's Catholicism, for example, poses a problem in a country with a majority Protestant population, as well as a history of hard-line commitment to the Protestant cause – but it is no less deeply felt for all that.

CONCLUSION

Sovereignty is one of the most fundamental of political issues, and nationalism continues to keep it in the forefront of the public consciousness. Disputes over sovereignty are rife and contribute significantly to political tension world wide: the former Yugoslavia remains a source of problems, and nationalist minorities are still trying to secede from the Russian federation, which may well shrink further in size. Outsiders can rarely understand the passion that lies behind such disputes or just how intractable they can be, but for the participants they are matters of overriding importance in which cultural identity is at stake. Nowhere is this more evident than in the Middle East, where the Palestinians and Israelis are locked in a seemingly interminable conflict that no third party is able to find an acceptable solution for, in spite of many attempts through the years. Neither side feels it can afford to make any significant concessions or indeed even to recognise the legitimacy of the other's claims: the search for a 'road map' continues, with little real progress to report to date. Add in competing religions, both of which are products of the region and believe that their presence there is divinely sanctioned, in fact divinely required, and it becomes an inflammatory mix. Even if a settlement were to be imposed, how many generations it would hold for is another question: the issue has an intrinsic capacity to remain emotive. Disputed sovereignty simply seems a fact of life for the populace of the Middle East.

Scott's treatment of a sovereignty dispute reveals its complex emotional landscape with great skill, and his conclusion harmonises well enough with the way Scots–English relations have worked out in general since the 1745 Rebellion (its bloody aftermath excepted). The two nations did indeed settle into their 'marriage' with reasonable success, although it does seem to be under considerable strain at present and a divorce cannot be ruled out. Scott suggests a nation willing to forgo its sovereignty over its own affairs for the benefits of a larger union, and there is no denying that most of the population has made that kind of calculation over the years, if only implicitly in going along with the system – again, until recently. The fanatical support provided by the Highlanders, however, ought to give us pause for thought. They become representative of an unreconstructed strain in Scottish life which cannot accept the loss of national sovereignty, and they have wider symbolic significance in this respect, indicating how sovereignty can never quite be repressed: in Freudian fashion it always manages to reassert itself, no matter how long it may have remained hidden. If it ever did become independent, Scotland might well have to face up to its own sovereignty dispute over the Shetland Isles, which retain a strong sense of their Norse heritage that would no doubt come to the fore if the Union were broken: another example of the return of the repressed in political terms.

What we might take away from Scott is the realisation that sovereignty disputes are immensely persistent, and that no amount of wishful thinking will make them go away. This is not to be critical of Scott personally, who is after all an author not a politician, but of the political class in general, who so often demonstrate a woeful lack of understanding of the emotional investment that national sovereignty can command. Almost every sovereignty dispute will have its equivalent of the

Highlanders somewhere within the mix, refusing to give up what they take to be their birthright. There are enough instances of similar disputes around the world to ensure that the issue remains near the top of the geopolitical agenda, taxing the political class to its limit. The virtue of Scott is that he makes us realise the disordering effect such disputes have on the emotional lives of those caught up in them. There are no easy answers, and many cases where the heart says one thing and the head another – to the confusion of the individual trying to decide where to commit himself. Scott is invariably sympathetic to those suffering such problems, and shows great insight as a writer in tracing their impact upon individual behaviour. We need to develop some of Scott's talent for seeing both sides of a dispute in our own engagement with the current crop of sovereignty problems, and to realise that they will not always respond to conventional political methods. Dual sovereignty may well prove to be worth further exploration, but its psychological ramifications must be very carefully considered: as Scott has so tellingly demonstrated, sovereignty is a matter of more than mere logic. That is the lasting message of a work like *Waverley*, rather than Scott's resolution of a sovereignty dispute by forcing it to submit to the dictates of a romance framework. In the real political world, situations and participants tend to be far less accommodating.

CHAPTER 11

Frankenstein, or, The Modern Prometheus and Artificial Life

THE ISSUE

Far-fetched though Mary Shelley's *Frankenstein* (1818) may have seemed to the audience in its day, we are now well into an era when life can be created in a variety of artificial ways.[1] Test-tube babies are a reality, and the manufacture of artificial life-forms – whether robotic or computer-bound – is something of a growth industry within science. Experiments in cloning and stem-cell research hold out the promise of ever-increasing scientific involvement in the manipulation of life processes, although public opposition to such projects suggests that many perceive this as a threat to our humanity, and that at the very least they wish to see it being monitored very closely by governments. There is unease as to where all of this will lead. In Jean-François Lyotard's opinion, for example, the further we go down this particular road the closer we come to the realm of the 'inhuman', where humanity finds itself in danger of being edged out of the picture in a computer-oriented universe that simply has no need of us. Lyotard feels moved to raise the question, 'what if what is "proper" to humankind were to be inhabited by the inhuman?', and does not much like the signs of this he sees when he looks around him, nor the general direction in which it is heading.[2]

One way in which the inhuman might well edge into our lives is through the development of the cyborg: an amalgam of human and machine. Theorists such as Donna Haraway have been very enthusiastic about this notion, seeing it as a means of enhancing the power of human beings by harnessing the far greater power and resilience of technology. For Haraway such hybrid identity is very desirable, especially if it helps women to break free from the domination of men, but for others it is a worrying prospect where we run the risk of losing our sense of humanity.[3] Film-makers have been particularly intrigued by cyborgs, and in films such as *Blade Runner* (1984) and *Terminator* (1991) have explored what one commentator has called 'the instability of the concept of the human' when 'the human becomes intertwined with the technologically reproduced image of the cyborg'.[4] Viewed from this perspective, cyborgs are a far more suspect phenomenon than Haraway finds them; the fear being that they will undermine the human instead of constituting an improved version of it to which we should all aspire.

The key objection to the development of artificial – or in any significant way, engineered – life (AL) is that humanity may not be able to retain control over it once it moves past a certain level of sophistication. That is certainly the problem exercising humanity in *Blade Runner*, with what is 'proper' to it not being respected – indeed, facing the prospect of invasion from humanoid 'replicants'. Cultural commentators wonder about future generations of robots taking on identities of their own in this way and resisting human commands. Then there is the worry that computer-generated 'life-forms' might also strive to escape human direction. Some computer viruses are already thought to have attained this capability, constantly and ingeniously mutating in a way that we cannot predict or prevent.[5] If that kind of autonomy becomes common, then the life-forms in question could at some point start competing with us for scarce resources, which would hardly be to humanity's benefit. The comments of some workers in the field does suggest that they expect such forms eventually to take on an independent identity. Christopher G. Langton, for example, has insisted that AL will 'be genuine life – it will simply be made of different stuff than the life that has evolved here on Earth', and is clearly looking forward to its imminent arrival.[6]

We are at an early stage of development as regards artificial life, and such scenarios are merely speculative, the material of science fiction rather than science fact for the time being; but the warning signs are there to be heeded as far as some critics are concerned. Not everyone wants share the world with life-forms made of 'different stuff', nor feels able to trust them. AI (Artificial Intelligence) and AL tend to polarise opinion, yet they clearly fascinate the scientific community. Projects in AI and AL are attracting substantial financial backing from both government and industry, and this shows every sign of being a very high-profile area of scientific research for the immediate future.

Proponents of AI and AL are generally quite sanguine about our relationship with the newly emerging life-forms, which they claim are designed to enhance our life experience rather than to create problems for us. Mark Ward, for example, has suggested that 'we will learn to live with ALife creations for a long time before we feel any kind of threat from them . . . . They will become familiar tools and possibly companions long before they are smart enough to think about doing away with us.'[7] We have to hope this is right, but the mere fact of such a prospect as conflict being mooted as possible is enough to give us pause for thought. What if such creations develop enough of an identity to want to become autonomous beings who can plan their own lives, instead of always being at the beck and call of humans? What if they learn to reproduce themselves without human aid? Science-fictional though such speculations may sound at present, they are within the realm of possibility as the enterprise of AI–AL research and experimentation progresses. And the question of how we shall relate to advanced AI or AL certainly looms large.

THE TEXT

Mary Shelley, *Frankenstein, or, The Modern Prometheus*

The fears about where such experiments in artificially created life might lead underpin Mary Shelley's *Frankenstein*, where the precocious young scientist Viktor Frankenstein discovers the secret of how to impart life to dead matter, thus creating a creature by artificial means. We never do know exactly how Frankenstein's creation comes to life (subsequent film adaptations provide their own suggested explanations, usually involving complicated machinery and lightning, or some other source of electrical power), but he soon turns into our worst fears of what artificial life might become: an alien life-form motivated by deep hatred for the human race, whom he feels, not unreasonably, has rejected him and must be punished for having done so. It is no accident that the story has exerted such an appeal over horror film-makers: the creature is the stuff of our nightmares, where we are so often helpless to protect ourselves against forces whose motivation we do not really understand. There is no reasoning with such forces, it is a case of a fight to the death against evil at its most sinister. As Chris Baldick has argued, the story has turned into a 'modern myth', whose 'various facets refer back to common and continuous anxieties, to genuine causes of alarm in the monstrous and uncontrollable tendencies of the modern world'.[8] In other words, *Frankenstein* nags away at our sense of vulnerability, just as contemporary developments in AI and AL are also doing.

The narrative charts the protagonist's development from a young man enthralled by the ideas behind medieval alchemy (as in the work of such notorious figures as Cornelius Agrippa, Paracelsus and Albertus Magnus), to a star pupil in the discipline of natural philosophy at the University of Ingolstadt, who then single-handedly cracks one of the greatest mysteries facing science. Having created life artificially, collecting the necessary body parts from 'among the unhallowed damps of the grave' in rather grisly fashion, he finds himself locked in conflict with his elusive creation, unable to cope with what he has done in bringing him into the world.[9] It is only when the creature turns into a murderer that Frankenstein is compelled to face up to his responsibilities in the matter and engage in some kind of dialogue with his creation, recognising that the latter's needs and desires, such as for a female companion to alleviate his solitude, are not after all unreasonable for one in his situation.

Although he reaches an advanced stage of work on the project, Frankenstein feels unable to carry it through to completion and destroys the unfinished creature. He justifies his refusal to produce the desired mate on the grounds that a new race would be the result, and one with superhuman powers as well, thus putting humanity's future in jeopardy. His secret of how to create life dies with him in the Arctic wastes where he is pursuing his creation, who vows to follow Frankenstein on into death: 'I shall die, and what I now feel be no longer felt. Soon these burning miseries will be extinct. I shall ascend my funeral pile triumphantly, and exult in the agony of the torturing flames.'[10] But what Frankenstein has discovered could no doubt be found by other researchers spurred on by the same drive of curiosity into the inner nature of things. Viktor is no unique figure in wanting to delve more deeply into the mystery of life processes – that is all but intrinsic to the scientific temperament. As he himself describes it: 'Whence, I often asked myself, did the principle of life proceed?'[11] It is unlikely that there are not several more young scientists in Viktor's world who are asking themselves the same question, and willing to follow wherever it may take them without much thought for the aftermath, just as keen, and foolhardy, as he was to uncover 'the secrets of heaven and earth'.[12]

The ethics of research into artificial life in general is an issue of considerable public concern, but Frankenstein never really addresses this while pursuing his experiments, with alarming enough consequences: 'his dream lacks moral content', as one critic has pointed out, while another condemns him as 'the pathetic victim of drives which he cannot control nor even acknowledge'.[13] Frankenstein's vision is restricted to the demands of the project and he never looks beyond those. Once engrossed by the technical problem the project sets he will continue on heedless of the outside world until he is able to report success in his endeavours: 'After days and nights of incredible labour and fatigue, I succeeded in discovering the cause of generation and life; nay, more, I became myself capable of bestowing animation upon lifeless matter.'[14] As he puts it in attempting to describe his state of mind during this period: 'None but those who have experienced them can conceive of the enticements of science.'[15] But whereas Shelley's fictional world had to deal with only one rogue scientist, ours has to deal with a host of multinational companies in pursuit of the potentially enormous profits that success in artificial intelligence, artificial life, cloning and stem-cell research could bring, and willing to invest vast sums of money in research to bring this about as rapidly as possible. Not surprisingly, scientists find such support very attractive. Whether the multinationals are any more to be trusted than Frankenstein remains an open question, but what is incontestable is that the enticements of profit will drive them on to ever greater efforts, regardless of what reservations society at large may have about their activities and where they may lead. The market dictates the course of events in such cases.

Frankenstein's original motivation for creating life artificially is not just a matter of scientific curiosity, however; he genuinely believes that it will be for the benefit of humankind generally: 'I thought, that if I could bestow animation upon lifeless matter, I might in process of time . . . renew life where death had apparently devoted the body to corruption.'[16] He imagines himself the lauded creator of a new species which will astonish the rest of humankind by its powers, but the reality he encounters on completion of his experiments is drastically different from his expectations:

> Oh! no mortal could support the horror of that countenance. A mummy again endued with animation could not be so hideous as that wretch. I had gazed on him while unfinished; he was ugly then; but when those muscles and joints were rendered capable of motion, it became a thing such as even Dante could not have conceived.[17]

After this classic instance of 'the failure of reality to match desire, of practice to match theory', Frankenstein flees the scene in disarray leaving the helpless creature to its own devices, totally abandoning any responsibility for his actions in bringing it into being.[18] His scientific curiosity has not extended far enough to consider the possible implications of his experiment, and he is revealed as emotionally inadequate to deal with the outcome. It is an indictment of the scientific temperament at its most blinkered. Frankenstein's moral failings are further revealed when his reaction to discovering that the creature has escaped overnight from his laboratory turns out to be elation rather than alarm. True, he does have a breakdown almost immediately afterwards and is clearly in a state of shock about the whole experience, but his desire simply to have the problem disappear, as if he had never been involved in it, does not speak well of his character or sense of social responsibility.

Since the creature is rejected by its creator it is forced to find a way of surviving on its own without any human help. He proves to be both adaptable and hungry for knowledge, as well as keen to be accepted by the human race. This he finally manages to achieve, although only very briefly, in striking up a conversation with a blind man, the father of the De Lacey family, whom he finds living in an isolated country cottage. The man converses with him and sympathises with his plight when his guest declares himself to be alone and friendless. When De Lacey goes on to say, 'I am blind, and cannot judge of your countenance, but there is something in your words, which persuades me that you are sincere', it carries the implication that the creature is mentally, if not physically, the same as the rest of the human race, which is a source of considerable encouragement to him.[19] The old man's family, whom he has been observing from a distance, keeping himself hidden, has also made a deep impression on him, and he feels himself very drawn towards their character: 'benevolence and generosity were ever present before me, inciting within me a desire to become an actor in the busy scene where so many admirable qualities were called forth and displayed.'[20]

This idyll only lasts until the rest of the De Lacey family cast eyes on him, when his appearance shocks and scares them into driving him away without even attempting to talk to him. He is simply treated as a monster. The predictable result of this unequivocal rejection is to embitter and alienate the creature, who vows vengeance on his creator for having failed to give him a physique and appearance that would render him acceptable to the rest of humanity:

> I will revenge my injuries: if I cannot inspire love, I will cause fear; and chiefly towards you my arch-enemy, because my creator, do I swear inextinguishable hatred. Have a care: I will work at your destruction, nor finish until I desolate your heart, so that you shall curse the hour of your birth.[21]

This objective he achieves by murdering some of those closest to Frankenstein, including, most shockingly, his wife on their wedding night: 'She was there, lifeless and inanimate, thrown across the bed, her head hanging down, and her pale and distorted features half covered by her hair.'[22] In the creature's mind he has exacted the same punishment on Frankenstein that his creator has inflicted upon him by denying him companionship.

Within a very short space of time the creature has moved, to use Mark Ward's terminology, from being a potential 'companion' to humanity, as the elder De Lacey is willing to consider him, to 'smart enough' not just 'to think about doing away with us' but to perform the deed several times over, effectively holding his creator to ransom to do his bidding. The creature's description of his reaction to his first murder, of Viktor's young brother William, is quite chilling:

> I gazed on my victim, and my heart swelled with exultation and hellish triumph: clapping my hands, I exclaimed, 'I, too, can create desolation; my enemy is not invulnerable; this death will

carry despair to him, and a thousand other miseries shall torment and destroy him'.[23]

Frankenstein's creation is now a fully-fledged menace to the human race in general, far outstripping it in power – he has more than something of the sublime about him in his larger-than-life physique and the stamina that goes with it, enabling him to survive in the most inhospitable of environments, such as the high Alps or the Arctic. The dilemma arises as to what might happen if he is allowed to establish a family line of his own with the companion he craves. Frankenstein himself is appalled at the prospect this opens up: 'a race of devils would be propagated upon the earth, who might make the very existence of the species of man a condition precarious and full of terror.'[24] The mutual antipathy, and thus incompatibility, of the two species becomes glaringly evident, and this is as much the fault of humankind as the new race. Humanity has failed to make the imaginative leap of seeing past the creature's appearance to his inner potential, with even the 'benevolent and generous' De Lacey siblings failing the test. Overall, Frankenstein has handled the entire issue disastrously, exposing both his family and humankind to mortal risk by his ill thought-out scientific undertaking.

Chris Baldick notes that 'the inhuman – whether mechanical or demonic – has figured very strikingly' in the Frankenstein myth and its various adaptations.[25] Shelley's narrative features both of these, with the body being assembled from spare parts much in the manner of a piece of machinery (putting us in mind of a cyborg creation too), and then turning into a demonic figure who terrorises the Frankenstein family in revenge for his fate. AI and AL creations take that mechanical aspect even further, and carry with them the possibility of the demonic, since they lack such human traits as conscience, which is one of the primary constraints on human behaviour. It is interesting to note that it is just such an absence that is presenting problems to current experiments into robotics, especially with regard to robot interaction with humans. Robots can be programmed to mimic our moods and emotional states, encouraging us to respond emotionally to them, thus making it easier for us to work together. But there are limits as to how far such simulations can go. Using robots to cooperate with humans in teams on designated projects has its drawbacks, as a *New Scientist* article has outlined:

[T]he idea of a robot as a teammate is rubbing some researchers up the wrong way. Because robots have no drive to protect themselves, they cannot protect the team and therefore humans cannot trust them, says Victoria Groom, a researcher in human–robot interaction at Stanford University in California. Nor do they have the ability to repair trust by feeling guilt and asking for forgiveness. This is a prerequisite for a team, so robotic teammates will fail to meet people's expectations.[26]

The nub of the matter is that we cannot expect AI and AL creations to have a sense of morality, thus undermining the possibility of properly human-style relations. There will be none of the psychological complexity that we associate with human beings to take into account.

The tragedy of Frankenstein's creation is that he suggests the capacity to develop the finer feelings of humanity, but is given no opportunity to do so. He is much taken by the work of Milton, Plutarch and Goethe, for example, describing it as reading which affords him 'extreme delight';[27] but the possession of such learning is no proof against rejection by the De Lacey family. For all his ability to appreciate such morally improving literature, however, it has to be worrying how easily the creature embraces violence as a means of resolving his anger and frustration at his condition. Conscience is not part of his make-up, and it remains a moot point whether he could come to experience this state of mind at all. Admittedly, there is a glimmer of it right at the end of the story when he is mourning his creator, and is moved to confess that 'it is true that I am a wretch. I have murdered the lovely and the helpless; I have strangled the innocent as they slept, and grasped to death his throat who never injured me or any other living thing'.[28] But this is rather late to have come to such a realisation.

Neither do guilt and a desire for forgiveness spontaneously emerge from the creature's character. When he displays emotion – such as his sense of despair at his isolation in the world – Frankenstein does start to empathise with him, as when he narrates his adventures after his abandonment by his creator at birth. Frankenstein's initial reaction at their encounter in the sublime landscape of the Alps is hostile: 'Begone! I will not hear you. There can be no community between you and me; we are enemies. Begone, or let us try our strength in a fight, in which one must fall.'[29] But he softens his stance when faced with the creature's pleas, and on hearing of his hopes of being accepted by humanity continually being dashed: 'I thought of the promise of virtues which he had displayed on the opening of his existence, and the subsequent blight of all kindly feeling by the loathing and scorn which his protectors had manifested towards him.'[30] Frankenstein is at least willing to consider the possibility that it is nurture rather than nature that has led to the creature's misdeeds. The outcome is that he agrees to fashion a mate for his creation, acknowledging his responsibility for his welfare; although he later decides to break the promise he has made, thus turning the creature even more firmly against him, with what will prove to be deadly consequences. In the final analysis, Frankenstein decides that he cannot trust the creature – or at least, that he cannot trust his descendants to keep the creature's bargain to remain strictly removed from the rest of the human race in what would be a parallel society. It is just such an aftermath to the creation of advanced AI and AL that exercises the minds of critics of the enterprise in general: will they pay any attention to our wishes?

Arguably the most worrying aspect of the creature is that he is not so much inhuman as too human for comfort: as Timothy Morton has argued, it 'is not the creature's difference from, but his *similarity* to human beings' that we find most disturbing.[31] It is a point also noted by Germaine Greer when she remarks that 'the monster is made as human as any other character; his depravity is the consequence of his miserable existence and his existence is Frankenstein's fault'.[32] Revenge is a powerful emotion with which humanity is well acquainted, and we can recognise our own propensity for this in the creature's reflex reactions to disappointment and the frustration of his desires. He lashes out at such points, but all of us are capable of doing so under certain circumstances. Frankenstein's creation could be said to represent the darker side of human nature, the side that resists civilising influences, and has few inhibitions about the use of violence in furthering its cause. If he were merely inhuman then he would be less psychologically disturbing than he turns out to be – but perhaps he is illustrative of the fact that we all contain the inhuman within us? He can arouse empathy in his creator, despite Viktor willing himself to be highly resistant to this response, and his words carry sincerity to the blind De Lacey father. There is a semblance in him of being 'proper' to humankind, therefore, even if the creature perceptively sums up the dilemma this poses: 'I found myself similar, yet at the same time strangely unlike to the beings concerning whom I read, and to whose conversation I was a listener.'[33]

The experience of Frankenstein and De Lacey suggests that the more AI–AL projects are designed to engender empathetic responses in us – mimicking or reflecting our moods, for example, so that we relax in the presence of robots – the more vulnerable we shall be as a species if they really do develop into independent entities. There will be a tendency, as the *New Scientist* article records, to treat those entities as human rather than the different species, with unknown motivations, that they have in reality become; to trust them rather than to be wary of them. In a way, the more inhuman AI–AL stays, the more vigilant we are likely to be at protecting the realm of the human from infiltration (the problem besetting humanity in *Blade Runner*).

What we will find it more difficult to be vigilant against is the 'enticements of science' that obsess figures like Frankenstein, driving them on in their quests to uncover 'the secrets of heaven and earth'. Frankenstein comes to recognise his folly as his end approaches, lying stricken by fever on the explorer Robert Walton's boat in the Arctic, concluding that it was 'a fit of enthusiastic madness' that led him on in his experiments.[34] Yet despite his apparent contrition, his last words indicate just how deep the enticements can go:

> Farewell, Walton! Seek happiness in tranquillity, and avoid ambition, even if it be only the apparently innocent one of distinguishing yourself in science and discoveries. Yet why do I say this? I have myself been blasted in these hopes, yet another may succeed.[35]

Even with the extensive catalogue of misery behind him that his scientific endeavours have generated, faith in science can still assert itself – somewhat ominously for the rest of humanity, we might well think. But Frankenstein is right, someone else undoubtedly will feel that they can succeed where others have failed: the lure of 'the secrets of heaven and earth' is too powerful to be resisted.

Frankenstein stands as a warning, therefore, about the dangers of scientific enquiry conducted for its own sake without regard to social consequences or moral codes. Unless science is contextualised in that way it can have outcomes which are against humanity's best interests – and there are those who would argue that this is a scenario which has happened too frequently for comfort in modern times. Nuclear power arguably has done more harm than good, for example, and the problem of how to dispose of nuclear waste is one that most societies would rather they did not have to face, given the risk it poses not just to the current generation but to generations for thousands of years into the future as the waste ever so slowly decays. The unintended consequences of scientific enquiry are only too evident in this instance, and, as so often is the case, it is only when it is too late to do anything to prevent these that such 'uncontrollable tendencies' are subjected to any really searching questions. The phenomenon of global warming, fuelled by a science and technology-led culture, is an even more depressing prospect to contemplate. Pursuing the metaphor, in global warming we have succeeded in creating our own uncontrollable monster, initiating a sequence of events which really does put human survival significantly at risk. With such examples before us it is only prudent to maintain a very sceptical attitude towards the claims made by the advocates of AI and AL, who are prone to let themselves be carried away by their enthusiasm. We cannot assume that everything will always turn out for the best when scientists are given their head.

CONCLUSION

We are so far advanced in the manufacture of both AL and AI that it is an all but inevitable part of our future: a combination of scientific curiosity and institutional hunger for profit and new markets will no doubt drive the enterprise ever onwards, with the ethical questions most likely being kept very much in the background or even suppressed altogether. This makes the need for careful monitoring imperative, as well as for public debate about the entire enterprise and its goals. The spectre of a process which escapes human control, as in the Frankenstein example, must always be borne in mind, especially given the scale on which science is conducted nowadays, going far beyond anything imaginable to such lone researchers as Viktor Frankenstein.

Cyborg experimentation will need to be kept under public surveillance too, as the more we move towards the machine end of the hybrid the more our sense of humanity is in danger of being eroded. Machine parts are already standardly inserted in human beings, as in the case of heart pacemakers; life-support machines can take over many of the body's main functions for significant periods; artificial organs will no doubt become more and more common as the technology becomes ever more sophisticated. The imperative behind such developments in medical technology is as high-minded as Fran kenstein's original vision: to extend human life and to ease suffering. But the more extreme voices on cyborgisation envisage something altogether more radical, to the extent of engineering what is almost a new species with vastly increased powers to those available to mere humanity. That presents a very different challenge to our conception of what it is to be human that could well become a source of friction between the general public and the scientific community. At what point would such hybrid beings cease to be technically human? And what if their worldview started to diverge significantly from that of the humanity at large? At least in part they are made of 'different stuff' and must in theory be confronted by a different reality. How might they react to us then? Might they see us a rival to be overcome?

One of the ways in which public concern about the direction of sci-entific research can be allayed is through adherence to a professional code of ethics. In the UK such a code has recently been unveiled by the government under the title of 'Rigour, Respect and Responsibility' (2007). In the words of the government's chief scientific adviser, Sir David King, the code sets out 'to foster ethical research, to encour-age active reflection among scientists on the implications and impacts of their work, and to support communication between scientists and the public on complex and challenging issues'.[36] King notes that '[t]he public increasingly demands that scientific developments are ethical and serve the wider public good, as evidenced by the debate on stem-cell research', and that a code is necessary because 'there have been numerous examples of what can go wrong in science' in recent years.[37] To prevent those negative examples from proliferating, King insists that scientists must keep asking themselves what the future impact of their work might be, rather than simply trusting to fate. This would be the exact opposite of how Frankenstein proceeded, where enthusiasm alone was allowed to dictate his course of action.

The 'enticements of science' cannot be allowed to override the public interest, therefore, or to jeopardise public safety in the manner that Frankenstein's successful round of experimentation did. The relationship between public safety and AI–AL must continue to be monitored very closely, lest Viktor's only too plausible fear of 'a race of devils' being unleashed on us becomes real. It is still a fanciful conceit, but by no means an impossible turn of events – even a new race of computer viruses could make life extremely difficult for a computer-dependent society such as ours – and we have already had several scares on that score in recent years. Who knows what even now is lurking in hyperspace? In that sense, Lyotard's warnings about the spread of the inhuman into our everyday lives need to be taken very seriously. If we really are on the verge of creating new species through AI and AL, then caution – perhaps even extreme caution – is surely called for.

CHAPTER 12

The Private Memoirs and Confessions of a Justified Sinner and Fundamentalist Terrorism

THE ISSUE

Fundamentalism-inspired terrorism is unquestionably one of the most pressing political problems of our age, and Western secular society has great difficulty in dealing with it. The idea that religious zealots can feel justified in killing non-believers is abhorrent to a democratic society, which expects debate rather than violence when ideological disputes occur. Yet increasingly, terrorist incidents are a part of our experience, most recently in the form of suicide bombings, which are all but impossible to defend against (although as we discussed in chapter 9, Western governments continue to insist that increased sur-veillance will act as a deterrent). 9/11 represents the practice of suicide bombing taken to its extreme, with a major world city being brought almost to a standstill, and a state of panic induced throughout an entire nation by just two attacks on the World Trade Center in New York and one on the Pentagon Building in Washington. In terms of global poli-tics we are still living with the backlash of that event, as it continues to inform US foreign policy, particularly with regard to the volatile Middle East. Secularists are baffled by the mind-set involved in fun-damentalist terrorism, but unless we begin to understand it we are unlikely to be successful in calling for its end. Religious fundamental-ism shows no signs of going away, and where fundamentalism exists the possibility of terrorism is always present.[1]

We can trace religious fundamentalism well back into history, in the sense that all monotheistic religions, by definition, are convinced that theirs is the only true God, but the term itself is of very recent origin. After the publication of a series of pamphlets called *The Fundamentals* by evangelical Christian theologians in America between 1910 and 1915, a journalist described adherents to the ideas they contained as 'fundamentalists'.[2] What the pamphlets outlined were the basic doctrines of Christianity that believers had to accept without question: doctrines such as the virgin birth of Christ, his resurrection and the reality of his miracles. All of these are reported in the Bible, and for Christian fundamentalists that text, as the word of God, is to be taken as literal truth.

The term itself stuck and is now widely used to refer to extremists across the religious spectrum, with Islamic fundamentalists being particularly prominent in the news of late given the actions of militant groups such as al-Qaeda. It is Islamic fundamentalism above all that the West fears, and it has taken over from communism as Western culture's major ideological enemy. Nevertheless, fundamentalism is also a significant factor in Judaism and Hinduism, with Islamic believers often being the target in return. The common feature is that all such groups consider themselves to be in possession of the ultimate truth. In consequence all are intolerant of other beliefs, which are treated as a threat to the purity of their own. The tendency is therefore to regard those outside one's own religion as non-believers. Islam historically may have allowed Christianity and Judaism to be practised within its domain, on the grounds of figures from those traditions being 'people of the book' (that is, mentioned in the Koran), but never on an equal footing: Islam was the only true way and other beliefs were at best misguided.

Fundamentalism seems to have become progressively more militant in our era, with terrorism being regarded by a substantial section of the faithful as an approved practice to assert the cause of religious belief. For this constituency, dialogue with one's opponents is felt to be largely pointless. The belief system in question invariably proves to have a political dimension as well. Islamic extremists want to keep the holy lands of Islam (Saudi Arabia, for example) completely free of non-believers to protect their purity. Jewish fundamentalists encourage an aggressive settlement policy in the West Bank and Gaza Strip in an effort to return Israel to its biblical geographical boundaries, driving out the 'alien' Palestinians from the Jewish holy land in the process. Christian fundamentalists in America are working hard to overturn much of the progressive social legislation of the last few decades (concerning women's rights, abortion, homosexuality, etc.), and have established elaborate networks of influence throughout the governmental system to expedite this objective. Hindu fundamentalists attack Moslems in India to keep them in a state of political subjection under the country's Hindu majority, with the government often turning a blind eye to violent incidents. We have to recognise that religious fundamentalism is a key player in twenty-first-century global politics, and that terrorism is an integral part of its method for many of its followers.

THE TEXT

James Hogg, *The Private Memoirs and Confessions of a Justified Sinner*

James Hogg's *Confessions of a Justified Sinner* (1824) takes us inside the mind of just such a fundamentalist terrorist, Robert Wringhim, a product of 'the rage of fanaticism' of his time:[3] Scotland in the early eighteenth century in the immediate aftermath of the bitter religious struggles of the seventeenth. In Scotland, as in England, religion was a major source of division that had a dramatic impact on political life, leading to substantial civil strife. The division was as much between the various sects of Protestantism as between Protestantism and Catholicism, and left a lasting mark on the national consciousness. Subtle theological differences were enough to turn one's neighbours, or even family, into sworn enemies, with each sectarian movement claiming the authority of the Bible in establishing their own position. It was particularly fertile territory for the growth of extremism, and in the person and career of Robert Wringhim that is what we observe. The authors of a recent survey of Scottish literary history have suggested that '[t]he central issue of the novel may simply be a satire on excessive Scottish presbyterianism; or it may be a much wider satirical attack on dogmatism and fundamentalism of any kind'.[4] The two are not disconnected of course, with the former representing a particular case of the latter; but it is the latter I want to develop here, particularly as it finds its expression in acts of terrorism.

Robert is brought up in a strict Calvinist faith that considers humanity to be divided into the elect (the 'justified', or saved) and the reprobate (the damned). He comes to believe that he is an agent of divine justice whose destiny is to punish the reprobate on God's behalf: 'I conceived it decreed, not that I should be a minister of the gospel, but a champion of it, to cut off the enemies of the Lord from the face of the earth'.[5] Several murders follow on from this realisation, but Robert rarely retains much memory of them, relying on the *doppelganger* figure of his companion, Gil-Martin, to inform him of what has taken place. The latter is either a projection of Robert's own character, his evil side, or an agent of the devil; but he clearly encourages Robert in all his religious enthusiasm, feeding his sense of being an agent of a higher power. We leave Robert apparently on the point of suicide, horrified at a satanic vision appearing before him ('who is yon that I see approaching furiously – his stern face blackened with horrid despair!'),[6] but not before leaving a trail of destruction behind him.

The narrative is told from the perspective of first the Editor, then the protagonist Robert (his 'Private Memoirs and Confessions'), then the Editor again. As the preliminary 'Editor's Narrative' makes evident, Robert's friends and acquaintances are just as baffled by his character, and what motivates him, as most of us in a secular society are by the actions of those religious zealots amongst us now. Taking it as a study of the complex machinations of the fundamentalist terrorist mind, and society's vulnerability to such ideological extremism, the *Confessions* is arguably unsurpassed in English literature, and certainly helps us to understand what we are up against when confronted by religious fanaticism. Robert proves impervious to all attempts to dissuade him from the righteousness of his mission, considering himself to be enagaged on his very own 'Pilgrim's Progress' through life guided by God's will, and thus a figure to be emulated rather than criticised.[7] A man 'sealed up in his repressive theology', Robert is a formidable adversary.[8]

Robert's background could have been expressly designed to promote the development of zealotry in the impressionable young individual. His mother is a devout believer who comes under the sway of a Calvinist minister, the Rev. Wringhim, a 'flaming predestinarian divine' in the Editor's memorable description, and it is hinted that he may even be Robert's father, so close do the two become through their common religious interests.[9] Robert is disowned by his legal father, the Laird of Dalcastle, baptised under the Reverend's name, and brought up by the latter to be convinced that he is one of the elect, chosen by God to be saved, thus 'justified' to all eternity:

[M]y reverend father one morning rose from his seat, and, meeting me as I entered the room, he embraced me, and welcomed me into the community of the just upon earth. . . . That I was now a justified person, adopted among the number of God's children – my name written in the Lamb's book of life, and that no bypast transgression, nor any future act of my own, or of any other men, could be instrumental in altering the decree.[10]

One reading of the narrative is that Robert is 'brainwashed' in his childhood, such that he will accept whatever the Rev. Wringhim tells him.[11] While one can see the rationale for such a judgement, it does run the risk of absolving Robert from responsibility for his actions as an adult – something he is only too willing to try to do himself. We do not want to find ourselves in the position of conceding that fundamentalist terrorists cannot help themselves, otherwise there is no point in campaigning against their belief system.

If election is a career-defining experience to Robert, then the encounter with the mysterious Gil-Martin runs it a close second in importance. Robert is astonished to find

that he was the same being as myself! The clothes were the same to the smallest item. the form was the same; the apparent age; the colour of the hair; the eyes; and, as far as recollection could serve me from viewing my own features in a glass, the features were the very same.[12]

This ought to strain even Robert's credibility, but as Kurt Wittig has pointed out, he 'tends to create his own subjective version of reality' and Gil-Martin is just what he needs post-election: a character to embody his own desires.[13] Gil-Martin certainly fulfils that, becoming a brilliantly effective metaphor for Robert's belief; visible to him, a living presence that informs his every thought and action, but either invisible or unidentifiable by others. If it is noted by some that Robert has a companion, none can agree as to who this person is: 'Having been so frequently seen in his company, several people happened to mention the circumstance to my mother and reverend father; but at the same time had all described him differently.'[14] Gil-Martin is an unfailing source of support to Robert, justifying his conduct and congratulating him on his singleness of purpose in being willing to 'shed blood in the cause of the true faith'.[15] Whatever opposition Robert may meet, Gil-Martin is there to reassure him, continually building up his ego and preventing him from having second thoughts as to the rightness of his choice to be a 'champion' of the gospel, doing the Lord's bidding by 'cutting off' his supposed enemies. Gil-Martin tells Robert precisely what he wants to hear; that he is a special being, superior to the rest of the human race, and with a divinely sanctioned mission to carry out.

In the Editor's Narrative all of Robert's actions appear in a very different light. He remains a source of mystery to his family and acquaintances, who, other than the Rev. Wringhim or his mother, simply cannot appreciate the depth of his zeal or how that shapes his behaviour, which is generally ungracious and lacking in basic respect for others. Robert is kept separate from his half-brother George until they meet by chance in Edinburgh, and there is an altercation between the two in which Robert is slightly hurt. After the affair blows up into a full-scale riot between supporters of the two men, who are on opposite sides of the political divide, Robert conceives a bitter hatred for George. He proceeds to stalk his brother, turning into 'a fiend of more malignant aspect . . . ever at his elbow', a running commentary on George's supposed lack of divine favour.[16]

Events turn much darker when George is murdered. Shortly afterwards the Laird dies too, broken-hearted at his loss, and Robert takes over the family estate as the new Laird of Dalcastle. Witness accounts of George's murder, initially very confused and contradictory, eventually point to Robert as the likely murderer, but when the authorities decide to bring him back to trial from Dalcastle he is not to be found, nor is his mother. We are left with a series of mysteries, with no clear understanding of what has actually happened, which only Robert's 'Private Memoirs and Confessions' will elucidate. Society simply has not identified how much of a menace Robert is, nor the depth of hatred he feels towards his fellow human beings, the majority of whom he has written off as reprobate. It is not expected that even religious extremists will go to the lengths that Robert has, but when he comes under suspicion the full extent of his activities remains unclear until he records them himself for posterity in his journal. Society's worrying vulnerability to the single-minded extremist registers forcefully.

Robert's retrospective account of his life reveals the steady development of a fundamentalist personality, with all the blindness to the rights of others this typically involves. His tone is from the start self-justifying and self-pitying, 'the outrage of a wronged man', as Robert Kiely has described it:[17]

> My life has been a life of trouble and turmoil; of change and vicis-
> situde; of anger and exultation; of sorrow and of vengeance. My
> sorrows have all been for a slighted gospel, and my vengeance has
> been wreaked on its adversaries.[18]

He proceeds to recount the details of his life, interpreting everything through the prism of a strict Calvinist theology based on predestinarian principles. His mother's adverse judgement of the Laird, for example, 'it so pleased Heaven, that, as a trial of her faith, she was married to one of the wicked; a man all over spotted with the leprosy of sin', is accepted at face value.[19] A precocious childhood interest in matters of theology, with Robert disputing in company the distinction between Effectual and Ineffectual Calling to the amazement of his adult hearers, indicates the success of the Rev. Wringhim's regimen. Robert is a bigot in the making, although even such as he have to undergo some psychological trials before being received into the realms of the elect:

> About this time, and for a long period afterwards, amounting to
> several years, I lived in a hopeless and deplorable state of mind;
> for I said to myself, 'If my name is not written in the book of life
> from all eternity, it is in vain for me to presume that either vows
> or prayers of mine, or those of all mankind combined, can ever
> procure its insertion now'.[20]

The Rev. Wringhim's announcement of his justified nature, and then the appearance of his 'spiritual guide' Gil-Martin, releases Robert from his fears about his fate. It should not do so, for reasons we shall go on to consider later; but for Robert, 'this time is a time of great rejoicing in spirit to me'.[21]

From rejoicing to terrorism proves to be a very short step, with Robert declaring open season on the reprobate:

> Seeing that God had from all eternity decided the fate of every
> individual that was to be born of woman, how vain was it in man
> to endeavour to save those whom their Maker had, by an unchange-
> able decree, doomed to destruction.[22]

Gil-Martin goes to work on Robert's pride, praising his intellectual ability in reaching such conclusions and engaging him in intense theological debate that persuades Robert he must become his disciple because of the subtlety of Gil-Martin's reasoning. As a disciple Robert is encouraged to develop the closed mind of the terrorist, where absolute conviction rules:

> he besought of me never to think it possible for me to fall from the truth, or the favour of him who had chosen me, else that misbelief would baulk every good work to which I set my face.[23]

Such arguments speak very directly to Robert's predestinarian beliefs, with their assumption that the justified cannot sin, since God's decree on their spiritual status is eternally binding: once justified, always justified. A further assumption growing from that would be that whatever one does, if one truly believes one has been justified, is therefore classifiable as a 'good work'. In seventeenth-century England this belief (antinomianism) led those called the 'Ranters' to feel they could sin as much as they wished, because, in effect, they were beyond sin: the actions of the justified could only be good in God's eyes. Ranters thus engaged enthusiastically in sexual and alcoholic excess, at least until they were suppressed by the authorities, who feared the threat that potentially they posed to social order.[24] Robert becomes a classic example of what one commentator has called the 'antinomian distortion' in action.[25]

To those opposed to predestinarian theology, antinomianism was a worrying indication of where extremism could lead, and the Laird of Dalcastle eloquently sums up their position when castigating the Rev. Wringhim for the influence he has attained over his wife:

> You are one, Sir, whose righteousness consists in splitting the doctrines of Calvin into thousands of undistinguishable films, and in setting up a system of justifying-grace against all breaches of all laws, moral or divine. In short, Sir, you are a mildew, – a cankerworm in the bosom of the Reformed Church, generating a disease of which she will never be purged, but by the shedding of blood.[26]

The last phrase is prophetic, because it is precisely what Robert will subject the Reformed Church to by his murders. It is also the activity to which fundamentalist terrorists seen inexorably drawn; their personal rite of passage.

The 'antinomian distortion' comes to the fore in the case of Mr Blanchard, a clergyman who takes a deep dislike to Gil-Martin, suggesting to Robert that he is a demonic figure sent to lead him astray. Robert's response is to decide to assassinate Blanchard. A sermon delivered by the latter in which he claims that men can save themselves by their actions, not needing to be predestined to salvation by God, merely serves to confirm Blanchard's reprobate status to Robert. No hard-line Calvinist could believe that our actions (or 'works') could have any effect whatsoever on our spiritual fate, since they emphasise that salvation comes by means of God's grace alone. To argue otherwise is to question the notion of predestination, whereby one's spiritual fate is decided before one's birth and cannot be altered thereafter. Gil-Martin is only too ready to support Robert's judgement on Blanchard: 'Can there be any doubt that it is the duty of one consecrated to God, to cut off such a mildew?'[27] Robert's career as a terrorist is now truly under way, and it is characteristic that it is based on a refusal to countenance an alternative interpretation of doctrine.

Blanchard is accordingly slaughtered by the two of them, with Gil-Martin manipulating the situation such that another preacher is accused and convicted of the crime. Rather than becoming suspicious of Gil-Martin's power in managing so astutely to deflect attention away from them, Robert is fired up to continue: 'Now, the ice being broke, I felt considerable zeal in our great work.'[28] Gil-Martin is soon urging Robert to murder both his brother and the Laird, arguing that this is a duty he owes the Lord. Such an argument weighs powerfully with Robert, although he should have noted the subtle distinction that Gil-Martin makes in his response to this declamation when he presses Robert 'to cleanse the sanctuary of thy God in this thy native land by the shedding of blood'.[29] The implication of 'thy God' is that Gil-Martin might worship a different one entirely. Such subtlety is lost on Robert, who hears only what he wants to hear – and what he wants to hear is that he is justified in continuing in his terrorist ways. As he remarks to his jailer at one point, while awaiting trial for his part in the riot that ensues after the dispute with his brother, 'if you belong to the unregenerate, I have a commission to slay you'.[30]

Once launched on a career as a terrorist, Robert finds confirmation for his intentions wherever he looks, becoming convinced that the

Rev. Wringhim, too, approves his plans to assassinate his father and brother. When he next encounters his brother's party at play, the fact that he strikes such terror in them that they break up in disarray is further proof to Robert that he is carrying out God's wishes. Self-reflection is not a prominent feature of Robert's personality and is a trait which any would-be terrorist needs to suppress if he is to be successful. The terrorist must remain totally focused on the objective at hand and deaf to all arguments for compromise. Gil-Martin plays a critical role in this respect, constantly reminding Robert to stay true to his ideals and not to lose his sense of divine mission. We note that Robert's only extended dialogue about theological matters after his 'election' is with a figure whose brief is to provoke him to extremes; he never subjects his core beliefs to real critique.

Robert eventually is almost entirely taken over by Gil-Martin, such that 'I generally conceived myself to be two people'.[31] Thinking himself to have been at home, he finds that others have reported him abroad stalking his brother and concludes that Gil-Martin has been impersonating him. When eventually he kills his brother, Robert has only a hazy notion of what has occurred, having to rely on the version given to him by Gil-Martin, claiming to have been an onlooker at the event. We have the impression of someone blanking out their actions in order to keep their humanitarian feelings at bay. This becomes a pattern after Robert moves back to Dalcastle to take possession of the family estate. There are long stretches of time of which Robert has no memory, yet he finds himself accused of a series of evil actions during these periods which leave him dumbfounded: 'Either I had a second self, who transacted business in my likeness, or else my body was at times possessed by a spirit over which it had no controul, and of whose actions my own soul was wholly unconscious.'[32]

This confusion is only felt in Gil-Martin's absence, and the latter's return brings the unwelcome news that Robert apparently has committed other murders in the interim, including that of his mother. Despite this, Gil-Martin is able to offer Robert a way of absolution for his crimes: 'I can prove them not to be so to the cause of pure Christianity, by the mode of which we have approved of it.'[33] In other words, election renders him innocent; the justified are exempt from conventional human laws. Robert has begun to question this notion in his own mind and he should push Gil-Martin further on the matter, but he allows himself to fall under his spiritual director's spell yet again. When Gil-Martin expounds the doctrine that '[w]e are all sub-jected to two distinct natures in the same person', it sums up the con-flict between good and evil that takes place in everyone's character, Robert's included. But we become aware that Robert has long since lost that battle, suppressing the humanitarian impulses within him (never very strong in his case, and never exactly fostered by the Rev. Wringhim in his upbringing). The dark side has taken over, erad-icating any better impulses he may ever have had: this is a character of whom it truly may be said that, '[i]n spiritual pride, sin and lies Robert is quite outstanding'.[34]

Gil-Martin reappears in Robert's grim last days, when he is in flight from capture. Despite all that has happened, Robert is once more taken in by Gil-Martin's arguments that nothing he has done can affect his spiritual state. No lasting expression of remorse over his actions is ever really forthcoming, and Robert reverts to type with alacrity. To the end he seeks confirmation of his beliefs at the expense of examin-ing them critically in terms of their effect on others. Perhaps the full horror of what he has done in the name of belief comes to him at the close – 'My hour is at hand. – Almighty God, what is this that I am about to do!'[35] – or is it just self-pity at his desperate state and the destruction of his belief system? Whether Robert has really learned anything from his actions and the pain and suffering they have caused is a moot point.

There are warning signs throughout Robert's narrative that all is not necessarily as it seems, that his spiritual condition is more problematic than he thinks. For a start, Robert's election is announced by his father, whereas readers of spiritual autobiography would recognise that the individual ought to become aware of this himself internally, the 'con-version experience' as this was called, taking the form of a spiritual epiphany, often of a psychologically shattering kind.[36] No one else can either bestow, or win, election for oneself; it is a deeply personal matter that has to be felt 'on the pulses'. Then there are several odd aspects to note about Gil-Martin's behaviour, such as his ability to take on the appearance of others when required and his reluctance to pray. On the latter point, as on other theological issues, he can be very uncon-ventional and even dangerously unorthodox. Although even Robert can recognise this on occasion, in the manner of the true zealot he is easily won over by Gil-Martin's often questionable explanations of his conduct:

He disapproved of prayer altogether, in the manner it was generally gone about, he said. Man made it merely a selfish concern,
and was constantly employed asking, asking, for every thing.
Whereas it became all God's creatures to be content with their lot,
and only to kneel before him in order to thank him for such benefits as he saw meet to bestow. In short, he argued with such
energy, that before we parted I acquiesced, as usual, in his position, and never mentioned prayer to him any more.[37]

The 'as usual' is very revealing: Robert is only too willing to be led by
Gil-Martin, especially if his arguments reaffirm Robert's sense of
being someone special, someone beyond the concerns of ordinary individuals. As a member of the elect he can easily be persuaded that he
has no need to prove himself by his actions, his destiny being fixed.
Robert is now existing in his own private world, where doubt is not to
be entertained and where conviction will always prevail. Gil-Martin
enables Robert to blank out whatever seems to call his destiny into
question: a process of 'depersonalisation', as Barbara Bloedé has
defined it.[38] All fundamentalist terrorists need to perform a similar
operation, reducing internal dialogue to acquiesence, 'as usual' as it
were, with their own version of Gil-Martin: the demon within that
directs them to sacrifice human life for their religious cause. Even
when Robert does briefly begin to wonder about *the infallibility of the
elect*, his 'backsliding' is soon overcome by 'the unwearied diligence'
of Gil-Martin's counsel.[39] The theological doctrine that Robert lives
by means that he is only too receptive to such diligence and only too
resistant to any arguments to the contrary.

John Carey has argued that '[t]he stern theology behind the
Confessions is, after all, not very different from Wringhim's , except that
he is the reprobate, not George'.[40] But Robert's actual spiritual status is
not the issue; rather it is the doctrine that encourages such bigoted zeal.
There is little comfort to be drawn from the fact of Robert's ultimate
punishment, especially for those enemies of the Lord whom he has 'cut
off'. Perhaps Hogg did want us to see this as a case of a man misled by the
devil, but we might be more likely nowadays to see the devil in the theology which thrives, in Carey's words, on 'the fear of exclusion'.[41] That
fear, especially if it is implanted firmly in early life, can be enough to lead
someone like Wringhim to operate his own act of exclusion on the rest of
the human race, with catastrophic consequences. Fundamentalism, after

all, is mainly about exclusion, with the vast majority of us being deemed to be outside the charmed circle of true believers: a point no less true in our own day than it was in Robert's.

CONCLUSION

Robert Wringhim is a chilling study of the fundamentalist mind and its ability to justify the most appalling acts in the name of belief. We can see that personality replicated across the religious spectrum today, with non-believers being treated as expendable by the fanatic faithful. It is as if non-believers hardly count as human, becoming mere excuses to 'shed blood in the cause of the true faith' and thus to prove the depth of one's commitment as a believer; mere means to a divinely ordained end to which the believer feels he has special access. What is most worrying in such cases, as with Robert, is the sheer conviction that fundamentalists can exhibit about their belief system; their ability to close off the critical side of their minds which might counsel tolerance towards other viewpoints. Doubt does not appear to come into their deliberations to any great extent after their conversion to the cause. Gil-Martin is always on hand to deflect doubt expertly with Robert, and even if the latter is perhaps experiencing something like that state of mind in his last moments, it is too late for all his unfortunate victims (for whom Robert never voices much regret).[42] Preventing conviction taking hold in such manner has to be one of the main priorities of any pluralist society committed to keeping difference a critical part of our everyday lives. Robert cannot bear difference, which he can only equate with non-belief.

Most believers are relatively moderate and probably willing to concede that others have the right to worship as they see fit – that is the multicultural ideal most of the West officially lives by anyway. Liberal democratic societies include the right to religious freedom, and all of us, believers and non-believers alike, are under an obligation to uphold this, difficult though it can be for many on either side of the divide. But extremism can surface even in a liberal democratic setting, and that is increasingly the case of late with fundamentalist views being asserted even in traditionally moderate religious settings such as the Anglican Church.[43] The more it does so, the more multicultural democracy is placed at risk, with theocracy rearing its ugly head. The prospect of Gil-Martin-inspired Robert Wringhims taking control of our destiny is not an attractive one. At the very least we might think again about the wisdom of allowing religions to have any significant input into the educational system, where Rev. Wringhim figures are only too likely to be found inculcating intolerant attitudes in their impressionable charges. 'Faith schools', which have become increasingly popular in Britain, even winning support in government circles, are a regressive step in this respect. Belief systems constantly have to be challenged, otherwise they are prone to slide into fundamentalism, and fundamentalism is the antithesis of the democratic ideal: a perpetual enemy to an open, pluralist society.

What is most depressing is that Wringhim's society was beginning to move away from 'the rage of fanaticism' and that our own world seems to have rediscovered a taste for it. The return of the Robert Wringhim personality remains to haunt the secularists among us.

Conclusion

The essays in this volume have, I trust, demonstrated the utility of the eighteenth-century novel in generating debate about some of the most pressing social issues of our time and giving us a new perspective on them. In the process, the eighteenth-century novel, from Aphra Behn to James Hogg, stands revealed as an outstandingly successful vehicle for social criticism from which we can still gain much in our reading today. This is one of the novel's strongest selling points and one of the major reasons for its development into the leading literary form of our time. I have been analysing the group of novels in this study through particular issues, but it is critical to note that they are issues which arise spontaneously from the narratives themselves, even if the terminology in which they are expressed may have changed over the centuries. Robinson Crusoe speaks of providence, we speak of intelligent design; Robert Wringhim of being God's agent to strike down the reprobate, we of fundamentalist terrorism; but the concepts, and the significance they have for us as individuals in our daily lives, are broadly the same. It is not imposing anything on these narratives to read them through contemporary concerns therefore; rather, it is to open up a dialogue with our predecessors. These are texts which continue to resonate for us now precisely because of their enthusiastic engagement with the critical socio-political problems of modernity, most notably the conflict between little narrative and grand narrative, a conflict that is inscribed in the very heart of modernity (and postmodernity too in its turn). It is a conflict which, then as now, reveals itself as a series of clashes: between individual and society, between the social classes, between the sexes, between family members, between the races, between us and our past.

It is time to summarise what have we learned from our dialogue with the eighteenth-century novel. In the area of religion, for example, it is that this activity can be a source of both comfort and of destructiveness; that it can both inspire and distort our individual psychology. We can still recognise the two aspects in our own world: born-again theology can instil a sense of inner security in the believer, but also make him intolerant of those who do not share his belief system; fundamentalist views can tip over into outright hatred of non-believers, to the point of seeing them as dispensable in the cause of one's religion. The heirs of both Robinson Crusoe and Robert Wringhim are amongst us, and we need to know how to differentiate them if we are to deal with them.

In terms of gender, there remains a huge gulf between the sexes on both sexual matters and relationships. Women are to this day worried by the Mister B syndrome; wary of being perceived as just another conquest in the sexual game, a game weighted towards males. Even when they enter into that game as men do they can still find themselves being subjected to the sexual double-standard, as happens to the women in *Tom Jones*. It is not Tom who is attacked by his peers, but the hapless Molly Seagrim, who carries the only too obvious signs of her sexual bravado in her pregnant state. Tom, on the other hand, is congratulated by Squire Western when he thinks Tom has fathered a bastard, as well he might have given his exuberant sexual history. The West may be more liberal nowadays, if still prone to a certain amount of hypocrisy with regard to women's sexual behaviour, but that is not the case in the Third World – and certainly not in the Muslim world. The male rake is still amongst us. Women in the Third World are oppressed and repressed by their families much in the way of a Radcliffe heroine too, with arranged marriages deemed an acceptable practice. The desire for personal development that marked out Arabella and Catherine Morland can still be difficult to satisfy, with many obstacles placed in the way of even the most determined seekers.

Social class can still divide us, as it does in *Caleb Williams*, and government can be just as oppressive an institution as the hero of that novel finds it to be – the little narrative of the individual is always at a severe disadvantage in such cases, unable to call on anything like the same forces that the ruling class can. Pamela is in a similar position with regard to Mister B, whose social position invests him with a power that someone in Pamela's class cannot match. It may end happily enough in this instance, but not before the heroine has been through severe trials that she would not have had to face had she been born higher up in the social scale. Equally, Caleb would not have been such an easy target for someone like Falkland had he been at a similar rank in the social hierarchy as his nemesis. Class and money continue to license similar conduct in our own world. Money also serves to drive on scientific enquiry, whether it is in the public interest or not, as we have seen in the case of artificial life, stem-cell research, etc. A contemporary Frankenstein would surely find backing from the drug multinationals for his researches.

The little narrative also finds itself at risk from the clash of grand narratives, as the hero of Scott's *Waverley* discovers. Sovereignty over ourselves is only ever partial and very much subsidiary to that wielded by ruling ideologies – and by their opponents. This can be a trial to individuals caught up in the conflict between competing versions of sovereignty, as we know from various extant examples around our world. Our political system prefers clear-cut solutions to problems of sovereignty, Hobbes being the ultimate standard for this outlook, and enforces these where it can. But it does not always work out that simply, to the detriment of individuals whose loyalties may well be split between warring factions. Dual sovereignty would be the rational solution, but as we can quickly determine from looking around us, neither politics nor nationalist loyalties are always the preserve of rationality; emotion gets in the way with monotonous regularity, leaving us confused as to what is the best course of action to take, which grand narrative to follow.

Family history also impacts significantly on individual sovereignty, as Tristram Shandy finds to his cost. None of us is a completely free agent, and we have to fashion ourselves out of materials that are given to us in largely predetermined shape. The extent to which we *can* fashion ourselves is still very much open to debate, with genetic determinists arguing that there is in fact very little scope for doing so. The little narrative of Tristram's present confronts his family past with some trepidation. It is a dialogue that all of us have to conduct, and no matter how strong our belief in the concept of free will it is a dialogue that can on occasion seem very one-sided. It is all too easy to feel as swamped by our family history as Tristram clearly does, battling to keep any sense of individual will alive against the odds. Tristram's adventures are both comic and deeply thought-provoking in this regard.

Race is very much with us too, yet another clash of narratives where individuals can find themselves exposed. Like gender relations, race relations generates a great deal of hypocrisy, and narratives such as *Oroonoko* bring these to the surface in a revealing way. Just as we can learn from narratives like *Gulliver's Travels* and *Tom Jones* how our nature can work against social harmony: the debate between nature and nurture is particularly well represented in the eighteenth-century novel and as topical now as it was then. We wrestle no less with Hobbes's bleak assessment of human nature than our eighteenth-century predecessors did.

This has been a very selective foray into the eighteenth-century novel, but a productive one I hope you will agree in terms of establishing common ground between our respective cultures. It is a sign of a vibrant literary tradition that it can keep speaking to us, keep challenging our beliefs and ideas across time, and that is a test I feel the eighteenth-century novel passes with honours. It is as relevant to our negotiations with our culture as it was in its own day and it deserves greater attention than it generally receives at present. The more dialogue we have with eighteenth-century novelists, the more we have to gain about understanding the moral dilemmas we both share.

Notes

Introduction

1. Daniel Defoe, *The Life and Strange Surprizing Adventures of Robinson Crusoe* (1719), ed. Thomas Keymer, Oxford: Oxford University Press, 2007; Henry Fielding, *The History of Tom Jones, A Foundling* (1749), eds John Bender and Simon Stern, Oxford: Oxford University Press, 1996.
2. James Hogg, *The Private Memoirs and Confessions of a Justified Sinner* (1824), ed. John Carey, Oxford: Oxford University Press, 1990.
3. William Godwin, *Caleb Williams, or, Things As They Are* (1794), ed. David McCracken, Oxford: Oxford University Press, 1970.
4. Mary Shelley, *Frankenstein, or, The Modern Prometheus* (1818), in *Four Gothic Novels*, Oxford: Oxford University Press, 1994.
5. Jane Austen, *Northanger Abbey and Other Works*, eds James Kinsley and John Davie, Oxford: Oxford University Press, 2003.
6. Charlotte Lennox, *The Female Quixote; or, The Adventures of Arabella* (1752), eds Amanda Gilroy and Will Verhoeven, London: Penguin Books, 2006.
7. Aphra Behn, *Oroonoko and Other Writings*, ed. Paul Salzman, Oxford: Oxford University Press, 1994; Jonathan Swift, *Gulliver's Travels* (1726), ed. Claude Rawson, Oxford: Oxford University Press, 2005.
8. E. M. Forster, *Aspects of the Novel* (1927), ed. Oliver Stallybrass, Harmondsworth: Penguin Books, 1976, p. 25.
9. See, for example, Philip Henderson, ed., *Shorter Novels: Seventeenth Century* (*Ornatus and Artesia, Oroonoko, The Isle of Pines, Incognita*), London: J. M. Dent, 1930.
10. Robert C. Elliott, *The Power of Satire: Magic, Ritual, Art*, Princeton, NJ: Princeton University Press, 1960, p. 184. For a detailed discussion of the genre issue in this instance, see Frederick N. Smith, ed., *The Genres of Gulliver's Travels*, London: Associated Universities Press, 1990.
11. Samuel Richardson, *Pamela; or, Virtue Rewarded* (1740), ed. Peter Sabor, Harmondsworth: Penguin Books, 1980; Laurence Sterne, *The Life and Opinions*

of Tristram Shandy, Gentleman (1759–67), ed. Ian Campbell Ross, Oxford: Oxford University Press, 1983; Ann Radcliffe, *The Mysteries of Udolpho: A Romance* (1794), ed. Bonamy Dobrée, Oxford: Oxford University Press, 1980; Sir Walter Scott, *Waverley; or, 'Tis Sixty Years Since* (1814), ed. Claire Lamont, Oxford: Oxford University Press, 1986.

12. The most detailed study of the rise of the novel is Michael McKeon, *The Origins of the English Novel 1600–1740*, 2nd edition, Baltimore, MD and London: Johns Hopkins University Press, 2002. Leonard J. Davies's *Factual Fictions: The Origins of the English Novel*, New York: Columbia University Press, 1983, is also very useful; while Ian Watt's *The Rise of the Novel*, London: Chatto and Windus, 1957, is still worth consulting even a half-century after its first publication.

13. John J. Richetti, *Defoe's Narratives: Situations and Structures*, Oxford: Clarendon Press, 1975, p. 22.

14. See Louis Althusser, *Lenin and Philosophy and Other Essays*, trans. Ben Brewster, London: NLB, 1971.

15. Such as Dale Spender's highly influential *Mothers of the Novel: One Hundred Good Women Writers before Jane Austen*, London: Pandora, 1986. Another classic text in this line is Ellen Moers's *Literary Women*, London: The Women's Press, 1978, which surveys women authors from the eighteenth through into the twentieth century. The chapter on 'Female Gothic' has contributed significantly to a revival of interest in this area of writing.

1   *Oroonoko, or, The History of the Royal Slave* and Race Relations

1. Quoted in Javeen Vasagar, 'Jade Evicted as Poll Reveals Public Anger with Channel 4', *The Guardian*, 20 January 2007, pp. 1–2.

2. Ibid., p. 2.

3. Steve Spencer, quoted in ibid., p. 2.

4. Aphra Behn, *Oroonoko and Other Writings*, ed. Paul Salzman, Oxford: Oxford University Press, 1994, p. 6.

5. Laura Brown, 'The Romance of Empire: *Oroonoko* and the Trade in Slaves', in Janet Todd, ed., *New Casebooks: Aphra Behn*, Basingstoke and London: Macmillan, 1999, pp. 180–208 (p. 181). Other critics are less convinced by the novel's anti-slavery credentials. Charlotte Sussman, for example, considers *Oroonoko* to be 'little concerned with the realities of slavery' ('The Other Problem with Women: Reproduction and Slave Culture in Aphra Behn's *Oroonoko*', in Heidi Hutner, ed., *Rereading Aphra Behn: History, Theory, and Criticism*, Charlottesville, VA and London: University Press of Virginia, 1993, pp. 212–33 (p. 227)).

6. Elaine Hobby also concedes that, when it comes to *Oroonoko* and its 'presentation of a slave rebellion and white racism', there is a need for feminist critics of Behn like herself 'to rethink our work on white women's writing to take account of these concerns' (Elaine Hobby, *Virtue of Necessity; English Women's Writings 1649–88*, London: Virago, 1988, p. 96). She proceeds to steer clear of the text for the rest of her analysis of Behn's fiction.

7. *Oronooko*, p. 11.
8. Ibid.
9. Ibid.
10. Brown, 'The Romance of Empire', p. 187.
11. *Oroonoko*, p. 12.
12. Ibid.
13. Ibid.
14. Ibid., p. 25.
15. Ibid., p. 14.
16. Ibid., p. 35.
17. Ibid., p. 40.
18. Ibid.
19. Ibid., p. 44.
20. Ibid., p. 9. Although at a later point the narrator speaks about being rowed between settlements by 'Indian slaves' (ibid., p. 56), suggesting a growing confidence in their power over this area by the European settlers.
21. Ibid., p. 58.
22. Ibid.
23. Ibid., p. 62.
24. Ibid., pp. 65–6.
25. S. J. Wiseman, *Aphra Behn*, Plymouth: Northcote House, 1996, p. 93.
26. Ros Ballaster, *Seductive Forms: Women's Amatory Fiction from 1684 to 1740*, Oxford: Clarendon Press, 1992, p. 82.
27. *Oroonoko*, p. 73.
28. Jane Spencer, *The Rise of the Woman Novelist: From Aphra Behn to Jane Austen*, Oxford: Basil Blackwell, 1986, p. 50.
29. *Oroonoko*, p. 73.
30. Wiseman, *Aphra Behn*, p. 100.
31. See, for example, the views expressed in Naomi Klein's *No Logo*, London: HarperCollins, 2001, which catalogues in extensive detail the scandalously unequal relationship that currently exists between the multinationals and the governments of impoverished Third World countries.
32. *Oroonoko*, p. 40.
33. Ballaster, *Seductive Forms*, p. 81.
34. Jacqueline Pearson, 'Gender and Narrative in the Fiction of Aphra Behn', in Todd, ed., *Aphra Behn*, pp. 111–42 (p. 135).
35. Ibid., p. 138.
36. Ibid., pp. 138–9.
37. The prominent psychologist Hans Eysenck was a particularly influential, as well as controversial, voice on this topic, arguing that IQ was linked to race. See, for example, his *Race, Intelligence and Education*, London: Temple Smith, 1971.
38. Georges Freche, quoted in Peter Beaumont, 'Top Socialist Sacked for Saying French Team is "Too Black"', *The Observer*, 28 January 2007, p. 32.
39. Brown, 'The Romance of Empire', p. 195.

2   *The Life and Strange Surprizing Adventures of Robinson Crusoe*,
     Born-Again Theology and Intelligent Design

1. For an analysis of this phenomenon and its historical background, see George M.
   Marsden, *Fundamentalism and American Culture. The Shaping of Twentieth-
   Century Evangelism: 1870–1925*, New York and Oxford: Oxford University
   Press, 1980, and *Reforming Fundamentalism: Fuller Seminary and the New
   Evangelicalism*, Grand Rapids, MI: William B. Eerdmans, 1987.
2. As reported in a 2004 Gallup Poll.
3. John Bunyan, *Grace Abounding to the Chief of Sinners* (1666), ed. W. R. Owens,
   Harmondsworth: Penguin Books, 1987, p. 59.
4. The extent to which this is so in Bunyan, and a significant part of his appeal to his
   readers over the centuries, is discussed in my 'Bunyan and His Fundamentalist
   Readers', in W. R. Owens and Stuart Sim, eds, *Reception, Appropriation,
   Recollection: Bunyan's* Pilgrim's Progress, Bern and Oxford: Peter Lang, 2007,
   pp. 213–28.
5. Martin Amis, 'The Palace of the End', *The Guardian*, 4 March 2003, p. 23.
6. There are two main strands of creationism: 'Young Earth' and 'Old Earth'. The
   former claims that the universe is somewhere between 6,000 and 8,000 years old,
   the latter that it is several billion, as most of the scientific community believes. In
   both cases, however, the argument is that the creation took six days, as Genesis
   asserts.
7. For a characteristic example of intelligent design, see Fazale Rana and Hugh Ross,
   Origins of Life: Biblical and Evolutionary Models Face Off, Colorado Springs, CO:
   NavPress, 2004. The authors espouse an Old Earth Creationist position.
8. G. A. Starr, *Defoe and Spiritual Autobiography*, Princeton, NJ: Princeton
   University Press, 1965, p. 15. See also J. Paul Hunter, *The Reluctant Pilgrim:
   Defoe's Emblematic Method and Quest for Form in* Robinson Crusoe, Baltimore,
   MD: Johns Hopkins University Press, 1966.
9. The links back to Bunyan's Giant Despair in *The Pilgrim's Progress* (1678), a fic-
   tionalised spiritual autobiography drawing in its turn on the author's own experiences in *Grace Abounding*, are all too obvious.
10. Daniel Defoe, *The Life and Strange Surprizing Adventures of Robinson Crusoe*,
    ed. Thomas Keymer, Oxford: Oxford University Press, 2007, pp. 82–3.
11. Ibid., p. 83.
12. Ibid.
13. John Allen Stevenson, *The British Novel, Defoe to Austen: A Critical History*,
    Boston, MA: Twayne, 1990, p. 12.
14. *Crusoe*, p. 97.
15. Ibid., p. 130.
16. Ibid., p. 132.
17. Ibid., p. 133.
18. Ibid.
19. Ibid.
20. Ibid., p. 182.
21. Ibid., p. 184.
22. Ibid.

23. Ibid., pp. 185–6.

24. Ibid., pp. 185, 186.

25. Ibid., p. 203.

26. Ibid.

27. David Trotter, *Circulation: Defoe, Dickens, and the Economies of the Novel*, Basingstoke and London: Macmillan, 1988, p. 37.

28. *Crusoe*, pp. 14–15.

29. Daniel Defoe, *The Farther Adventures of Robinson Crusoe* (1719), Oxford: Shakespeare Head Press, 1927.

30. For more on the contradictions and complexities of Crusoe's belief system, see my *Negotiations with Paradox: Narrative Practice and Narrative Form in Bunyan and Defoe*, Hemel Hempstead: Harvester Wheatsheaf, 1990.

31. Maximilian E. Novak, *Economics and the Fiction of Daniel Defoe*, Berkeley, CA: University of California Press, 1962, p. 48; John Bunyan, *The Pilgrim's Progress* (1678), ed. J. B. Wharey, revd. Roger Sharrock, Oxford: Clarendon Press, 1928, 1960.

32. Bishop Simon Patrick, *Fifteen Sermons upon Contentment and Resignation to the Will of God*, London, 1719, Sermon X, p. 247.

33. Ian A. Bell, *Defoe's Fictions*, London: Croom Helm, 1985, p. 108.

34. Ibid., p. 98.

35. John Milton, *Paradise Lost* (1667), ed. Alastair Fowler, London and New York: Longman, 1971.

36. For one such prominent scientific convert to intelligent design, see Michael J. Behe, *Darwin's Black Box: The Biochemical Challenge to Evolution*, New York: Simon & Schuster, 1996.

37. See Karl Marx, *Capital* (1867), vol. I, trans. Eden and Cedar Paul, London: J. M. Dent, 1930, revd. 1972, pp. 50–2.

3   *Gulliver's Travels,* **Multiculturalism and Cultural Difference**

1. Pascal Bruckner, 'Enlightenment Fundamentalism or Racism of the Anti-Racists?', http://www.signandsight.com, 24 January 2007.

2. Ibid.

3. Jonathan Swift, *The Correspondence of Jonathan Swift*, ed. Harold Williams, vols I–V, Oxford: Clarendon Press, 1963–5, vol. III, p. 103.

4. Frances D. Louis, *Swift's Anatomy of Misunderstanding: A Study of Swift's Epistemological Imagination in* A Tale of a Tub *and* Gulliver's Travels, London: George Prior, 1981, p. xxv.

5. Jonathan Swift, *Gulliver's Travels*, ed. Claude Rawson, Oxford: Oxford University Press, 2005, p. 276.

6. Ibid., p. 43.

7. Ibid., p. 29.

8. Kathleen Williams, *Jonathan Swift and the Age of Compromise*, Lawrence, KA: University of Kansas Press, 1958, p. 158.

9. *Gulliver's Travels*, p. 43.

10. Ibid.

11. Here I diverge sharply from Williams's reading of Swift's works, that they are designed to show the virtues of 'practical and fruitful compromise' (*Jonathan Swift and the Age of Compromise*, p. vi). Swift to me seems to demonstrate just how unlikely this is to occur.

12. *Gulliver's Travels*, p. 42.

13. Ibid.

14. Ibid., p. 108.

15. Ibid., p. 60.

16. Ibid., p. 47.

17. Ibid., p. 69.

18. Ibid., p. 96.

19. Ibid.

20. Kathleen Williams, 'Gulliver's Voyage to the Houyhnhnms', in Richard Gravil, ed., *Swift, Gulliver's Travels: A Casebook*, London and Basingstoke: Macmillan, 1974, pp. 136–47 (p. 137). Critics are very divided on how to read the Houyhnhnms: for an analysis of the spectrum of opinion on the topic, see James L. Clifford, 'Gulliver's Fourth Voyage: "Hard" and "Soft" Schools of Interpretation', in Larry S. Champion, ed., *Quick Springs of Sense: Studies in the Eighteenth Century*, Athens, GA: University of Georgia Press, 1974, pp. 33–49. For a recent positive interpretation of the Houyhnhnms see Ian Higgins, *Jonathan Swift*, Tavistock: Northcote House, 2004, chapter 4.

21. *Gulliver's Travels*, p. 122.

22. Ibid., p. 123.

23. Ibid., p. 146.

24. Ibid., p. 150.

25. Ibid., p. 179.

26. Ibid., p. 165.

27. Williams, *Jonathan Swift and the Age of Compromise*, 1958, p. 17.

28. *Gulliver's Travels*, p. 163.

29. Ibid., p. 193.

30. Ibid., p. 195.

31. Ibid., p. 190.

32. Ibid., p. 242.

33. Ibid.

34. Ibid., p. 271.

35. Ibid., p. 276.

36. Claude Rawson has suggested that author and narrator are not all that easy to separate from each other in a general sense in the narrative, arguing that Gulliver is not 'sufficiently independent from Swift' to be a true 'novel-character' (C. J. Rawson, *Gulliver and the Gentle Reader: Studies in Swift and Our Time*, London and Boston, MA: Routledge & Kegan Paul, 1973, p. 27).

37. Louis, *Swift's Anatomy*, p. 123.

38. In a notorious case, the Dutch politician Pim Fortuyn, who espoused such views very strongly through the political party he founded ('Pym Fortuyn's List'), arousing considerable controversy in doing so, was assassinated in 2002 by someone opposed to his position.

4 *Pamela; Or, Virtue Rewarded* and Sexual Abstinence

1. A Columbia University survey of 12,000 young Americans aged 12–18 found that 99 per cent of non-pledgers went on to have sex before marriage, and 88 per cent of pledgers ('How Effective Are Abstinence Pledges?', BBC News Magazine, International Version, Tuesday, 29 June 2004; http://news.bbc.co.uk/1/hi/magazine/3846687.stm (accessed 1 May 2007)).

2. See, for example, Ellen Fein and Sherrie Schneider, *The Complete Book of Rules: Everything You Need to Know to Capture the Heart of Mr Right*, New York: HarperCollins, 2000.

3. Zoe Williams, 'Gatekeepers of Sex', *The Guardian*, 24 January 2007, p. 31. For a recent pro-chastity argument, see Kate Taylor, *Not Tonight, Mr Right*, Harmondsworth: Penguin Books, 2007.

4. Williams, 'Gatekeepers of Sex'.

5. Samuel Richardson, *Pamela; or, Virtue Rewarded*, ed. Peter Sabor, Harmondsworth: Penguin Books, 1980, p. 505.

6. This was also recognised by Richardson's contemporaries, with the Danish dramatist Ludvig Holberg raising the spectre of Pamela as a 'crafty Girl, in her Courtship; who understands the Art of bringing a Man to her Lure' (quoted in A. D. McKillop, *Samuel Richardson, Printer and Novelist*, Chapel Hill, NC: University of North Carolina Press, 1936, pp. 101–2).

7. *Pamela*, p. 45.

8. Ibid., p. 43.

9. Ibid., p. 45.

10. Ibid., p. 46.

11. Ibid., p. 52.

12. Ibid., p. 55.

13. See, for example, Mark Kinkead-Weekes, for whom Mister B is a 'clumsy schoolboy impossibly miscast as a rake' (*Samuel Richardson: Dramatic Novelist*, London: Methuen, 1973, p. 20). Kinkead-Weekes is disinclined to see Mister B as a villain, and argues that it is the author's 'failure to give us access to the hero's mind' that has led to such an assessment (ibid., p. 96). Whether this is enough to excuse Mister B's abuse of his power over the heroine is another matter.

14. *Pamela*, p. 95.

15. Ibid., p. 96.

16. Ibid., p. 211.

17. Ibid., p. 213.

18. Kinkead-Weekes, *Samuel Richardson*, p. 47.

19. *Pamela*, pp. 229, 230.

20. Ibid., p. 231.

21. Quoted in Williams, 'Gatekeepers of Sex'.

22. Samuel Richardson, *Clarissa, or, The History of a Young Lady*, ed. Angus Ross, Harmondsworth: Penguin Books, 1985.

23. *Pamela*, p. 242.

24. Ibid.

25. Ibid., p. 232.

26. Margaret A. Doody, *A Natural Passion: A Study of the Novels of Samuel Richardson*, Oxford: Oxford University Press, 1974, p. 49.

27. *Pamela*, p. 392.

28. Ibid., pp. 467, 470. At least one critic is willing to give Mister B the benefit of the doubt, with Roy Roussel claiming that he genuinely 'wants love to act as a unifying element' between himself and his wife, such that there is some kind of equality in their marriage (*The Conversation of the Sexes: Seduction and Equality in Selected Seventeenth- and Eighteenth-Century Texts*, New York: Oxford University Press, 1986, p. 84).

29. *Pamela*, p. 467.

30. Doody, Introduction to *Pamela*, pp. 7–20 (p. 9).

31. Rita Goldberg, *Sex and Enlightenment: Women in Richardson and Diderot*, Cambridge: Cambridge University Press, 1984, p. 25.

32. Patricia Meyer Spacks, *Desire and Truth: Functions of Plot in Eighteenth-Century English Novels*, Chicago and London: University of Chicago Press, 1990, p. 90.

33. *Pamela*, p. 510.

34. Ibid., p. 497.

35. Ibid., p. 505.

36. Ibid., pp. 500, 505.

37. Samuel Richardson, *The History of Sir Charles Grandison*, ed. Jocelyn Harris, Oxford: Oxford University Press, 1972.

38. *Pamela*, p. 505.

39. *Pamela*, vol. II, London: J. M. Dent, 1962, pp. 184–5.

5   *The History of Tom Jones, A Foundling* and Anti-Social Behaviour

1. Lynne Truss, *Talk to the Hand: The Utter Bloody Rudeness of Everyday Life (or Six Good Reasons to Stay Home and Bolt the Door)*, London: Profile Books, 2005, pp. 2–3.

2. Alan Duncan, quoted in 'Britain Becoming Decivilised, Minister Says', *The Guardian*, 16 February 2007, p. 12.

3. The case of Baltimore, estimated to have around 47,000 empty properties in its inner city suburbs, has been one of the most talked about in the US of late, partly through the impact of the cult television series *The Wire*, which has been much praised for its realistic portrayal of the widespread drug culture in the city.

4. 'The Western financial system is rapidly coming to resemble nothing as much as a vast casino' (Susan Strange, *Casino Capitalism*, Oxford: Blackwell, 1986, p. 1).

5. Thomas Hobbes, *Leviathan, or The Matter, Forme, and Power of a Common-wealth Ecclesiasticall and Civill* (1651), ed. Richard Tuck, Cambridge: Cambridge University Press, 1991, p. 89.

6. Claude Rawson, *Henry Fielding and the Augustan Ideal Under Stress: 'Nature's Dance of Death' and Other Studies*, London and Boston, MA: Routledge & Kegan Paul, 1972, p. 21.

7. Henry Fielding, *The History of Tom Jones, A Foundling*, eds John Bender and Simon Stern, Oxford: Oxford University Press, 1996, pp. 870–1.

8. Hobbes, *Leviathan*, p. 89.

9. For an analysis of the influence of Hobbes on intellectuals of the period like Fielding, see Stuart Sim and David Walker, *The Discourse of Sovereignty from Hobbes to Fielding; The State of Nature and the Nature of the State*, Aldershot and Burlington, VT: Ashgate, 2003.

10. *Tom Jones*, p. 154.

11. Ibid., p. 163.

12. Ibid.

13. Ibid., p. 870.

14. Ibid., p. 417.

15. Ibid., p. 500.

16. Ibid., p. 531.

17. Ibid., p. 604.

18. Ibid., pp. 392–3.

19. Ibid., p. 404.

20. Ibid., p. 417.

21. Ibid., p. 420.

22. Against this, Gillian Skinner argues that *Tom Jones* 'has a broad spectrum of understanding hearts'; but I am not convinced this can be applied to society at large in Fielding, nor that it is enough to keep rampant self-interest at bay (Gillian Skinner, *Sensibility and Economics in the Novel, 1740–1800: The Price of a Tear*, Basingstoke and London: Macmillan, 1999, p. 16).

23. *Tom Jones*, p. 420.

24. Ibid., p. 417.

25. Ibid., p. 33.

26. Ibid., p. 280.

27. Ibid., p. 502.

28. Jenny Uglow, *Henry Fielding*, Plymouth: Northcote House, 1995, p. 66.

29. *Tom Jones*, p. 721.

30. Ibid., p. 722.

31. Ibid., p. 728.

32. Ibid., p. 871.

33. Ian A. Bell, *Henry Fielding: Authorship and Authority*, London and New York: Longman, 1994, p. 210.

34. *Tom Jones*, p. 114.

35. Sarah Fielding, *The Adventures of David Simple* (1744, 1753), ed. Malcolm Kelsall, Oxford: Oxford University Press, 1987 (this edition includes *Volume the Last*). I discuss this in *The Discourse of Sovereignty*, chapter 12.

36. Henry Fielding, *The Life of Mr Jonathan Wild the Great* (1743), ed. Hugh Amory, Oxford: Oxford University Press, 2003; Henry Fielding, *Amelia* (1751), ed. Martin C. Battestin, Oxford: Oxford University Press, 1983.

6 *The Female Quixote; or, The Adventures of Arabella* and *Northanger Abbey*: **The Power of the Media and Popular Culture**

1. For an analysis of the rise of the novel as popular culture, see William B. Warner, *Licensing Entertainment: The Elevation of Novel Reading in Britain, 1684–1750*, Berkeley, Los Angeles and London: University of California Press, 1998.

2. It has been argued that the eighteenth-century reading public was considerably more sophisticated than might have been once thought, so that 'these fears were exaggerated', but that does not mean they were perceived so at the time (Moyra Haslett, *Pope to Burney, 1714–1779*, Basingstoke and New York: Palgrave Macmillan, 2003, p. 72).

3. Plato, *The Republic*, trans. Desmond Lee, Harmondsworth: Penguin Books, 2nd edition, 1974, p. 157.

4. Janet Todd, *The Sign of Angellica: Women, Writing and Fiction, 1660–1800*, London: Virago, 1989, p. 152.

5. Although it should be noted that the popularity of such heroic romances was waning by Lennox's day; on this see Amanda Gilroy, Introduction to Charlotte Lennox, *The Female Quixote; or, The Adventures of Arabella*, eds Amanda Gilroy and Wil Verhoeven, London: Penguin Books, 2006, pp. xviii–xix.

6. Ibid., p. 19. Janet Todd suggests that the bad translation makes the books sound even more bombastic than they should, thus affecting Arabella's discourse in turn (see *The Sign of Angellica*, p. 155). It is not just the language which renders Arabella ridiculous, however, but her belief in the events being portrayed.

7. *The Female Quixote*, p. 28.

8. Ibid., pp. 71, 353.

9. Ibid., p. 220.

10. Ibid., pp. 228, 229.

11. Peter Knox-Shaw, *Jane Austen and the Enlightenment*, Cambridge: Cambridge University Press, 2004, p. 198.

12. *The Female Quixote*, p. 405.

13. Ibid., p. 408.

14. Ibid., p. 424.

15. Ibid.

16. Warner, *Licensing Entertainment*, p. 287.

17. Todd, *The Sign of Angellica*, p. 156.

18. *The Female Quixote*, p. 300.

19. Ibid., p. 304.

20. Ibid., p. 316.

21. Gilroy, Introduction to *The Female Quixote*, p. xxv.

22. Jane Austen, *Northanger Abbey and Other Works*, eds James Kinsley and John Davie, Oxford: Oxford University Press, 2003, p. 7.

23. Ann Radcliffe, *The Mysteries of Udolpho, A Romance* (1794), ed. Bonamy Dobrée, Oxford: Oxford University Press, 1980.

24. Knox-Shaw, *Jane Austen and the Enlightenment*, p. 110.

25. *Northanger Abbey*, p. 145. Tony Tanner suggests there is a kind of poetic truth in Catherine's speculations about the general, arguing that he has a deadening effect on the emotional development of those around him: 'there are various ways of denying and destroying life, and in his brutal and repressive way the General does work to block the budding life, not only of Catherine, but also of his children' (Tony Tanner, *Jane Austen*, Basingstoke and London: Macmillan, 1968, p. 68).

26. *Northanger Abbey*, p. 146.

27. Ibid., p. 147.

28. Ibid.
29. Mary Waldron, *Jane Austen and the Fiction of Her Time*, Cambridge: Cambridge University Press, 1999, p. 30.
30. *Northanger Abbey*, p. 152.
31. Ibid., p. 77.
32. Ibid., p. 79.
33. Knox-Shaw, *Jane Austen and the Enlightenment*, p. 127.
34. Sandra Shulman, Introduction to Charlotte Lennox, *The Female Quixote*, London, Henley and Boston, MA: Pandora, 1986, p. xiii.
35. 'In *Northanger Abbey*, her irony is too often in excess of the immediate need' (Marvin Mudrick, *Jane Austen: Irony as Defense and Discovery*, Princeton, NJ: Princeton University Press, 1952, pp. 37–59). Mudrick goes so far as to accuse Austen of occasional 'flippancy' in the treatment of her characters (ibid.).
36. John Wiltshire, *Jane Austen and the Body: 'The Picture of Health'*, Cambridge: Cambridge University Press, 1992, p. 31.
37. *Northanger Abbey*, p. 175.
38. John Cleland, *Memoirs of a Woman of Pleasure* (1748–9), ed. Peter Sabor, Oxford: Oxford University Press, 1985; Matthew Lewis, *The Monk: A Romance* (1796), eds James Kinsley and Howard Anderson, Oxford: Oxford University Press, 1973.
39. Gilroy, Introduction to *The Female Quixote*, p. xii.

7   *The Life and Opinions of Tristram Shandy, Gentleman* and Genetic Inheritance

1. Richard Strohman, 'Toward a New Paradigm for Life: Beyond Genetic Determinism', http://www.psrast.org/strohmnewgen.htm, 22 March 2001.
2. Hans Eysenck, *Race, Intelligence and Education*, London: Temple Smith, 1971, p. 11.
3. See, for example, Strohman, 'Toward a New Paradigm'.
4. James E. Swearingen, *Reflexivity in* Tristram Shandy: *An Essay in Phenomenological Criticism*, New Haven, CT and London: Yale University Press, 1977, p. 78. The point Swearingen is making is that theories such as Locke's *tabula rasa* conception of the self have greater currency at the time.
5. Laurence Sterne, *The Life and Opinions of Tristram Shandy, Gentleman*, ed. Ian Campbell Ross, Oxford: Oxford University Press, 1983, p. 233.
6. Ibid., p. 61.
7. Wolfgang Iser, *Tristram Shandy*, trans. David Henry Wilson, Cambridge: Cambridge University Press, 1988, p. 109.
8. D. W. Jefferson, '*Tristram Shandy* and the Tradition of Learned Wit', in John Traugott, ed., *Laurence Sterne: A Collection of Critical Essays*, Englewood Cliffs, NJ: Prentice-Hall, 1968, pp. 148–67 (p. 165).
9. *Tristram Shandy*, p. 233.
10. Ibid., p. 235.
11. Ibid., p. 10.
12. David Hume, *A Treatise of Human Nature* (1739), ed. D. G. C. Macnabb, Glasgow: William Collins, 1962, p. 302.

13. I take issue here with Melvyn New, for whom *Tristram Shandy* is essentially a satire on sentimentalism (see *Laurence Sterne as Satirist: A Reading of 'Tristram Shandy'*, Gainesville, FL: University of Florida Press, 1969). New's argument is very persuasive, but I think he overestimates the satirical intent of the author, arguing that Sterne is in effect holding his characters up to ridicule much of the time. Granted there is, as he says, 'a hollowness pervading the sentiment of *Tristram Shandy*', but I do not believe this is always meant satirically (ibid., p. 131).

14. I discuss the implications of this combination of forces in the characters' lives in ' "All that Exist are 'Islands of Determinism' " ': Shandean Sentiment and the Dilemma of Postmodern Physics', in David Pierce and Peter de Voogd, eds, *Laurence Sterne in Modernism and Postmodernism*, Amsterdam and Atlanta, GA: Rodopi, 1996, pp. 109–21; and in 'Sterne • Chaos • Complexity', in Susan Spencer, ed., *The Eighteenth-Century Novel, 1*, New York: AMS Press, 2001, pp. 201–15.

15. *Tristram Shandy*, p. 178.

16. Ibid., p. 5.

17. Ibid., p. 6.

18. Manfred Pfister, *Laurence Sterne*, Tavistock: Northcote House, 2001, p. 19.

19. *Tristram Shandy*, pp. 379–80.

20. Gabriel Josipovici, *Writing and the Body*, Brighton: Harvester, 1982, p. 29.

21. John Traugott speaks of Sterne's 'wry development of the philosophy of John Locke' endowing the author with 'a dramatic formula for the endless rhetorical inventions which demonstrate his conception of reality. These opinions of Tristram Shandy bespeak a philosophy' (*Tristram Shandy's World: Sterne's Philosophical Rhetoric*, Berkeley and Los Angeles: University of California Press, 1954, p. 4).

22. *Tristram Shandy*, p. 8.

23. John Locke, *An Essay Concerning Human Understanding* (1690), ed. Peter H. Nidditch, Oxford: Clarendon Press, 1979, p. 395.

24. *Tristram Shandy*, p. 10.

25. Ibid., p. 226.

26. Ibid., p. 47.

27. In chaos theory, the strange attractor is 'the trajectory towards which all other trajectories converge' (James Gleick, *Chaos: Making a New Science*, London: Sphere, 1988, p. 150); in other words, a hidden pattern within natural systems, dictating their outcomes in what to human beings at any rate are mysterious ways.

28. *Tristram Shandy*, p. 9.

29. Ibid., pp. 54–5.

30. Ibid., p. 68.

31. Robert C. Gordon, *Under Which King? A Study of the Scottish Waverley Novels*, Edinburgh and London: Oliver & Boyd, 1969, p. 15.

32. *Tristram Shandy*, p. 301.

33. Josipovici, *Writing the Body*, p. 6.

34. *Tristram Shandy*, p. 175.

35. Ibid.

36. Ibid., p. 174.

37. Ibid., p. 175.

38. Ibid., p. 300.

39. Laurent Milesi, ' "Have You Not Forgot to Wind Up the Clock?" Tristram Shandy and Jacques Le Fataliste on the (Post?)Modern Psychoanalytic Couch', in Pierce and de Voogd, eds, *Laurence Sterne in Modernism and Postmodernism*, pp. 179–95 (p. 179).

40. *Tristram Shandy*, p. 53.

41. Carol Watts, 'The Modernity of Sterne', in Pierce and de Voogd, eds, *Laurence Sterne in Modernism and Postmodernism*, pp. 19–38 (p. 38).

42. David Hume, *Moral and Political Philosophy*, ed. Henry D. Aiken, New York: Hafner, 1972, p. 184.

43. Ibid., p. 214.

44. *Tristram Shandy*, p. 178.

45. James A. Work, ed., Introduction to Laurence Sterne, *The Life and Opinions of Tristram Shandy, Gentleman*, New York: Odyssey, 1940, p. lx.

46. James Hogg, *The Private Memoirs and Confessions of a Justified Sinner* (1824), ed. John Carey, Oxford: Oxford University Press, 1990.

8   *The Mysteries of Udolpho, A Romance* and Family Values

1. R. D. Laing and the anti-psychiatry movement were particularly critical of the effect of the family on the individual psyche. See, for example, R. D. Laing and A. Esterson, *Sanity, Madness and the Family*, Harmondsworth: Penguin Books, 1964.

2. Ann Radcliffe, *The Mysteries of Udolpho, A Romance*, ed. Bonamy Dobrée, Oxford: Oxford University Press, 1980, p. 270.

3. See Ellen Moers, *Literary Women*, London: Women's Press, 1978, chapter 7. For Moers, Radcliffe's particular forte is 'travelling heroinism', whereby her heroines are enabled to experience a wide range of cultures and lifestyles, and thus have exciting adventures (ibid., p. 127).

4. Also see Ellena Rosalba in *The Italian* (1797).

5. Maggie Kilgour, *The Rise of the Gothic Novel*, London and New York: Routledge, 1995, p. 115.

6. For the link between character and landscape in Radcliffe, see Daniel Cottom, *The Civilized Imagination: A Study of Ann Radcliffe, Jane Austen, and Sir Walter Scott*, Cambridge: Cambridge University Press, 1985, chapter 2. Not everyone appreciates the landscape descriptions, however, with Coleridge speaking for many when he complains that 'there is too much of sameness' in them (Samuel Taylor Coleridge, Review in *Critical Review*, 2nd series, 11 (August 1794), pp. 361–72; reprinted in Deborah D. Rogers, ed., *The Critical Response to Ann Radcliffe*, Westport, CT and London: Greenwood Press, 1994, pp. 17–18 (p. 17)).

7. *Udolpho*, p. 139.

8. Ibid., p. 251. Moers, on the other hand, chooses to see the interior of such Gothic castles as 'freely female space' (*Literary Women*, p. 126).

9. *Udolpho*, p. 6.

10. Cottom, T*he Civilized Imagination*, p. 35.

11. *Udolpho*, p. 224.
12. Ibid., p. 358.
13. Ibid., p. 376.
14. Ibid., p. 381.
15. Ibid., p. 264.
16. Kilgour, *The Rise of the Gothic Novel*, p. 118.
17. I am not persuaded by Robert Kiely's view that 'the reader is never for a moment allowed to believe that Emily could be raped' (*The Romantic Novel in England*, Cambridge, MA: Harvard University Press, 1972, p. 73). Radcliffe is too decorous a writer to bring this out into the open, but it seems inconceivable that someone in Emily's position would not have had that fear – or that it would not have come to the audience's mind either.
18. *Udolpho*, p. 383.
19. Matthew Lewis, *The Monk: A Romance* (1796), eds James Kinsley and Howard Anderson, Oxford: Oxford University Press, 1973; Charlotte Dacre, *Zofloya, or, The Moor* (1806), ed. Kim Ian Michasiw, Oxford: Oxford University Press, 1997.
20. There is also the question of how much Emily is drawn to Montoni's sexual allure to be considered. For Kenneth W. Graham, for example, Montoni turns into the heroine's 'smouldering, passionate demon-lover' ('Emily's Demon-Lover: The Gothic Revolution and *The Mysteries of Udolpho*', in Kenneth W. Graham, ed., *Gothic Fictions: Prohibition/Transgression*, New York: AMS Press, 1989, pp. 163–71 (p. 163)).
21. *Udolpho*, p. 494.
22. Ibid., p. 286.
23. Ibid., p. 672.
24. Ibid., p. 329.
25. Kilgour, *The Rise of the Gothic Novel*, p. 115.
26. *Udolpho*, p. 576.
27. Ann Radcliffe, *The Italian, or, The Confessional of the Black Penitents* (1797), ed. Frederick Garber, Oxford: Oxford University Press, 1981, p. 410.
28. Hence the rise of a home schooling movement in the US, where creationism and intelligent design can be taught by parents; thus circumventing what from a fundamentalist perspective are to be considered uncooperative school boards.

9   *Caleb Williams, or, Things As They Are* and the Surveillance Society

1. George Monbiot, 'When it Won't Need a Tyranny to Deprive Us of Our Freedom', *The Guardian*, 21 February 2006, p. 29.
2. William Godwin, *Caleb Williams* (1794), ed. David McCracken, Oxford: Oxford University Press, 1970, Preface, p. 1 (this Preface was withdrawn from the first edition, although restored in the 1795 edition).
3. Gary Kelly, *The English Jacobin Novel 1780–1805*, Oxford: Clarendon Press, 1976, p. 193.
4. William Godwin, *Enquiry Concerning Political Justice* (1793), ed. Isaac Kramnick, Harmondsworth: Penguin Books, 1985, p. 556.
5. See Isaac Kramnick, Introduction to ibid., p. 24.

6. *Caleb Williams*, p. 554.

7. Ibid., p. 313.

8. Identifying a critical trend seeking to separate Godwin's political philosophy from his fictional *oeuvre*, Pamela Clemit reasserts the case for a unity of ideas across the author's work (see *The Godwinian Novel: The Rational Fictions of Godwin, Brockden Brown, Mary Shelley*, Oxford: Clarendon Press, 1993). I follow in that line here, arguing that in both cases a debate is being set up between the values of the old and new political orders.

9. Burton Ralph Pollin, *Education and Enlightenment in the Works of William Godwin*, New York: Las Americas Publishing, 1962, p. 38.

10. *Caleb Williams*, p. 6.

11. Ibid., p. 4.

12. Clemit notes the influence of spiritual autobiography in Caleb's quest, which certainly does lend it an air of self-aggrandizing drama (see *The Godwinian Novel*, p. 55).

13. *Enquiry Concerning Political Justice*, p. 251.

14. David Fleischer, *William Godwin: A Study in Liberalism*, London: George Allen and Unwin, 1951, p. 27.

15. *Enquiry Concerning Political Justice*, p. 70.

16. *Caleb Williams*, p. 96.

17. Ibid., p. 107.

18. Ibid., p. 135.

19. Ibid., p. 136.

20. Ibid., p. 3.

21. Patricia Meyer Spacks, *Desire and Truth: Functions of Plot in Eighteenth-Century English Novels*, Chicago and London: University of Chicago Press, 1990, p. 179.

22. *Caleb Williams*, pp. 153, 154.

23. Ibid., p. 181.

24. Ibid., p. 235.

25. Ibid., p. 281.

26. Jacqueline T. Miller, 'The Imperfect Tale: Articulation, Rhetoric, and Self in *Caleb Williams*', *Criticism*, 20 (1978), pp. 366–82 (p. 368). William D. Brewer has also suggested that Caleb is 'unreliable as an interpreter of his life story' (*The Mental Anatomies of William Godwin and Mary Shelley*, Cranbury, NJ and London: Associated University Presses, 2001, p. 43).

27. *Caleb Williams*, p. 284.

28. Ibid., p. 302.

29. Ibid., p. 313.

30. Ibid., p. 3.

31. George Woodcock, *William Godwin: A Biographical Study*, London: Porcupine Press, 1946, p. 120.

32. *Caleb Williams*, Appendix I, p. 331.

33. Ibid., Appendix I, p. 334. Clemit, on the other hand, finds an 'unconvincing passivity' about the character's conduct in the first ending (*The Godwinian Novel*, p. 64).

34. *Caleb Williams*, p. 324.

35. Ibid.
36. Our contemporary surveillance society claims innocent lives too, as in the case of the Brazilian, Jean Charles de Menezes, mistakenly identified as a terrorist suspect and shot and killed by police in London in 2005: a notorious example of a surveillance operation gone badly wrong.
37. *Enquiry Concerning Political Justice*, p. 247.
38. *Caleb Williams*, p. 325.
39. Ibid., p. 326.
40. Essentially the point made by Slavoj Žižek in *The Sublime Object of Ideology*, when discussing how totalitarian Marxist regimes in Europe managed to survive as long as they did, despite their citizens eventually being well aware of their many ideological failings: 'they [the people] know that, in their activity, they are following an illusion, but still, they are doing it' (London and New York: Verso, 1989, p. 33). It is only when that complicity ceases that real political change can occur, as we saw in the case of the Soviet empire in the 1980s. Godwin's success at capturing that complicity can be gauged by the critical comment that the novel 'has a more moving character in the noble persecutor, Falkland, than in the working class hero' (Pollin, *Education and Enlightenment*, p. 205).
41. David McCracken, Introduction to *Caleb Williams*, p. xxi.

10 *Waverley, or, 'Tis Sixty Years Since* and Disputed Sovereignty

1. All federal systems feature a measure of dual sovereignty. The nature of this is still a source of much debate in American political life, in terms of the relationship between individual states and the national government in Washington. For a discussion of the issues involved, see Kalypso Nicolaidis and Robert Howse, eds, *The Federal Vision: Legitimacy and Levels of Governance in the United States and Europe*, Oxford: Oxford University Press, 2001.
2. Most notably after the death of Elizabeth I and then the Protector, Oliver Cromwell. The accession of the Catholic James II to the throne in 1685 was widely unpopular, and a critical element in the 'Glorious Revolution' of 1688–9, which brought in William of Orange as the new king.
3. See Claire Lamont's Introduction to Sir Walter Scott, *Waverley, or, 'Tis Sixty Years Since*, ed. Claire Lamont, Oxford: Oxford University Press, 1986, for a discussion of Scott's Jacobite sympathies.
4. *Waverley*, p. 6.
5. Henry Fielding, *The History of Tom Jones, A Foundling*, eds John Bender and Simon Stern, Oxford: Oxford University Press, 1996, p. 292.
6. Sir Walter Scott, *Rob Roy* (1817), ed. Ian Duncan, Oxford: Oxford University Press, 1998.
7. Sir Walter Scott, *Redgauntlet: A Tale of the Eighteenth Century* (1824), ed. Kathryn Sutherland, Oxford: Oxford University Press, 1985.
8. Jane Millgate, *Walter Scott: The Making of the Novelist*, Toronto, Buffalo and London: University of Toronto Press, 1984, p. 36.
9. *Waverley*, p. 128.
10. Ibid., p. 219.

11. Robert C. Gordon, *Under Which King? A Study of the Scottish Waverley Novels*, Edinburgh and London: Oliver & Boyd, 1969.

12. John Sutherland, *The Life of Walter Scott: A Critical Biography*, Oxford: Blackwell, 1995, p. 174. A kinder assessment of Waverley's conduct is that, being neither 'hero' nor 'anti-hero', he is not given to grand gestures (Douglas Gifford, Sarah Dunnigan and Alan MacGillivray, eds, *Scottish Literature in English and Scots*, Edinburgh: Edinburgh University Press, 2002, p. 237).

13. *Waverley*, p. 207.

14. Ibid., p. 280.

15. Ibid., p. 196.

16. See John Locke, *Second Treatise of Government*: 'The end of Government is the good of Mankind, and which is *best for Mankind*, that the People should be always expos'd to the boundless will of Tyranny, or that the Rulers should be sometimes liable to be oppos'd, when they grow exorbitant in the use of their Power, and imploy it for the destruction, and not the preservation of the Properties of the People? . . . [I]t is lawful for the people, in some Cases, to *resist* their King' (John Locke, *Two Treatises of Government* (1690), ed. Peter Laslett, 2nd edition, Cambridge: Cambridge University Press, 1970, pp. 417, 419).

17. *Waverley*, p. 340.

18. James Kerr, *Fiction Against History: Scott as Storyteller*, Cambridge: Cambridge University Press, 1989, p. 3.

19. *Waverley*, p. 302.

20. Ibid., p. 336.

21. See chapter 2, 'The Reemplotment of Rebellion: *Waverley* and *Old Mortality*', of James Kerr, *Fiction Against History*. Kerr takes over the notion of 'reemplotment' from the historian Hayden White.

22. Claire Lamont, Introduction *Waverley*, p. xiv.

23. *Waverley*, p. 318.

24. Ibid., pp. 289–90.

25. Ibid., p. 151.

11   *Frankenstein, or, The Modern Prometheus* and Artificial Life

1. Although it is worth noting that in the work's preface the author remarks that '[t]he event on which this fiction is founded, has been supposed, by Dr Darwin, and some of the physiological writers of Germany, as not of impossible occurrence' (Mary Shelley, *Frankenstein, or, The Modern Prometheus*, in *Four Gothic Novels*, Oxford: Oxford University Press, 1994, p. 459).

2. Jean-François Lyotard, *The Inhuman: Reflections on Time*, trans. Geoffrey Bennington and Rachel Bowlby, Oxford: Basil Blackwell, 1991, p. 2.

3. See my *Lyotard and the Inhuman*, Cambridge: Icon Press, 2001, for more discussion of this issue. Haraway's major work on the topic is *Simians, Cyborgs, and Women: The Reinvention of Nature*, New York: Routledge, 1991.

4. Forest Pyle, 'Making Cyborgs, Making Humans: Of Terminators, and Blade Runners', in Jim Collins, Hilary Radner and Ava Preacher Collins, eds, *Film Theory Goes to the Movies*, New York and London: Routledge, 1993, pp. 227–41 (p. 231).

5. As an example, there was the infamous 'love bug' virus in 2000, which created chaos to the extent of closing down 10 per cent of the world's email servers within just a few hours. A spokesperson for the computer industry described it as 'one of the most aggressive and nastiest I've ever seen' (see 'Love Bug Creates Worldwide Chaos', *The Guardian*, 5 May 2000, p. 1).

6. Christopher G. Langton, 'Artificial Life', in Christopher G. Langton, ed., *Artificial Life*, Redwood City, CA: Addison-Wesley, 1989, pp. 1–47 (p. 33).

7. Mark Ward, *Virtual Organisms: The Startling World of Artificial Life*, London: Macmillan, 1999, p. 280.

8. Chris Baldick, *In Frankenstein's Shadow: Myth, Monstrosity, and Nineteenth-Century Writing*, Oxford: Clarendon Press, 1987, pp. 1, 9.

9. *Frankenstein*, p. 488.

10. Ibid., pp. 605–6.

11. Ibid., p. 486.

12. Ibid., p. 476.

13. Frederick R. Karl, *A Reader's Guide to the Development of the English Novel in the Eighteenth Century*, London: Thames & Hudson, 1975, p. 267; William Veeder, *Mary Shelley and Frankenstein: The Fate of Androgyny*, Chicago and London: University of Chicago Press, 1986, p. 204.

14. *Frankenstein*, p. 487.

15. Ibid., p. 485.

16. Ibid., p. 488.

17. Ibid., p. 491.

18. Gary Kelly, *English Fiction of the Romantic Period 1789–1830*, London and New York: Longman, 1989, p. 188.

19. *Frankenstein*, p. 544.

20. Ibid., p. 539.

21. Ibid., p. 551.

22. Ibid., p. 586.

23. Ibid., p. 550.

24. Ibid., p. 565.

25. Chris Baldick, *In Frankenstein's Shadow*, p. 8.

26. Celeste Biever, 'If You're Happy the Robot Knows It', *New Scientist*, 24 March 2007, pp. 30–1 (p. 31).

27. *Frankenstein*, p. 539.

28. Ibid., p. 605.

29. Ibid., p. 520.

30. Ibid., p. 553.

31. Timothy Morton, ed., *A Routledge Literary Sourcebook on Mary Shelley's Frankenstein*, London and New York: Routledge, 2002, p. 46.

32. Germaine Greer, 'Yes, Frankenstein Really Was Written by Mary Shelley. It's Obvious – Because the Book is So Bad', *The Guardian*, G2 Section, 9 April 2007, p. 28. The title of the article refers to a claim made by an American academic, John Lauritsen, that *Frankenstein* was really the work of Mary's husband, Percy Bysshe Shelley (see *The Man Who Wrote Frankenstein: Percy Bysshe Shelley*, Provincetown, MA: Pagan Press, 2007). Greer is dismissive of *Frankenstein*, arguing that it 'hardly

merits the attention it has been given' ('Yes, Frankenstein'). Most feminist critics, on the other hand, regard it as a landmark work in the history of women's literature, with Ellen Moers, for example, seeing its importance lying in its being a particularly powerful 'birth myth' (*Literary Women*, London: The Women's Press, 1978, p. 92).

33. *Frankenstein*, pp. 539–40.
34. Ibid., p. 601.
35. Ibid., p. 602.
36. Sir David King, 'An Ethical Code Will Secure Public Support for Science', *The Guardian*, Education Section, 20 March 2007, p. 12.
37. Ibid.

12 The Private Memoirs and Confessions of a Justified Sinner and Fundamentalist Terrorism

1. I discuss fundamentalism as a general cultural phenomenon of recent times in my *Fundamentalist World: The New Dark Age of Dogma*, Cambridge: Icon Press, 2004. For a study of the historical development of religious fundamentalism, see Malise Ruthven, *Fundamentalism: The Search for Meaning*, Oxford: Oxford University Press, 2004.
2. Curtis Lee Laws, quoted in George M. Marsden, *Fundamentalism and American Culture: The Shaping of Twentieth-Century Evangelism, 1870–1925*, New York and Oxford: Oxford University Press, 1980, p. 159.
3. James Hogg, *The Private Memoirs and Confessions of a Justified Sinner*, ed. John Carey, Oxford: Oxford University Press, 1990, p. 93.
4. Douglas Gifford, Sarah Dunnigan and Alan MacGillivray, eds, *Scottish Literature: In English and Scots*, Edinburgh: Edinburgh University Press, 2002, p. 307. For an interesting reworking of the story in terms of contemporary Scottish culture, see James Robertson, *The Testament of Gideon Mack*, London: Hamish Hamilton, 2006.
5. *Confessions*, p. 122.
6. Ibid., p. 240.
7. Ibid., p. 221.
8. David Groves, *James Hogg: The Growth of a Writer*, Edinburgh: Scottish Academic Press, 1988, p. 121.
9. *Confessions*, p. 2.
10. Ibid., p. 115.
11. Douglas Gifford, *James Hogg*, Edinburgh: Ramsay Head Press, 1976, p. 157.
12. *Confessions*, pp. 116–17.
13. Kurt Wittig, *The Scottish Tradition in Literature*, Westport, CT: Greenwood Press, 1958, p. 249. In Douglas Gifford's reading, Robert 'creates' Gil-Martin 'to offer him relief from repression of the desires which his faith sees as evil' (*James Hogg*, p. 158).
14. *Confessions*, p. 128.
15. Ibid., p. 157.
16. Ibid., p. 35.
17. Robert Kiely, *The Romantic Novel in England*, Cambridge, MA: Harvard University Press, 1972, p. 224.

18. *Confessions*, p. 97.
19. Ibid..
20. Ibid., p. 100.
21. Ibid., p. 117.
22. Ibid., p. 123.
23. Ibid., p. 127.
24. The existence of Ranterism as any kind of organised movement tends to be disputed by historians nowadays, but clearly such ideas were in circulation at the time and had enough impact to be thought of as dangerous by the authorities (see J. C. Davis, *Fear, Myth and History*, Cambridge: Cambridge University Press, 1986).
25. Thomas Crawford, 'James Hogg: The Play of Region and Nation', in Douglas Gifford, ed., *The History of Scottish Literature. Volume 3: The Nineteenth Century*, Aberdeen: Aberdeen University Press, 1988, pp. 89–106 (p. 101).
26. *Confessions*, p. 15.
27. Ibid., p. 137.
28. Ibid., p. 143.
29. Ibid., p. 148.
30. Ibid., p. 150.
31. Ibid., p. 154.
32. Ibid., p. 182.
33. Ibid., p. 191.
34. Gifford, Dunnigan and MacGillivray, *Scottish Literature: In English and Scots*, p. 303.
35. *Confessions*, p. 240.
36. A point noted by Barbara Bloedé, in '*The Confessions of a Justified Sinner*: The Paranoiac Nucleus', in Gillian Hughes, ed., *Papers Given at the First Conference of the James Hogg Society*, Stirling: James Hogg Society, 1983, pp. 15–28. In Bloedé's reading, Robert has a residual anxiety about the conversion experience that he 'projects . . . onto his Double' (p. 19). For a famous example of the conversion experience, see John Bunyan's spiritual autobiography, *Grace Abounding to the Chief of Sinners* (1666), ed. Roger Sharrock, Oxford: Clarendon Press, 1962.
37. *Confessions*, p. 128.
38. Bloedé, 'The Paranoiac Nucleus', p. 21.
39. *Confessions*, p. 147.
40. John Carey, Introduction to ibid., p. xviii. Douglas Gifford, on the other hand, argues for a humanist dimension to Hogg's outlook (see *James Hogg*, pp. 180–1).
41. Carey, Introduction, *Confessions*, p. xvii.
42. I discuss the critical role of doubt in countering uncritical belief in my *Empires of Belief: Why We Need More Scepticism and Doubt in the Twenty-First Century*, Edinburgh: Edinburgh University Press, 2006.
43. The row over gay priests, for example, is being fought largely on fundamentalist grounds by the opposition ('against the Bible', etc.). It has even been suggested that the leader of the Anglican Church, the Archbishop of Canterbury Dr Rowan Williams, is 'a virtual prisoner of the religious right' over such issues (Giles Fraser and William Whyte, 'Don't Hand Religion to the Right', *The Guardian*, 18 March 2005, p. 26).

Bibliography

Althusser, Louis, *Lenin and Philosophy and Other Essays*, trans. Ben Brewster, London: NLB, 1971.

Amis, Martin, 'The Palace of the End', *The Guardian*, 4 March 2003, p. 23.

Austen, Jane, *Northanger Abbey and Other Works*, eds James Kinsley and John Davie, Oxford: Oxford University Press, 2003.

Baldick, Chris, *In Frankenstein's Shadow: Myth, Monstrosity, and Nineteenth-Century Writing*, Oxford: Clarendon Press, 1987.

Ballaster, Ros, *Seductive Forms: Women's Amatory Fiction from 1684 to 1740*, Oxford: Clarendon Press, 1992.

Beaumont, Peter, 'Top Socialist Sacked for Saying French Team is "Too Black"', *The Observer*, 28 January 2007, p. 32.

Behe, Michael J., *Darwin's Black Box: The Biochemical Challenge to Evolution*, New York: Simon & Schuster, 1996.

Behn, Aphra, *Oroonoko and Other Writings*, ed. Paul Salzman, Oxford: Oxford University Press, 1994.

Bell, Ian A., *Defoe's Fictions*, London: Croom Helm, 1985.

—, *Henry Fielding: Authorship and Authority*, London and New York: Longman, 1994.

Biever, Celeste, 'If You're Happy the Robot Knows It', *New Scientist*, 24 March 2007, pp. 30–1.

'Britain Becoming Decivilised, Minister Says', *The Guardian*, 16 February 2007, p. 12.

Bloedé, Barbara, '*The Confessions of a Justified Sinner*: The Paranoiac Nucleus', in Gillian Hughes, ed., *Papers Given at the First Conference of the James Hogg Society*, Stirling: James Hogg Society, 1983.

Brewer, William D., *The Mental Anatomies of William Godwin and Mary Shelley*, Cranbury, NJ and London: Associated University Presses, 2001.

Brown, Laura, 'The Romance of Empire: *Oroonoko* and the Trade in Slaves', in Janet Todd, ed., *New Casebooks: Aphra Behn*, Basingstoke and London: Macmillan, 1999, pp. 180–208.

Bruckner, Pascal, 'Enlightenment Fundamentalism or Racism of the Anti-Racists?', http://www.signandsight.com, 24 January 2007.

Bunyan, John, *Grace Abounding to the Chief of Sinners* (1666), ed. W. R. Owens, Harmondsworth: Penguin Books, 1987.

—, *The Pilgrim's Progress* (1678), ed. J. B. Wharey, Rev. Roger Sharrock, Oxford: Clarendon Press, 1928, 1960.

Champion, Larry S., ed., *Quick Springs of Sense: Studies in the Eighteenth Century*, Athens, GA: University of Georgia Press, 1974.

Cleland, John, *Memoirs of a Woman of Pleasure* (1748–9), ed. Peter Sabor, Oxford: Oxford University Press, 1985.

Clemit, Pamela, *The Godwinian Novel: The Rational Fictions of Godwin, Brockden Brown, Mary Shelley*, Oxford: Clarendon Press, 1993.

Clifford, James L., 'Gulliver's Fourth Voyage: "Hard" and "Soft" Schools of Interpretation', in Larry S. Champion, ed., *Quick Springs of Sense: Studies in the Eighteenth Century*, Athens, GA: University of Georgia Press, 1974, pp. 33–49.

Coleridge, Samuel Taylor, Review in *Critical Review*, 2nd series, August 1794, pp. 361–72, in Deborah D. Rogers, ed., *The Critical Response to Ann Radcliffe*, Westport, CT and London: Greenwood Press, 1994, pp. 17–18.

Collins, Jim, Radner, Hilary and Collins, Ava Preacher, eds, *Film Theory Goes to the Movies*, New York and London: Routledge, 1993.

Cottom, Daniel, *The Civilized Imagination: A Study of Ann Radcliffe, Jane Austen, and Sir Walter Scott*, Cambridge: Cambridge University Press, 1985.

Crawford, Thomas, 'James Hogg: The Play of Region and Nation', in Douglas Gifford, ed., *The History of Scottish Literature. Volume 3: The Nineteenth Century*, Aberdeen: Aberdeen University Press, 1988, pp. 89–106.

Dacre, Charlotte, *Zofloya, or, The Moor* (1806), ed. Kim Ian Michasiw, Oxford: Oxford University Press, 1997.

Davies, Leonard J., *Factual Fictions: The Origins of the English Novel*, New York: Columbia University Press, 1983.

Davis, J. C., *Fear, Myth and History*, Cambridge: Cambridge University Press, 1986.

Defoe, Daniel, *The Life and Strange Surprizing Adventures of Robinson Crusoe* (1719), ed. Thomas Keymer, Oxford: Oxford University Press, 2007.

—, *The Farther Adventures of Robinson Crusoe* (1719), Oxford: Shakespeare Head Press, 1927.

Doody, Margaret A., *A Natural Passion: A Study of the Novels of Samuel Richardson*, Oxford: Oxford University Press, 1974.

Elliott, Robert C., *The Power of Satire: Magic, Ritual, Art*, Princeton, NJ: Princeton University Press, 1960.

Eysenck, Hans, *Race, Intelligence and Education*, London: Temple Smith, 1971.

Fein, Ellen and Schneider, Sherrie, *The Complete Book of Rules: Everything You Need to Know to Capture the Heart of Mr Right*, New York: HarperCollins, 2000.

Fielding, Henry, *The Life of Mr Jonathan Wild the Great* (1743), ed. Hugh Amory, Oxford: Oxford University Press, 2003.

—, *The History of Tom Jones, A Foundling* (1749), eds John Bender and Simon Stern, Oxford: Oxford University Press, 1996.

—, *Amelia* (1751), ed. Martin C. Battestin, Oxford: Oxford University Press, 1983.

Fielding, Sarah, *The Adventures of David Simple* (1744, 1753), ed. Malcolm Kelsall, Oxford: Oxford University Press, 1987.

Fleischer, David, *William Godwin: A Study in Liberalism*, London: George Allen and Unwin, 1951.

Forster, E. M., *Aspects of the Novel* (1927), ed. Oliver Stallybrass, Harmondsworth: Penguin Books, 1976.

Four Gothic Novels, Oxford: Oxford University Press, 1994.

Fraser, Giles and Whyte, William, 'Don't Hand Religion to the Right', *The Guardian*, 18 March 2005, p. 26.

Gifford, Douglas, *James Hogg*, Edinburgh: Ramsay Head Press, 1976.

—, ed., *The History of Scottish Literature. Volume 3: The Nineteenth Century*, Aberdeen: Aberdeen University Press, 1988.

—, Dunnigan, Sarah and MacGillivray, Alan, eds, *Scottish Literature: In English and Scots*, Edinburgh: Edinburgh University Press, 2002.

Gleick, James, *Chaos: Making a New Science*, London: Sphere, 1988.

Godwin, William, *Enquiry Concerning Political Justice* (1793), ed. Isaac Kramnick, Harmondsworth: Penguin Books, 1985.

—, *Caleb Williams, or, Things As They Are* (1794), ed. David McCracken, Oxford: Oxford University Press, 1970.

Goldberg, Rita, *Sex and Enlightenment: Women in Richardson and Diderot*, Cambridge: Cambridge University Press, 1984.

Gordon, Robert C., *Under Which King? A Study of the Scottish Waverley Novels*, Edinburgh and London: Oliver & Boyd, 1969.

Graham, Kenneth W., ed., *Gothic Fictions: Prohibition / Transgression*, New York: AMS Press, 1989.

—, 'Emily's Demon-Lover: The Gothic Revolution and *The Mysteries of Udolpho*', in Kenneth W. Graham, ed., *Gothic Fictions: Prohibition / Transgression*, New York: AMS Press, 1989, pp. 163–71.

Gravil, Richard, ed., *Swift*, Gulliver's Travels: *A Casebook*, London and Basingstoke: Macmillan, 1974.

Greer, Germaine, 'Yes, Frankenstein Really Was Written by Mary Shelley. It's Obvious – Because the Book is So Bad', *The Guardian*, G2 Section, 9 April 2007, p. 28.

Groves, David, *James Hogg: The Growth of a Writer*, Edinburgh: Scottish Academic Press, 1988.

Haraway, Donna, *Simians, Cyborgs, and Women: The Reinvention of Nature*, New York: Routledge, 1991.

Haslett, Moyra, *Pope to Burney, 1714–1779*, Basingstoke and New York: Palgrave Macmillan, 2nd edition, 1974.

Henderson, Philip, ed., *Shorter Novels: Seventeenth Century (Ornatus and Artesia, Oroonoko, The Isle of Pines, Incognita)*, London: J. M. Dent, 1930.

Higgins, Ian, *Jonathan Swift*, Tavistock: Northcote House, 2004.

Hobbes, Thomas, *Leviathan, or The Matter, Forme, and Power of a Common-wealth Ecclesiasticall and Civill* (1651), ed. Richard Tuck, Cambridge: Cambridge University Press, 1991.

Hobby, Elaine, *Virtue of Necessity: English Women's Writings 1649–88*, London: Virago, 1988.

Hogg, James, *The Private Memoirs and Confessions of a Justified Sinner* (1824), ed. John Carey, Oxford: Oxford University Press, 1990.

'How Effective Are Abstinence Pledges?', BBC News Magazine, International Version, 29 June 2004; http://news.bbc.co.uk/1/hi/magazine/3846687.stm (accessed 1 May 2007).

Hughes, Gillian, ed., *Papers Given at the First Conference of the James Hogg Society*, Stirling: James Hogg Society, 1983.

Hume, David, *A Treatise of Human Nature* (1739), ed. D. G. C. Macnabb, Glasgow: William Collins, 1962.

—, *Moral and Political Philosophy*, ed. Henry D. Aiken, New York: Hafner, 1972.

Hunter, J. Paul, *The Reluctant Pilgrim: Defoe's Emblematic Method and Quest for Form in Robinson Crusoe*, Baltimore, MD: Johns Hopkins University Press, 1966.

Hutner, Heidi, ed., *Rereading Aphra Behn: History, Theory, and Criticism*, Charlottesville, VA and London: University Press of Virginia, 1993.

Iser, Wolfgang, *Tristram Shandy*, trans. David Henry Wilson, Cambridge: Cambridge University Press, 1988.

Jefferson, D. W., '*Tristram Shandy* and the Tradition of Learned Wit', in John Traugott, ed., *Laurence Sterne: A Collection of Critical Essays*, Englewood Cliffs, NJ: Prentice-Hall, 1968, pp. 148–67.

Josipovici, Gabriel, *Writing and the Body*, Brighton: Harvester, 1982.

Karl, Frederick R., *A Reader's Guide to the Development of the English Novel in the Eighteenth Century*, London: Thames & Hudson, 1975.

Kelly, Gary, *The English Jacobin Novel 1780–1805*, Oxford: Clarendon Press, 1976.

—, *English Fiction of the Romantic Period 1789–1830*, London and New York: Longman, 1989.

Kerr, James, *Fiction Against History: Scott as Storyteller*, Cambridge: Cambridge University Press, 1989.

Kiely, Robert, *The Romantic Novel in England*, Cambridge, MA: Harvard University Press, 1972.

Kilgour, Maggie, *The Rise of the Gothic Novel*, London and New York: Routledge, 1995.

King, Sir David, 'An Ethical Code Will Secure Public Support for Science', *The Guardian*, Education Section, 20 March 2007, p. 12.

Kinkead-Weekes, Mark, *Samuel Richardson: Dramatic Novelist*, London: Methuen, 1973.

Klein, Naomi, *No Logo*, London: HarperCollins, 2001.

Knox-Shaw, Peter, *Jane Austen and the Enlightenment*, Cambridge: Cambridge University Press, 2004.

Laing, R. D., and Esterson, A., *Sanity, Madness and the Family*, Harmondsworth: Penguin Books, 1964.

Langton, Christopher G., ed., *Artificial Life*, Redwood City, CA: Addison-Wesley, 1989.

—, 'Artificial Life', in Christopher G. Langton, ed., *Artificial Life*, Redwood City, CA: Addison-Wesley, 1989, pp. 1–47.

Lauritsen, John, *The Man Who Wrote Frankenstein: Percy Bysshe Shelley*, Provincetown, MA: Pagan Press, 2007.

Lennox, Charlotte, *The Female Quixote; or, The Adventures of Arabella* (1752), London, Henley and Boston, MA: Pandora, 1986.

—, *The Female Quixote; or, The Adventures of Arabella* (1752), eds Amanda Gilroy and Will Verhoeven, London: Penguin Books, 2006.

Lewis, Matthew, *The Monk: A Romance* (1796), eds James Kinsley and Howard Anderson, Oxford: Oxford University Press, 1973.

Locke, John, *An Essay Concerning Human Understanding* (1690), ed. Peter H. Nidditch, Oxford: Clarendon Press, 1979.

—, *Two Treatises of Government* (1690), ed. Peter Laslett, 2nd edn, Cambridge: Cambridge University Press, 1970.

Louis, Frances D., *Swift's Anatomy of Misunderstanding: A Study of Swift's Epistemological Imagination in* A Tale of a Tub *and* Gulliver's Travels, London: George Prior, 1981.

'Love Bug Creates Worldwide Chaos', *The Guardian*, 5 May 2001, p. 1.

Lukács, Georg, *The Historical Novel*, trans. Hannah and Stanley Mitchell, London: Merlin Press, 1962.

Lyotard, Jean-François, *The Inhuman: Reflections on Time*, trans. Geoffrey Bennington and Rachel Bowlby, Oxford: Basil Blackwell, 1991.

McKeon, Michael, *The Origins of the English Novel*, 2nd edition, Baltimore, MD and London: Johns Hopkins University Press, 2002.

McKillop, A. D., *Samuel Richardson, Printer and Novelist*, Chapel Hill, NC: University of North Carolina Press, 1936.

Marsden, George M., *Fundamentalism and American Culture. The Shaping of Twentieth-Century Evangelism: 1870–1925*, New York and Oxford: Oxford University Press, 1980.

—, *Reforming Fundamentalism: Fuller Seminary and the New Evangelicalism*, Grand Rapids, MI: William B. Eerdmans, 1987.

Marx, Karl, *Capital* (1867), vol. I, trans. Eden and Cedar Paul, London: J. M. Dent, 1930, rev. 1972.

Milesi, Laurent, '"Have You Not Forgot to Wind Up the Clock?": Tristram Shandy and Jacques Le Fataliste on the (Post?)Modern Psychoanalytic Couch', in David Pierce and Peter de Voogd, eds, *Laurence Sterne in Modernism and Postmodernism*, Amsterdam and Atlanta, GA: Rodopi, 1996.

Miller, Jacqueline T., 'The Imperfect Tale: Articulation, Rhetoric, and Self in *Caleb Williams*', *Criticism*, 20 (1978), pp. 366–82.

Millgate, Jane, *Walter Scott: The Making of the Novelist*, Toronto, Buffalo and London: University of Toronto Press, 1984.

Milton, John, *Paradise Lost* (1667), ed. Alastair Fowler, London and New York: Longman, 1971.

Moers, Ellen, *Literary Women*, London: The Women's Press, 1978.

Monbiot, George, 'When It Won't Need a Tyranny to Deprive Us of Our Freedom', *The Guardian*, 21 February 2006, p. 29.

Morton, Timothy, ed., *A Routledge Literary Sourcebook on Mary Shelley's* Frankenstein, London and New York: Routledge, 2002.

Mudrick, Marvin, *Jane Austen: Irony as Defense and Discovery*, Princeton, NJ: Princeton University Press, 1952.

New, Melvyn, *Laurence Sterne as Satitrist: A Reading of 'Tristram Shandy'*, Gainesville, FL: University of Florida Press, 1969.

Nicolaidis, Kalypso and Howse, Robert, eds, *The Federal Vision: Legitimacy and Levels of Governance in the United States and Europe*, Oxford: Oxford University Press, 2001.

Novak, Maximilian E., *Economics and the Fiction of Daniel Defoe*, Berkeley, CA: University of California Press, 1962.

Owens, W. R. and Sim, Stuart, eds, *Reception, Appropriation, Recollection: Bunyan's Pilgrim's Progress*, Bern and Oxford: Peter Lang, 2007.

Patrick, Bishop Simon, *Fifteen Sermons upon Contentment and Resignation to the Will of God*, London, 1719.

Pearson, Jacqueline, 'Gender and Narrative in the Fiction of Aphra Behn', in Janet Todd, ed., *New Casebooks: Aphra Behn*, Basingstoke and London: Macmillan, 1999.

Pfister, Manfred, *Laurence Sterne*, Tavistock: Northcote House, 2001.

Pierce, David, and de Voogd, Peter, eds, *Laurence Sterne in Modernism and Postmodernism*, Amsterdam and Atlanta, GA: Rodopi, 1996.

Plato, *The Republic*, trans. Desmond Lee, Harmondsworth: Penguin Books, 2nd edn, 1974.

Pollin, Burton Ralph, *Education and Enlightenment in the Works of William Godwin*, New York: Las Americas Publishing, 1962.

Pyle, Forest, 'Making Cyborgs, Making Humans: Of Terminators, and Blade Runners', in Jim Collins, Hilary Radner and Ava Preacher Collins, eds, *Film Theory Goes to the Movies*, New York and London: Routledge, 1993.

Radcliffe, Anne, *The Mysteries of Udolpho, A Romance* (1794), ed. Bonamy Dobrée, Oxford: Oxford University Press, 1980.

—, *The Italian, or, The Confessional of the Black Penitents* (1797), ed. Frederick Garber, Oxford: Oxford University Press, 1981.

Rana, Fazale, and Ross, Hugh, *Origins of Life: Biblical and Evolutionary Models Face Off*, Colorado Springs, CO: NavPress, 2004.

Rawson, Claude, *Henry Fielding and the Augustan Ideal Under Stress: 'Nature's Dance of Death' and Other Studies*, London and Boston, MA: Routledge & Kegan Paul, 1972.

—, *Gulliver and the Gentle Reader: Studies in Swift and Our Time*, London and Boston, MA: Routledge & Kegan Paul, 1973.

Richardson, Samuel, *Pamela; or, Virtue Rewarded* (1740), ed. Peter Sabor, Harmondsworth: Penguin Books, 1980.

—, *Pamela*, vol. 2 (1741), London: J. M. Dent, 1962.

—, *Clarissa, or, The History of a Young Lady* (1747–8), ed. Angus Ross, Harmondsworth: Penguin Books, 1985.

—, *Sir Charles Grandison* (1753–4), ed. Jocelyn Harris, Oxford: Oxford University Press, 1972.

Richetti, John J., *Defoe's Narratives: Situations and Structures*, Oxford: Clarendon Press, 1975.

Rogers, Deborah D., ed., *The Critical Response to Ann Radcliffe*, Westport, CT and London: Greenwood Press, 1994.

Roussel, Roy, *The Conversation of the Sexes: Seduction and Equality in Selected Seventeenth- and Eighteenth-Century Texts*, New York: Oxford University Press, 1986.

Ruthven, Malise, *Fundamentalism: The Search for Meaning*, Oxford: Oxford University Press, 2004.

Scott, Sir Walter, *Waverley; or, 'Tis Sixty Years Since* (1814), ed. Claire Lamont, Oxford: Oxford University Press, 1986.

—, *Rob Roy* (1817), ed. Ian Duncan, Oxford: Oxford University Press, 1998.

—, *Redgauntlet: A Tale of the Eighteenth Century* (1824), ed. Kathryn Sutherland, Oxford: Oxford University Press, 1985.

Shelley, Mary, *Frankenstein, or, The Modern Prometheus* (1818), in *Four Gothic Novels*, Oxford: Oxford University Press, 1994.

Sim, Stuart, *Negotiations with Paradox: Narrative Form and Narrative Practice in Bunyan and Defoe*, Hemel Hempstead: Harvester Wheatsheaf, 1990.

—, ' "All that Exist are 'Islands of Determinism' ": Shandean Sentiment and the Dilemma of Postmodern Physics', in David Pierce and Peter de Voogd, eds, *Laurence Sterne in Modernism and Postmodernism*, Amsterdam and Atlanta, GA: Rodopi, 1996, pp. 109–21.

—, 'Sterne • Chaos • Complexity', in Susan Spencer, ed., *The Eighteenth-Century Novel, I*, New York: AMS Press, 2001, pp. 201–15.

—, *Lyotard and the Inhuman*, Cambridge: Icon Press, 2001.

—, *Fundamentalist World: The New Dark Age of Dogma*, Cambridge: Icon Press, 2004.

—, *Empires of Belief: Why We Need More Scepticism and Doubt in the Twenty-First Century*, Edinburgh: Edinburgh University Press, 2006.

—, 'Bunyan and His Fundamentalist Readers', in W. R. Owens and Stuart Sim, eds, *Reception, Appropriation, Recollection: Bunyan's* Pilgrim's Progress, Bern and Oxford: Peter Lang, 2007, pp. 213–28.

— and Walker, David, *The Discourse of Sovereignty from Hobbes to Fielding: The State of Nature and the Nature of the State*, Aldershot and Burlington, VT: Ashgate, 2003.

Skinner, Gillian, *Sensibility and Economics in the Novel, 1740–1800: The Price of a Tear*, Basingstoke and London: Macmillan, 1999.

Smith, Frederick N., ed., *The Genres of Gulliver's Travels*, London: Associated Universities Press, 1990.

Spacks, Patricia Meyer, *Desire and Truth: Functions of Plot in Eighteenth-Century English Novels*, Chicago and London: University of Chicago Press, 1990.

Spencer, Jane, *The Rise of the Woman Novelist: From Aphra Behn to Jane Austen*, Oxford: Basil Blackwell, 1986.

Spencer, Susan, *The Eighteenth-Century Novel, I*, New York: AMS Press, 2001.

Spender, Dale, *Mothers of the Novel: One Hundred Good Women Writers before Jane Austen*, London: Pandora, 1986.

Starr, G. A., *Defoe and Spiritual Autobiography*, Princeton, NJ: Princeton University Press, 1965.

Sterne, Laurence, *The Life and Opinions of Tristram Shandy, Gentleman* (1759–67), ed. James A. Work, New York: Odyssey, 1940.

Sterne, Laurence, *The Life and Opinions of Tristram Shandy, Gentleman* (1759–67), ed. Ian Campbell Ross, Oxford: Oxford University Press, 1983.

Stevenson, John Allen, *The British Novel, Defoe to Austen: A Critical History*, Boston, MA: Twayne, 1990.

Strange, Susan, *Casino Capitalism*, Oxford: Basil Blackwell, 1986.

Strohman, Richard, 'Toward a New Paradigm for Life: Beyond Genetic Determinism', http://www.psrast.org/strohmnewgen.htm, 22 March 2001.

Sussman, Charlotte, 'The Other Problem with Women: Reproduction and Slave Culture in Aphra Behn's *Oroonoko*', in Heidi Hutner, ed., *Rereading Aphra Behn: History, Theory, and Criticism*, Charlottesville, VA and London: University Press of Virginia, 1993, pp. 212–33.

Sutherland, John, *The Life of Walter Scott: A Critical Biography*, Oxford: Blackwell, 1995.

Swearingen, James E., *Reflexivity in* Tristram Shandy*: An Essay in Phenomenological Criticism*, New Haven, CT and London: Yale University Press, 1977.

Swift, Jonathan, *Gulliver's Travels* (1726), ed. Claude Rawson, Oxford: Oxford University Press, 2005.

—, *The Correspondence of Jonathan Swift*, ed. Harold Williams, vols I–V, Oxford: Clarendon Press, 1963–5.

Tanner, Tony, *Jane Austen*, Basingstoke and London: Macmillan, 1968.

Taylor, Kate, *Not Tonight, Mr Right*, Harmondsworth: Penguin Books, 2007.

Todd, Janet, *The Sign of Angellica: Women, Writing and Fiction, 1660–1800*, London: Virago, 1989.

—, ed., *New Casebooks: Aphra Behn*, Basingstoke and London: Macmillan, 1999.

Traugott, John, *Tristram Shandy's World: Sterne's Philosophical Rhetoric*, Berkeley and Los Angeles: University of California Press, 1954.

—, ed., *Laurence Sterne: A Collection of Critical Essays*, Englewood Cliffs, NJ: Prentice-Hall, 1968.

Trotter, David, *Circulation: Defoe, Dickens, and the Economies of the Novel*, Basingstoke and London: Macmillan, 1988.

Truss, Lynn, *Talk to the Hand: The Utter Bloody Rudeness of Everyday Life (or Six Good Reasons to Stay Home and Bolt the Door)*, London: Profile Books, 2005.

Uglow, Jenny, *Henry Fielding*, Plymouth: Northcote House, 1995.

Vasagar, Javeen, 'Jade Evicted as Poll Reveals Public Anger with Channel 4', *The Guardian*, 20 January 2007.

Veeder, William, *Mary Shelley and Frankenstein: The Fate of Androgyny*, Chicago and London: University of Chicago Press, 1986.

Waldron, Mary, *Jane Austen and the Fiction of Her Time*, Cambridge: Cambridge University Press, 1999.

Ward, Mark, *Virtual Organisms: The Startling World of Artificial Life*, London: Macmillan, 1999.

Warner, William B., *Licensing Entertainment: The Elevation of Novel Reading in Britain, 1684–1750*, Berkeley, Los Angeles and London: University of California Press, 1998.

Watt, Ian, *The Rise of the Novel*, London: Chatto and Windus, 1957.

Watts, Carol, 'The Modernity of Sterne', in David Pierce and Peter de Voogd, eds, *Laurence Sterne in Modernism and Postmodernism*, Amsterdam and Atlanta, GA: Rodopi, 1996.

Williams, Kathleen, *Jonathan Swift and the Age of Compromise*, Lawrence, KA: University of Kansas Press, 1958.

—, 'Gulliver's Voyage to the Houyhnhnms', in Richard Gravil, ed., *Swift*, Gulliver's Travels: *A Casebook*, London and Basingstoke: Macmillan, 1974, pp. 136–47.

Williams, Zoe, 'Gatekeepers of Sex', *The Guardian*, 24 January 2007, p. 31.

Wiltshire, John, *Jane Austen and the Body: 'The Picture of Health'*, Cambridge: Cambridge University Press, 1992.

Wiseman, S. J., *Aphra Behn*, Plymouth: Northcote House, 1996.

Wittig, Kurt, *The Scottish Tradition in Literature*, Westport, CT: Greenwood Press, 1958.

Woodcock, George, *William Godwin: A Biographical Study*, London: Porcupine Press, 1946.

Žižek, Slavoj, *The Sublime Object of Ideology*, London and New York: Verso, 1989.

Index